PRACTICAL SOCIAL WORK

Series Editor: Jo Campling

Social work is at an important stage in its development. All professions must be responsive to changing social and economic conditions if they are to meet the needs of those they serve. This series focuses on sound practice and the specific contribution which social workers can make to the well-being of our society.

The British Association of Social Workers has always been conscious of its role in setting guidelines for practice and in seeking to raise professional standards. The conception of the Practical Social Work series arose from a survey of BASW members to discover where they, the practitioners in social work, felt there was the most need for new literature. The response was over-whelming and enthusiastic, and the result is a carefully planned, coherent series of books. The emphasis is firmly on practice set in a theoretical frame-work. The books will inform, stimulate and promote discussion, thus adding to the further development of skills and high professional standards. All the authors are practitioners and teachers of social work representing a wide variety of experience.

JO CAMPLING

A list of published titles in this series follows overleaf

Practical Social Work
Series Standing Order ISBN 0–333–69347–7

You can receive future titles in this series as they are published by placing a standing order. Please contact your bookseller or, in the case of difficulty, write to us at the address below with your name and address, the title of the series and the ISBN quoted above.

Customer Services Department, Macmillan Distribution Ltd
Houndmills, Basingstoke, Hampshire RG21 6XS, England

PRACTICAL SOCIAL WORK

Robert Adams *Social Work and Empowerment*

Sarah Banks *Ethics and Values in Social Work (2nd edn)*

James G. Barber *Beyond Casework*

James G. Barber *Social Work with Addictions*

Peter Beresford and Suzy Croft *Citizen Involvement*

Suzy Braye and Michael Preston-Shoot *Practising Social Work Law (2nd edn)*

Helen Cosis Brown *Social Work and Sexuality*

Alan Butler and Colin Pritchard *Social Work and Mental Illness*

Cressy Cannan, Lynne Berry and Karen Lyons *Social Work and Europe*

Roger Clough *Residential Work*

David M. Cooper and David Ball *Social Work and Child Abuse*

Veronica Coulshed and Audrey Mullender *Management in Social Work (2nd edn)*

Veronica Coulshed and Joan Orme *Social Work Practice: An Introduction (3rd edn)*

Paul Daniel and John Wheeler *Social Work and Local Politics*

Peter R. Day *Sociology in Social Work Practice*

Lena Dominelli *Anti-Racist Social Work (2nd edn)*

Celia Doyle *Working with Abused Children (2nd edn)*

Angela Everitt and Pauline Hardiker *Evaluating for Good Practice*

Angela Everitt, Pauline Hardiker, Jane Littlewood and Audrey Mullender *Applied Research for Better Practice*

Kathy Ford and Alan Jones *Student Supervision*

David Francis and Paul Henderson *Working with Rural Communities*

Alison Froggatt *Family Work with Elderly People*

Danya Glaser and Stephen Frosh *Child Sexual Abuse (2nd edn)*

Gill Gorell Barnes *Working with Families*

Cordelia Grimwood and Ruth Popplestone *Women, Management and Care*

Jalna Hanmer and Daphne Statham *Women and Social Work (2nd edn)*

Tony Jeffs and Mark Smith (eds) *Youth Work*

Michael Kerfoot and Alan Butler *Problems of Childhood and Adolescence*

Joyce Lishman *Communication in Social Work*

Carol Lupton and Terry Gillespie (eds) *Working with Violence*

Mary Marshall and Mary Dixon *Social Work with Older People (3rd edn)*

Paula Nicolson and Rowan Bayne *Applied Psychology for Social Workers (2nd edn)*

Kieran O'Hagan *Crisis Intervention in Social Services*

Michael Oliver and Bob Sapey *Social Work with Disabled People (2nd edn)*

Joan Orme and Bryan Glastonbury *Care Management*

John Pitts *Working with Young Offenders (2nd edn)*

Michael Preston-Shoot *Effective Groupwork*

Peter Raynor, David Smith and Maurice Vanstone *Effective Probation Practice*

Steven Shardlow and Mark Doel *Practice Learning and Teaching*

Carole R. Smith *Social Work with the Dying and Bereaved*

David Smith *Criminology for Social Work*

Christine Stones *Focus on Families*

Neil Thompson *Anti-Discriminatory Practice (3rd edn)*

Neil Thompson, Michael Murphy and Steve Stradling *Dealing with Stress*

Derek Tilbury *Working with Mental Illness*

Alan Twelvetrees *Community Work (3rd edn)*

Hilary Walker and Bill Beaumount (eds) *Working with Offenders*

Ethics and Values in Social Work

Second Edition

Sarah Banks

palgrave

First edition 1995
Reprinted seven times
Second edition 2001

Published by
PALGRAVE
Houndmills, Basingstoke, Hampshire RG21 6XS and
175 Fifth Avenue, New York, N.Y. 10010
Companies and representatives throughout the world

PALGRAVE is the new global academic imprint of St. Martin's Press LLC
Scholarly and Reference Division and Palgrave Publishers Ltd (formerly
Macmillan Press Ltd).

ISBN 0–333–94798–3

This book is printed on paper suitable for recycling and made from fully
managed and sustained forest sources.

10 9 8 7 6 5 4
10 09 08 07 06 05 04 03

Printed in China

To past and present community and youth work and social work students at the Universities of Durham and York

Contents

List of Figures and Tables

Figures

Tables

Preface to the Second Edition

Changing social work

The Introduction to the first edition of this book started with the statement: 'Social work is currently in a period of change'. This statement remains in the second edition and is as true in the year 2000 as it was in 1995. The editorial comment in the magazine *Community Care* (1999/2000) ushered in the new millennium with the headline 'A new century of uncertainty', commenting that: 'Few professions have changed more than social work in a decade.' This comment relates to Britain, but similar shifts in the organisation and practice of social work are also occurring in many other countries as the introduction of market principles, the mixed economy of welfare and the increasing concern with quality assurance and standards take hold (see Donati and Folgheraiter, 1999; Soulet, 1997). These changes are having profound effects on the nature of the roles and tasks performed by social workers and on the status and identity of social work as a profession. What this means for professional ethics is one of the questions the book has to address, even more so now than five years ago.

At the time of writing, in Britain, there are major initiatives under way in the field of social work, social care and social services generally. These include the establishment of General Councils as regulatory bodies in the countries of the UK which will register practitioners and have a role in developing and enforcing new codes of ethics and practice for the profession. There are also new requirements on social services departments to develop quality standards for their services. These developments have inevitably informed some of the changes that have been made to the first edition of this book, although they have not been dwelt upon in depth, as by the time the book is published, another new policy initiative will probably be in place and it is the broader trends that are more important when looking at ethics and values.

Some of the trends towards fragmentation and specialisation of the work, the growth of procedures and protocols, and the concern to involve service users as partners in decision-making noted in Chapters 6 and 7 are still there and intensifying. More literature is emerging on 'postmodern social work', which takes account of this fragmentation of practice and recognises the diversity of the values and needs of service users. Whilst ethics is only just beginning to be considered in the context of this literature (for example, Rossiter *et al.*, 2000), the implications for professional ethics could be profound, depending on whether a 'sceptical' or 'affirmative' view is taken, to use the distinction made by Rosenau (1992, pp. 15–16). There are those who announce the 'end of ethics' as a system of universal principles of right/wrong, good/bad (see McBeath and Webb, 1991), others who argue that certain value choices are superior to others and see the possibility of emancipatory action for social change (Ife, 1999; Leonard, 1997). Some of this literature on postmodern perspectives on social work has been incorporated into Chapter 4.

The 'ethics boom'

In addition to the changes in social work practice, there has also been what Davis (1999) has termed an 'ethics boom', particularly in the field of professional ethics. Some of this has to do with changes in technology, particularly in the field of medical ethics, where new issues relating to genetics, for example, are subject to intense debate. But there is also a much broader concern in all professions with 'standards in public life' as a number of high-profile cases of corruption, lying or malpractice have come to light. Ethical issues in social work are no exception, with many more publications coming out in recent years than previously with a specific focus on ethics (for example, Clark, 2000; Hunt, 1998; Payne and Littlechild, 2000; Wilmot, 1997).

While the focus of professional ethics in the past tended to be on developing lists of principles and how to handle conflict between principles (say between respecting the self-determination of a service user and promoting her welfare), an interest in what I have called character- and relationship-based ethics ('virtue ethics' and 'the ethic of care') has now begun to emerge. I have therefore included a new chapter (Chapter 3) in this edition which focuses specifically on these approaches to ethics and how they might relate to social work.

Changes in the second edition

The Introduction and Chapter 1 remain broadly the same, although a more detailed discussion of the nature of ethics is now included in the Introduction. This was felt necessary partly because the growth of literature in the field of professional ethics has created a confusing range of meanings of terms such as 'ethics', 'morals' and 'morality'.

In the first edition, Chapter 2 included an overview of the changing nature of values in social work and brief coverage of three approaches to ethics: Kantian, utilitarian and an 'ethic of care'. Some of the material on changing social work values has now been moved to Chapter 4, while Chapter 2 focuses on 'principle-based' approaches to ethics, and a completely new Chapter 3 has been added to discuss the relevance of virtue ethics and an ethic of care for professional ethics, and social work in particular. A more explicit 'moral pluralism' is advocated at the end of this chapter, suggesting that our moral judgements are based not just on weighing up and implementing ethical principles, but also on character traits and particular commitments and responsibilities.

Chapter 4 includes discussion of the relationship of social work values to the 'knowledge base', taking account of some of the recent literature on social work practice and theories, including the postmodernist critique of social work knowledge. Chapter 5, on codes of ethics, has been substantially revised to take account of the latest versions of codes of ethics from twenty professional associations in the membership of the International Federation of Social Workers. A number of the codes have become longer and more prescriptive, and some emergent new themes are noted, although codes of ethics are notoriously slow to reflect actual changes in practice. For example, in one or two cases the concern with the rights of citizens and service users is now beginning to encompass the notion of their reciprocal responsibilities, and several codes have extended their sections on confidentiality, sometimes explicitly to take account of multidisciplinary work.

The structure of the next two chapters (6 and 7) on service users' rights and social workers' responsibilities is broadly the same as in the first edition, taking into account some of the intensifying trends towards service user responsibility, 'consumerist' approaches, user participation in decision-making, increasing standardisation and regulation of the social work task and a concern with 'evidence-based' practice.

In Chapter 8, a brief account of the nature of ethical decision-making is included at the beginning, to set the scene for the discussion of ethical problems and dilemmas experienced by practitioners. This section on ethical decision-making has been moved from Chapter 1 and modified to take some account of character- and relationship-based approaches to ethics, as well as the role of ethical principles. A couple of new ethical dilemmas have been included in this chapter, in particular the last example, from a team manager, which is analysed both in terms of principle-based and relationship/care-based approaches to ethics. As in the first edition, the main aim of the book is to encourage critical thinking and reflection on the ethical problems and dilemmas encountered in social work practice, hence this last chapter is one of the most important in the book. It highlights the importance for both trainee and experienced social workers of discussing and debating ethical issues in their practice with others, and the usefulness of a variety of types of case examples to stimulate this process.

Acknowledgements

The main stimulus for writing this book has been the dialogue and discussion generated through teaching ethics to trainee social workers and community and youth workers, both at the University of Durham and especially the many cohorts of University of York Master of Social Work students.

I would like to thank the social workers who were prepared to discuss their ethical dilemmas with me – particularly trainee social workers from the Universities of York and Durham, and social workers from several social services departments in the north of England. I am also grateful to the International Federation of Social Workers and the professional associations across the world that sent copies of their ethical codes; to Kate Boardman, Lieve van Espen, Marie Sanders and Mea Wilkins for their translations; and to the *International Journal of Youth and Adolescence* for permission to use sections in Chapter 3 from a forthcoming article concerning virtue ethics and the ethics of care. Many colleagues and friends have offered encouragement and been prepared to discuss aspects of both the first and second edition of the book with me, including: Margaret Bell, Tim Bond, Lorna Durrani, Ken Fairless, Umme Imam, Tony Jeffs, Juliet Koprowska, Kate Leonard, Una McCluskey, Audrey Mullender, Alf Ronnby, Muriel Sawbridge, Mark Smith, Fritz-Rudiger Volz and Robin Williams. I have also benefited from Jo Campling's enthusiastic support and the helpful comments of two anonymous referees on the first edition.

Finally, I would like to thank my colleagues at the University of Durham for giving me space to complete a large part of the book during a period of research leave, and Fred Banks for first pointing me in the direction of moral philosophy.

SARAH BANKS

Introduction

The current context of social work

The occupation of social work is currently in a period of change – both in Britain and in many other western countries – as the role of the state as a direct provider of services declines, resources for welfare are being reduced and new styles of management and accountability are introduced. This makes it not only difficult to look at the ethics and values of social work (because old values may be becoming irrelevant and new ones are beginning to emerge) but also particularly important. Social work has always been a difficult occupation to define because it has embraced work in a number of different sectors (public, private, independent, voluntary), a multiplicity of different settings (residential homes, area offices, community development projects) with workers taking on a range of different tasks (caring, controlling, empowering, campaigning, assessing, managing) for a variety of different purposes (redistribution of resources to those in need, social control and rehabilitation of the deviant, prevention or reduction of social problems). This diversity, or 'fragmentation' as some have called it, is increasing, which raises the question of whether the occupation can retain the rather tenuous identity it was seeking to develop in the 1970s and 1980s.

In such a climate of fragmentation, there are some who argue that it is the values of social work that should hold it together. Yet the values traditionally stated – self-determination of the service user, acceptance, non-judgementalism and confidentiality, for example – are neither unique to social work, nor do they seem to be complete for social work. Similar statements of values or ethical principles are made for medicine, nursing and counselling, for example. It is precisely because these values are so broad-ranging that they can encompass the variety of tasks and settings which come under the umbrella of 'social work'. They are relevant to the 'caring professional' who is in a relationship of trust with a service user in need of help. Yet this description has never adequately characterised social work, which is also about controlling people in the interests of social order. So, not only do the traditional social work values fail to characterise social

1

work uniquely, they also fail to encompass social work itself completely. Other values also seem relevant, such as fairness in the distribution of resources and the promotion of the public good. As local
authority social work changes, with the emphasis less on the individual helping relationship and more on the distribution of resources
and on social control, this is becoming more apparent. Local authority social workers who are involved in the criminal justice system,
community care, child protection and mental health are finding themselves increasingly working to legal, governmental and agency procedures and guidelines and hence ethical issues around justice and
fairness are prominent. At the same time, workers in some of the new
specialist services that are being set up largely in the voluntary sector,
such as child advocacy or AIDS/HIV counselling, can operate more
easily within the traditional casework value system which emphasises
user self-determination (or its modern development, 'empowerment')
and the rights and welfare of the individual user.

Terminology: 'social workers' and 'users'

The term 'social worker' is used in this book to refer to people who
are paid in a professional capacity to undertake the tasks of counselling and/or social care planning as defined by the Barclay Report
(1982, pp. xiv–xv). Although the report was written some years ago,
these two aspects of the social work task provide a useful starting
point for considering what social workers do. According to the
report:

> By *counselling* we mean the process (which has often been known
> as 'social casework') of direct communication and interaction
> between clients and social workers, through which clients are
> helped to change, or to tolerate, some aspects of themselves or
> their environment . . . *Social care planning* covers plans designed
> to solve or alleviate existing problems and plans which aim to
> prevent the development of social problems in the future or to
> create or strengthen resources to respond to those which do arise.

These activities may be carried out by people who are not social
workers (volunteers, family members, other welfare professionals),
but it would be expected that all those calling themselves social

workers should be able to carry out, or organise the carrying out of, such functions (ibid., p. 34). However, since the Barclay Report was written, the roles of counselling and social care planning have become more distinct, with many workers specialising much more in one than the other. Is this book equally relevant to a care manager, an approved mental health social worker, a residential social worker, a family therapist, a youth justice worker or a community social worker? The answer is 'yes' in so far as they all regard themselves as social workers. Indeed many of the issues covered are generic – including discussion of the professional code of ethics. However, in so far as the context in which people work is regarded as important (and I believe it is in relation to ethical and value issues), then inevitably this book cannot take account of all the different types of work settings and their impact on social workers' values. It is mainly concerned with the ethical problems and dilemmas faced by social workers working face to face, or organising care for individual users, rather than those faced by managers of social workers or developers of services and communities.

I have tended to adopt the term 'user' to refer to the people who use social work services. I prefer this to 'customer' or 'consumer' as these terms have connotations of choice and market-based relationships which are not necessarily appropriate in social work. Occasionally the term 'client' is used, as this was until the last decade in common usage and much of the social work literature, including the codes of ethics, uses this term. I have tended to use 'she' when I am referring to a social worker instead of the more cumbersome 'he/she'.

Terminology: 'ethics' and 'values'

It is also important to clarify the terms in the title of the book – 'ethics' and 'values'. People use the term 'ethics' in a number of different ways, but perhaps the most important distinction to make is between ethics as synonymous with moral philosophy and ethics as moral norms or standards. Within each of these two broad types of usage there are also many variations, depending on what aspects of moral philosophy are stressed and whether 'moral norms' are seen as habits, preferences, rules, standards, principles or character traits, for example.

If we take the first usage of ethics, as moral philosophy, it is a

singular term, used to describe a branch of philosophy concerned
with the study of 'morality, moral problems and moral judgements'
(Frankena, 1963, p. 3). This is the way most moral philosophers
writing on ethics use the term. For example, Warnock (1998, p.
7) talks of 'ethics (or moral philosophy, as I prefer to call it)'.
Exactly what is the nature and remit of moral philosophy is, of course, dis-
puted. But often philosophers distinguish three types of ethics as
follows:

1. *Metaethics* – comprises critical and analytical thinking about the
   meaning and use of moral terms such as 'right', 'good' or 'duty',
   about whether moral judgements can be justified or what is the
   nature of morality, for example.
2. *Normative ethics* – attempts to give answers to moral questions
   and problems regarding, for example, what is the morally right
   course of action in a particular case, whether someone is a
   morally good person, or whether lying is always wrong.
3. *Descriptive ethics* – studies what people's moral opinions and
   beliefs are and how they act in relation to these – for example,
   whether people in Britain believe abortion is always morally
   wrong.

Some philosophers confine moral philosophy to metaethics only
(for example, Urmson, 1975, p. 99), but generally it is regarded as
comprising both metaethics and normative ethics, although some
philosophers may inevitably spend more of their time on the former
than the latter. Descriptive ethics, however, is usually regarded as
outside the realm of moral philosophy, although not irrelevant, in
that it comprises the kinds of empirical and historical inquiries that
might be conducted by anthropologists, sociologists or historians.
Clearly in the context of professional ethics, we are interested in all
three aspects of ethics, including descriptive ethics (what moral views
social workers actually hold and how they behave in practice),
although the purpose of this book is not to conduct an empirical
inquiry.

The second usage of the term 'ethics' is as a plural term referring
to the norms or standards of behaviour people follow concerning
what is regarded as good or bad, right or wrong. Commentators vary
according to whether they regard ethics as norms, standards, rules,
principles or character traits, and whether they regard them as inter-

nally developed by the moral agent, or externally imposed by an outside authority. A common use of this second sense of ethics is in the expression 'code of ethics' – which is usually regarded as a set of principles, standards or rules of conduct for ethical practice. A variant on this usage of ethics is to use the term synonymously with 'morality' to mean a system of moral norms or standards.

In English we often use the terms 'ethics' and 'morals' interchangeably in this second sense. Indeed, as Edwards (1998, p. 41) points out, 'morals' is derived from the Latin (*mores*) and 'ethics' from the Greek (*ethos*), both meaning habits or customs. It is in this interchangeable sense that I will use the terms 'ethics' and 'morals' in this book, along with the adjectives 'ethical' and 'moral'. However, it is important to point out that some commentators do distinguish between the two. Osborne (1998, pp. 221–2) makes the following distinction:

> Moral systems are systems of interdiction; they are ideologies, codes to which individuals must relate themselves. Ethics, on the other hand, might be considered in a more positive sense, not as codes of interdiction, not as external norms to which individuals must relate themselves, but as constructed norms of 'internal consistency' (cf. Deleuze, 1988: 23; Foucault, 1984). Morality, one could say, is about doing one's duty to others or doing one's duty by some moral norm; ethics is about doing one's duty to oneself.

This has resonances with the distinction made in some of the French literature between 'la morale' and 'l'éthique'. Bouquet (1999, p. 27) defines 'la morale' as 'a set of universalisable values, absolute and imperative; it comprises duties'. She suggests that the term has become discredited through being confused with moralising and through the recent rejection of a prescriptive morality, of dogmatism and universalism. Common usage is now substituting the term 'éthique' for 'morale'. She regards 'l'éthique' as equally normative, but not categorical. It is principally associated with the Subject and interior to the Subject (that is, the moral agent) who is autonomous, free and responsible to herself for her acts. Bouquet defines 'l'éthique' as 'the set of principles which are at the foundation of each person's conduct'.

However, such distinctions in the English-speaking literature are relatively rare, and great care must be taken to ascertain how commentators are distinguishing 'ethics' and morals', if at all, since they do not all follow the same broad distinctions made by Osborne and Bouquet. For example, Bauman frequently talks of 'ethics' as the externally imposed codes prescribing correct behaviour universally (1995, p. 11) and the 'moral impulse' or 'morality' as internal and 'autonomous' (1993, p. 46). No such distinctions will be made in this book.

The term 'values' is equally problematic. 'Social work values', 'the value-base of social work, 'social work as a value-laden activity' are all common phrases in the social work literature. Yet what is meant by 'the values of social work'? 'Values' is one of those words that tend to be used rather vaguely and have a variety of different meanings. In everyday usage, 'values' is often used to refer to one or all of religious, moral, political or ideological principles, beliefs or attitudes. In the context of social work, however, it seems frequently to be used to mean a set of fundamental moral/ethical principles to which social workers are/should be committed. According to the Central Council for Education and Training in Social Work (CCETSW, 1995, p. 18), such values include a willingness to 'respect and value uniqueness and diversity' and 'promote people's rights to choice, privacy, confidentiality and protection', for example. For the purpose of this discussion, while noting that the term 'values' is used in many different and conflicting ways, I will use it to refer to the fundamental moral/ethical principles of social work. Other commentators on social work ethics use the terminology differently (for example, Levy, 1993; Clark, 2000). The reason for including both 'ethics' and 'values' in the title of the book is that 'ethics' in its first meaning emphasises that the book is very much about *the study and analysis* of what is regarded as good or bad, right or wrong in social work practice.

Rationale and aims of the book

The discussion above suggests that it is both timely and difficult to explore the nature of the ethical and value issues inherent in social work practice. It is timely not just because the old values are under threat, but also because social workers themselves are increasingly under moral attack from the press and public for the outcomes of their actions. Controversies over the handling of child abuse cases, for example, raise ethical questions about the duties and rights of social workers, and the extent to which they should be blamed if a child dies, or if children are removed from their families unnecessarily. Many social workers feel a sense of guilt and anxiety when having to make a difficult ethical decision. While such feelings are inevitable for anyone who makes difficult decisions and has a sense of moral responsibility, should social workers take all the blame for bad outcomes? One of the purposes of this book is to encourage social workers to be clear about their own value positions, and hence to reduce some of the unnecessary feelings of guilt, blame and anxiety in making difficult ethical decisions.

In the course of collecting material for this book, I have found that when social workers are asked to describe ethical dilemmas in their practice, there is never any shortage of examples, and there is no need even to define what is meant by an 'ethical dilemma'. If we do define what is meant by the term 'ethical dilemma' – a choice between two equally unwelcome alternatives relating to human welfare – then it is immediately apparent that the occurrence of ethical dilemmas in social work is serious and common. There is never any shortage of cases where the rights of parents have to be balanced against the rights of children or the social worker's duty to the agency conflicts with a duty to the user, for example.

There are no easy answers to the ethical problems and dilemmas in social work practice. It is not possible (or desirable) to produce a rulebook which would enable social workers easily and quickly to resolve these dilemmas. Even if it were, the resolution of the dilemma will still entail making a choice between two unwelcome alternatives, perhaps by careful consideration and deciding that one alternative is less unwelcome than the other. Having made the choice, the impact of the dilemma does not go away, for even the least unwelcome alternative is still unwelcome. This is where some of the main stresses for social workers lie; not just in having to make difficult choices and decisions, but having to take responsibility for the unwelcome nature or outcomes of the decisions. For example:

> there is a 10-year-old boy whose parents are still barely able to control him after a lot of support from the social worker and other agencies. Should the social worker recommend that the boy be removed from the parental home which would go against the

wishes of the parents and the boy and risk further disruptive
behaviour as a result of the move, or should she recommend that
he should stay at home which is contrary to the demands coming
from neighbours and the school and risks further violent and disruptive behaviour towards other children and neighbours?

Both solutions have unwelcome consequences. The process of investigation, noting the legal and moral rights of different parties, the
risks involved in both courses of action, and taking into account
the legal and procedural responsibilities of the social worker is a
complex one. Whatever course of action is taken, somebody's rights
may be compromised and some of the consequences may be
unwelcome.

The aim of this book is not to tell social workers how to make
such choices – because I believe that would be both impossible and
undesirable. It is impossible because of the complexity of social work
decision-making; no rulebook could cover the variety of situations.
It would be undesirable because it would suggest that social workers
would simply have to follow the prescribed rules applying in each
case and could in effect abrogate their individual responsibility for
decision-making. Rather, the book aims to encourage critical thinking and reflection through exploring what is the nature of the ethical
problems and dilemmas in social work, how and why they arise, and
what might be some alternative ways of tackling them according to
different ethical theories and approaches. Through gaining a clearer
understanding of what the problems and dilemmas are about, hope-
fully social workers can decide where they stand on some of the
important ethical issues in the work and will have more confidence
in justifying the decisions they have made, and may feel less obliged
to take the blame for the inevitable unwelcome outcomes of social
work intervention.

At the end of some of the chapters exercises have been included
which can be used by readers to focus their thoughts around particular issues, or by tutors/facilitators teaching or working with
groups of social workers. Case studies from social work practitioners have also been used, mainly in Chapter 8, to illustrate how ethical
problems and dilemmas arise and can be tackled in practice. Details
of the cases and all names of people involved have been changed to
preserve anonymity.

1
Ethical Issues in Social Work

There is general agreement amongst social work practitioners and academics that questions of ethics, morals and values are an inevitable part of social work. The majority of social workers, when asked, have no difficulty in offering examples of ethical problems and dilemmas. The literature of social work is also very clear: 'Moral issues haunt social work', says Jordan (1990, p. 1); according to Pinker, 'social work is, essentially, a moral enterprise' (Pinker, 1990, p. 14); the Central Council for Education and Training in Social Work (CCETSW) states: 'practice must be founded on, informed by and capable of being judged against a clear value base' (CCETSW, 1995, p. 18); and the International Federation of Social Workers comments that 'Ethical awareness is a necessary part of the practice of any social worker' (IFSW, 1994, p. 1).

This chapter will explore the nature of the ethical issues inherent in social work, and how and why questions of ethics arise. It will also consider the guilt and anxiety felt by social workers and whether the blame allocated to them for outcomes of what are essentially moral decisions is justified.

The ethical, the technical and the legal

Frequently in the social work literature values are distinguished from knowledge, and ethical/moral issues from legal and technical matters. Such distinctions can be useful, as long as it is not implied that knowledge can be value-free, or that legal and technical decisions can be made without recourse to ethics. We might say, 'it is essentially a legal question whether to detain this person in hospital under the Mental Health Act'. Yet, as Braye and Preston-Shoot

9

(1997) point out, the law is rarely clear, and has to be interpreted by the social worker. For example, the Mental Health Act 1983 talks of: 'mental disorder of a nature or degree which warrants the detention of the patient in a hospital – in the interest of his own health or safety or with a view to the protection of others'. The law tells us that if we make the technical (and ethical) judgement that the disorder is such that it is in the patient's interest to be detained in hospital, then we have the legal powers to bring that about. The law does not tell us what we ought to do, just what we can do. The law itself reflects certain values and norms in society – some of which we may regard as immoral, for example immigration laws. Most decisions in social work involve a complex interaction of ethical, political, technical and legal issues which are all interconnected. Our ethical principles or values will influence how we interpret the law.

Giving another example, we might say, 'it is a technical matter to decide whether this person is eligible for a disabled car parking badge'. We assess the person according to the defined criteria and make a decision using our professional skill and judgement. We might only judge that moral issues were involved if we had to consider whether we ought to give the person a permit although she did not quite meet the criteria. This is a helpful distinction between the technical and the ethical. However, a decision might be regarded as a technical one not because only technical questions of measurement and assessment were involved, but because the social worker chose to see it in that way – as she might if it were a relatively straightforward case which did not present any ethical problems or dilemmas. The process itself, assessing needs for a parking permit, is not devoid of ethical content. The criteria of need which determine who should get permits will be based on ethical judgements about social duties to reduce some of the disadvantages caused by disability, or about how to distribute a scarce resource efficiently and fairly, for example. The social worker may judge that the criteria are not fair or do not result in resources being allocated to the most needy people.

In the light of the discussion above, it may be useful to distinguish between ethical issues, ethical problems and ethical dilemmas as follows:

- *Ethical issues* – pervade the social work task (including what appear to be 'legal' or 'technical' matters) in that social work takes place in the context of the welfare state premised on principles of social justice and public welfare and the social worker has professional power in the relationship with the user. So, although deciding whether to give a parking permit to a person with a disability in a case which is straightforward may not involve the social worker in agonising over a moral dilemma, it is not devoid of ethical content.

- *Ethical problems* – arise when the social worker sees the situation as involving a difficult moral decision, for example, when she has to turn down the application of a very needy person because this person does not quite fit the criteria.
- *Ethical dilemmas* – occur when the social worker sees herself as faced with a choice between two equally unwelcome alternatives which may involve a conflict of moral principles and it is not clear which choice will be the right one. For example, should she bend the criteria for issuing parking permits in order to help a very needy person, or stick to the rules and refuse a permit to someone who really needs it. She is faced with a conflict between the interests of this individual and the public interest in having rules and criteria which apply to everyone.

Thus what is a technical matter for one person (simply applying the rules) may be an ethical problem for another (a difficult decision, but it is clear what decision should be made) or a dilemma for a third person (there appears to be no solution). It depends on how each person sees the situation, how experienced they are at making moral decisions and how they prioritise their ethical principles.

What are the ethical issues in social work?

From talking to qualified and trainee social workers there seem to be three main types of issues, which frequently result in ethical problems and dilemmas:

- *Issues around individual rights and welfare* – a user's right to make her own decisions and choices; the social worker's responsibility to promote the welfare of the user.
- *Issues around public welfare* – the rights and interests of parties other than the user; the social worker's responsibility to her employing agency and to society; the promotion of the greatest good of the greatest number of people.

- *Issues around inequality and structural oppression* – the social worker's responsibility to challenge oppression and to work for changes in agency policy and in society.

Any categorisation is obviously artificial, and does not do justice to the complexity of the issues within each category and the overlap between them. Frequently there are conflicts between rights, responsibilities and interests both within and between these categories. However, this framework may be a useful starting point for exploring issues of values and ethics in social work practice. Quotations from three social workers talking about their practice may illuminate our discussion.

1. Rights/welfare of the individual

A social worker talking about an 80-year-old woman recently referred to the social services department by a local hospital after a fall at home said:

> It was difficult to know how far to try to persuade or even coerce Mrs Brown to accept the offer of a home help or whether just to leave her alone and hope she would manage to survive.

Here the focus of the worker's concern is the user's welfare. The social worker wants to respect Mrs Brown's own choices about how to live her life, yet the worker also wants to ensure Mrs Brown feeds herself properly and is checked regularly in case she falls again. There is a conflict between the promotion of the user's welfare and the user's right to make her own choices.

2. Public welfare

A residential social worker spoke about Sally, a 12-year-old girl who had recently come into care because her parents felt her behaviour was out of control. She had been having sexual relations with a 50-year-old man who supplied her with money in return for sexual favours:

the police were near to catching the man, and asked staff to lift restrictions on Sally leaving the unit in the hope of catching him in the act. Should we have refused because we were allowing Sally to put herself at risk, or was catching the culprit and preventing further risk to herself and other girls a priority?

The social worker sees that it will be in the best interests of everyone if this man is caught, yet feels uneasy about using the young girl in this way, because of both the deception involved, and the responsibility if any harm comes to Sally when she is allowed out. This is a case of deciding whether the public interest in catching the man outweighs the deception involved and the short-term risk to the girl.

3. *Structural oppression*

A social worker visited a travelling family who had requested that their children attend a local playgroup. When she arrived to discuss how to provide financial support, she was told that the children had been refused access on the grounds that it may cause other local families to remove their children and hence threaten the viability of the playgroup. During the visit the social worker noticed that the children had been playing with an electric fire and plugs while the worker was talking to their parents:

> I realised that in another situation I may well have challenged the parents in allowing their children to play with such a dangerous appliance. Given that I felt they were being treated very shabbily by the wider community, I found it very difficult to challenge any of the ways in which they cared for their children.

The social worker is aware that the travellers are being discriminated against by the local community, and by wider society. She does not want to collude in this, but is not sure how to react. This is a case of a social worker recognising she is working with members of an oppressed group, not wishing to oppress them further by challenging their standards of childcare, yet concerned about the safety of children.

The descriptions above have simplified the issues arising in each case. In many cases issues in all three categories arise, and some of the dilemmas workers face are about balancing different ethical principles and relationships – different sets of rights, interests, responsibilities and commitments. Social work is a complex activity, with many layers of duties and responsibilities (for example, to one's own moral integrity, to the user, to the agency and to society). These often conflict and have to be balanced against each other. There are no easy answers to questions such as these. They are part of the everyday life of social workers. Some will handle them more easily than others – depending on experience, moral sensitivity and their own value positions. In the following sections we will explore how and why questions of ethics are an integral part of social work practice.

Social work as a human services profession

Social work may be regarded as a 'human services' profession along with the health care, teaching and legal professions. The social worker has special knowledge and expertise and must be trusted by service users to act in their best interests. The relationship between social worker and user is an unequal one, in that the social worker is more powerful. Social work, therefore, along with law, medicine, nursing, counselling, and other similar professions has a code of ethics which is designed, among other things, to protect the user from exploitation or misconduct. Some commentators describe the social worker–user relationship as a 'fiduciary' one – that is, based on a relationship of trust (Levy, 1976, pp. 55ff.; Kutchins, 1991).

While there are many similarities between social work and professions like law and medicine, there are also several ways in which social work is different. Some have argued that social work is a 'semi-profession', partly because the individual autonomy of social workers is more limited than that of doctors and lawyers. Many social workers are either directly or indirectly employed by local authorities; they have a social control function and therefore their primary aim is not straightforwardly to work in the best interests of the user. The social worker also functions as part of the welfare state which is itself based on contradictory principles and which is undergoing a process of questioning and change (Langan, 1993), as is the role of the professions generally (Southon and Braithwhaite, 2000).

Social work and the welfare state

Social work is part of a state-organised and state-funded system for distributing goods and services to meet certain types of social needs of individuals, families, groups and communities and to cure, contain or control behaviour that is regarded as socially problematic or deviant. It is part of a welfare state which organises and funds a range of other social services, including education, health, social security and housing, and other public services such as the police, the army, roads and refuse collection. These are collective services which, in principle, benefit the whole community. However, social services are often regarded as different from public services in that they are seen as a means of transferring resources to people who are dependent – through sickness, old age, childhood, unemployment, disability, for example. Welfare states are allied to capitalist economies and have a redistributive role through taxation, compulsory social insurance and direct provision of services. They can be seen as compensating for defects in the market system in the allocation of goods and services.

Many commentators have analysed the nature of the welfare state in terms of contradictions. Marshall (1972) saw the tensions inherent in welfare capitalism between the values of social justice and equality and the competitive individualism of the market, though he recognised that the aim of the welfare state is not to remove inequality of income, rather it is to eradicate poverty and give everyone equal status as citizens in society. According to O'Connor (1973, p. 6) the welfare state has two contradictory functions in capitalist societies – accumulation (enabling private capital to remain profitable) and legitimation (of the existing economic and social order). Moon succinctly summarises the contradictory principles upon which the welfare state is based as follows:

> The welfare state embraces the market, but at the same time seeks to limit and control it; it incorporates ideas of rights, especially rights to property and the fruits of one's labor, but asserts a right to welfare, a right to have one's basic needs met; it is based on a conception of the person as a responsible agent but recognizes as well that many of the conditions of one's life are due to circumstances beyond one's control; it is premised upon sentiments of sociability and common interest, but its very success may under-

mine those sentiments; it seeks to provide security, but embraces as well a commitment to liberty. (Moon, 1988, p. 12)

Moon suggests that this is one reason why the welfare state appears to be so vulnerable to criticism. Others might disagree that it is the contradictions *per se* that make it vulnerable (Offe, 1984, ch. 5), but there is no doubt that the whole concept of the welfare state – its aims, its functions, its methods and its outcomes – is the subject of questioning and criticism from various quarters, both right and left (Pierson, 1998; Roger, 2000). The economic recession of the mid-1970s gave rise to a sustained critique of the welfare state from right-wing politicians and theorists, and this was reinforced by the recession of the late 1980s/early 1990s. First, the burden of taxation and regulation imposed on capital is claimed to serve as a disincentive to investment. Second, welfare benefits and the collective power of trades unions amount to a disincentive to work. The argument has also been made from a communitarian perspective that family values and responsibilities, a sense of community and moral obligation may, in fact, be undermined by the welfare state (Etzioni, 1995, 1997). Criticisms from the left tend to focus on the ineffectiveness and inefficiency of the welfare bureaucracies, which have done little to redistribute income between classes and do not tackle the fundamental causes of poverty and unemployment. Feminist and anti-racist critiques have been increasingly vocal as many aspects of the welfare state have been shown to reinforce gender and race stereotyping, discrimination and oppression. The welfare state is also seen as a repressive instrument of social control (through individualising problems and distinguishing between the deserving and undeserving).

This discussion of social work as part of the welfare state is important as it helps us understand how some of the ethical issues are inherent in the role of the social worker. As part of the welfare state it is based on contradictions and societal ambivalence. Social work contributes towards expressing society's altruism (care) and enforcing societal norms (control); it champions individual rights as well as protecting the collective good. Social workers are regarded as wimps (caring for those who do not deserve it) and as bullies (wielding too much power over individuals and families). As the welfare state is questioned, undermined and reformed, so the role of social work is also subject to question and change.

Blame and guilt in social work

The position of social workers in the welfare state not only places them at the heart of the contradictions of the welfare state itself, but also leads to them bearing the brunt of the blame for certain unpalatable societal problems such as child abuse. One of the most publicised areas of social work is child protection. In this context, if a bad outcome occurs, social workers usually get the blame. A bad outcome can be either that children left at home suffer or die, or that children are removed from home unnecessarily. Franklin (1989) demonstrates how the press often portray social workers either as indecisive wimps who fail to protect children from death, or as authoritarian bullies who unjustifiably snatch children from their parents. Either way, the social workers are to blame. As Franklin comments:

> Press reporting of child abuse, paradoxically, rarely focuses upon the abuse of children. It quickly regresses into an attack on welfare professionals, particularly social workers who, in their turn, seem to have become a metaphor for the public sector. (Franklin, 1989, p. 1)

Social workers can be seen as symbols of the welfare state, simultaneously representing two of its much criticised facets – bungling inefficiency and authoritarian repression. Although Aldridge (1994, p. 70) argues that 'social work and its vicissitudes are not singled out for vilification' by the press, it nevertheless offers a soft target when its interventions fail. Social workers, Franklin claims, seem to have a unique place among professionals in being regarded as culpable by the press for the fate of their users. This may be partly connected with the more ambivalent and morally charged role that social workers play in society. For example, doctors treat people who are sick; and sickness might be regarded as an unfortunate state which generally affects individuals through no fault of their own. Social workers are often working with people whom society regards as 'undeserving', idle, feckless or deviant. They have a control as well as a care function. It is their job to protect society from deviant or morally dangerous people; if they fail to do this job, they are committing a moral crime. Physical and sexual abuse of children, particularly by their parents, is a threat to social stability and the idea of the family as a good and caring setting. Child abuse in families, therefore, must not happen. It must either be prevented by social workers (and therefore barely exist) or not exist at all. Social workers' vilification by the press and public is partly due to their role as welfare professionals in a society that is ambivalent about the welfare state and also the particular role they play within the welfare state which includes both the care and control of people whom the family or other state agencies cannot help and who may be regarded as difficult or deviant.

Social workers tend to feel that they should not always take the blame in cases where children are abused or die. The situation is complex: resource constraints mean that social workers cannot always provide the services required; decisions regarding how to handle children at risk are usually taken by interprofessional groups at case conferences and are a shared responsibility; assessing the nature of risk of child abuse is an uncertain art and even the most skilled and competent professionals who follow all the guidelines and procedures may find a child dies. Obviously if workers fail to follow the procedures correctly or neglect to carry out specified duties, then they are culpable. Yet if a worker does the best she can in the circumstances, surely she should not be blamed? This is certainly the line taken by Macdonald (1990) and seems to make sense to most social workers. However, it is not the view of Hollis and Howe, who claim that it is justifiable to blame social workers for bad outcomes (such as child deaths) even if they have done their well-intentioned best. Social workers must accept this as part of their role, which involves a high level of moral risk. They suggest that:

> the social worker would receive better sympathy, if her responsibility for bad outcomes was understood to be personal yet, at the same time, a function of the role rather than of self-evident personal incompetence. (Hollis and Howe, 1990, p. 548)

Their view, they suggest, helps explain why professional social workers are troubled by guilt even when they have done their best.

Hollis and Howe are, in a sense, putting social work decision-making back into the sphere of the moral, suggesting that the more comfortable retreat into the bureaucratic and technical (following

procedures and making technical 'risk assessments') is not an appropriate response to public blame. Yet, in order to do this, is it necessary for Hollis and Howe to go so far as to say that social workers
should always be blamed for a bad outcome? Their view depends
upon accepting the premise that the outcomes of an action/decision
determine the nature of the action/decision. If the child survives and
thrives, the action was morally right; if the child dies, the action was
morally wrong. It appears that such decisions are what Nagel would
describe as 'decisions under uncertainty' (Nagel, 1976, p. 143), where
the overall moral judgement can shift from positive to negative
depending on the outcome. While we might agree that the death of
a child is a negative outcome, and that the social worker involved in
the case might have made a technically wrong decision not to remove
the child from the family, was it also a morally wrong decision?
Surely not, if the social worker gained as much information as possible, assessed the risk and made the judgement that the risk to the
child was low. We might even question whether the decision was
'technically' wrong. The social worker may have been right – the risk
was one in a hundred and the fact that this case was the one in a
hundred does not prove the social worker wrong – one might say
she was unlucky. Risk assessment in social work is not a precise,
scientific or straightforward business. It might be the case that
the technical decision is a 'decision under uncertainty', so we
would, in fact, say that the social worker's assessment was correct
or incorrect according to the outcome. However, to say that it is
morally right or wrong according to the outcome is surely going
too far.

That social workers feel 'guilt' for a bad outcome is not surprising. Yet in the same way that my friends would tell me not to feel
guilty for running over a young child who unexpectedly leapt out in
front of my car, surely we would say the same to the social worker.
We may torment ourselves by blaming ourselves and thinking 'if
only I had reacted more quickly; if only I had visited the family an
hour earlier', but what we should feel is regret, not guilt. I imagine
Hollis and Howe would respond that the cases are not analogous. In
fact, they liken the social worker to the driver of a car who nevertheless drives knowing the brakes are faulty. If I had run over the
child while driving with faulty brakes, then I would have been
morally blameworthy.

According to Hollis and Howe, in taking on the job of social worker, the worker knows that she is being asked to drive a car with faulty brakes. Therefore she must expect and accept moral blame when bad outcomes occur (as they inevitably will). Yet this analogy does not capture the complexity of social work practice. First, while this may not exonerate the social worker, it is important to note that it is not her job to service the car. Second, while she may be in the driving seat, there are plenty of others in the car map-reading or directing. Third, while objective observers like Hollis and Howe may claim that the brakes are faulty, the rest of society regards such a state as the norm, and is certainly not prepared to pay to improve the brakes. If social workers take moral responsibility, they are, in effect, allowing others to scapegoat them and avoid taking blame, and hence to avoid recognising the variety of contributing factors that caused the child's death and the need to change some of these factors. Also, if social workers take the blame, they become personally and professionally undermined and stressed. To allow oneself to be blamed for outcomes of which many of the causes are outside one's control is debilitating and draining. It may be appropriate to take some responsibility, and hence blame, but certainly not all of it. The retreat into 'defensive' social work (following rules and procedures) becomes even more necessary and appealing as a survival strategy.

One of the purposes of this book is to enable social workers to gain an understanding of the nature of ethical decision-making and hence to feel less guilt and blame for the outcomes of decisions and actions with which they are involved. Very often in connection with moral and ethical issues in social work (and indeed the caring professions generally) the term 'dilemma' is used. As has already been noted, a dilemma is usually defined along the lines of 'a choice between two equally unwelcome alternatives' – which seems to sum up quite well how it often feels to be a social worker in a 'no win' situation. For example, in a child protection case, if the child is removed from the family both the child and the mother will be unhappy and the child may have to spend some time in institutional care, which may be damaging. Yet if the child remains with the family, there is a chance that the child will suffer physical abuse from the father and may be injured or even die. The way to resolve the dilemma is to try to work out whether one of the alternatives is more unwelcome than the other and then act on that. Of course, we also need to try to work out how likely it is that each of the unwelcome outcomes will occur. We might decide that it is more unwelcome (indeed it would be tragic) for the child to die, than to be unhappy. But it is thought to be highly unlikely that the father will seriously injure or kill the child. So, on balance, it is decided to leave the child with the family. We know it is a risk – a moral risk as well as a technical one – which was why we described the situation as a dilemma. There are not welcome outcomes, only less unwelcome ones; when the choice is the lesser of two evils, whichever one chooses is an 'evil'. This is a constant problem for the social worker. If the social worker has carefully thought through all aspects of the dilemma, and made a decision to act in order to try to avoid the worst outcome, she has acted with moral integrity.

We will return to this important issue of the guilt and blame felt by social workers and will explore further how these can be counteracted at the end of the book, in the light of the more detailed discussion of ethical and value issues in the next few chapters.

Conclusions

In this chapter we have set the scene for our discussion of questions of ethics in social work. We have argued that ethical problems and dilemmas are inherent in the practice of social work. The reasons for this arise from its role as a public service profession dealing with vulnerable users who need to be able to trust the worker and be protected from exploitation; and also from its position as part of the welfare state which is itself based on contradictory aims and values (care and control; capital accumulation and legitimation; protection of individual rights and promotion of public welfare) which cause tensions, dilemmas and conflicts. The current 'crises' of the welfare state, which entail a questioning of both its legitimation function and its capital accumulation function, are increasing the tensions and dilemmas for social workers, who very often find themselves the victims of media attacks and public blame. We argued that this blame is often unjustified and it is important that social workers both understand their role at the sharp end of the contradictions of the welfare state and consider how moral decisions are actually made in social work, in order that they are not consumed by unnecessary guilt about the unfortunate, tragic, or unwanted outcomes of cases in which they have been involved.

Exercise 1

Aims of the exercise – to encourage readers to identify ethical issues in their own practice and to reflect on and clarify their own ethical stance.

1. Briefly describe a situation/incident/event in your experience as a practitioner which raised ethical issues for you.
2. List the ethical issues.
3. What does your view of this situation/event tell you about the important values/ethical principles that underpin your practice as a social worker?

2

Principle-based Approaches to Social Work Ethics

This chapter and the next will explore a number of approaches that have been or could be taken to theorising about ethics and social work. There are many ways of categorising approaches to ethics. For the purposes of this discussion I will divide the approaches into two broad kinds: those that focus on principles of action, which will be the subject of this chapter; and those that pay more attention to the character of the moral agents and their relationships with each other, which will be covered in the next chapter. I will draw on some of the theories of ethics developed by moral philosophers and on literature in other areas of professional ethics, particularly health care, to develop ideas as yet underexplored in the context of social work. Some caution must be exercised in relating theories of moral philosophy to professional ethics. When writers on professional ethics talk of 'Kantian' or 'utilitarian' approaches, they are not necessarily taking on board the whole of the ethical theories of Kant or utilitarianism, but rather suggesting that their approaches to professional ethics have connections with some of the basic orientations to morality found in those theories. The aim of these two chapters is to point out some of these connections to help to clarify the nature of different approaches to social work ethics.

Principles

The most common approach to professional ethics is to articulate a set of general ethical principles which give guidance about how we should act. According to Beauchamp (1996, pp. 80–1), a principle is:

a fundamental standard of conduct on which many other standards and judgements depend. A principle is an essential norm in a system of thought or belief, forming a basis of moral reasoning in that system.

It is important to distinguish a principle from a rule, which is much more specific and narrower in scope. For example, 'respect people's rights to self-determination' would count as a principle because its scope is broad, in that it applies to all people in all circumstances, whereas 'respect the rights of service users to consult files' is more specific in that it applies to people in a social work context who wish to see their files and would therefore be regarded as a rule. Principle-based theories of ethics usually construe ethical reasoning and decision-making as a rational process of applying principles and derived rules to particular cases and/or justifying action with reference to relevant rules and principles (for clear examples of such approaches in medical and nursing ethics see Beauchamp and Childress, 1994, pp. 14–17; Edwards, 1996). We will briefly look at three principle-based approaches which can be loosely linked with Kantian, utilitarian and common-morality approaches in moral philosophy.

Respect and autonomy in the social work relationship: Kantian principles

Much of the literature on social work values and ethics has focused on lists of principles about how the social worker ought to treat the individual service user. Such lists of principles are often underpinned by one basic or ultimate principle formulated as 'respect for persons', which, it has been argued, is the foundation of social work ethics, and, indeed, any system of moral thinking (Plant, 1970). This principle is derived from Kant, the eighteenth-century German philosopher, who formulated it as a categorical imperative (that is, a command that must be adhered to), one version of which is: 'So act as to treat humanity, whether in your own person or that of any other, never solely as a means but always also as an end' (Kant, 1964, p. 96). By this he meant that we should treat others as beings who have ends (that is, choices and desires), not just as objects or a means to our own ends. The individual person is intrinsically worthy of respect simply because she or he is a person, regardless of whether we like the person, whether they are useful to us or whether they have behaved badly towards us. According to Kantian philosophy, a 'person' is a being who is capable of rational thought and self-determined action, where 'rational' means the ability to give reasons for actions; and 'self-determining' entails acting according to one's own choices and desires and having the ability to make decisions. 'Respect' can be regarded as an 'active sympathy' towards another human being (Downie and Telfer, 1969, 1980).

It is this aspect of Kantian moral philosophy, the principle of respect for persons, that has been the most influential in social work ethics. It focuses on the content of morality, explicitly stating how we should treat other people. Other features of Kant's theory are also important in relation to professional ethics. He did, in fact, formulate several other versions of his categorical imperative, one of which focuses on the importance of consistency and universalisability in the form of moral judgements: 'Act only on that maxim through which you can at the same time will that it should become a universal law' (Kant, 1964, p. 88). The example of promise-keeping can be used to illustrate this point. In order to get a loan, I may be tempted to promise to repay the money borrowed, although I have no intention of doing so. The maxim I might act on in this case might be something along the lines of: 'I will make a false promise if it will get me out of difficulty'. However, if I ask whether I could consistently will that this should become a universal principle applying to everybody, Kant's answer would be 'no'. For if everybody made false promises, the whole institution of promise-keeping would collapse and there would be no basis for getting loans at all. So if I could not will that everybody should do this, then such an action would be morally wrong. It is important to stress that for Kant, making false promises is not wrong because of the consequences if everyone did so, but rather that it would be logically inconsistent to will that everyone should do it, because I would then be making a promise in a world where promise-keeping no longer existed. This highlights a very important feature of Kantian ethics, the stress on rationality and the importance of the will. According to Kant, the only good action is that which is done from a sense of duty (as opposed to inclination). We work out what is our duty through a process of logical reasoning. We are, like all our fellow human beings, rational and autonomous – that is, we are free to make our own decisions and choices; we ourselves make the moral law and give it to ourselves.

There have been numerous criticisms as well as many defences and developments of Kantian ethics (for brief summaries see Arrington, 1998, pp. 262–94; Norman, 1998, pp. 70–91; for the debate in social work see Downie, 1989; Webb and McBeath, 1989, 1990). Many of the criticisms have tended to focus on Kant's formalism (his stress on the form of moral judgements as universalisable and consistent) at the expense of the content of morality, and on his moral absolutism (for example, that lying is always wrong) and his stress on doing one's duty for its own sake as the only morally worthy motive. However, few have developed in any detail a wholly Kantian approach to social work ethics – although Bowie's (1999) application of Kantian moral philosophy to business ethics gives some idea of how it might be achieved. In social work, as I said earlier, the main element of Kantian moral philosophy that has been influential is the principle of respect for persons which has been used to underpin a set of general principles relating to the relationship between the individual social worker and service user.

The lists of principles of the social worker–user relationship developed for social work are often adaptations or modifications of the seven principles developed by Biestek, an American Catholic priest, in the late 1950s (Biestek, 1961). These principles have been surprisingly influential, especially given two factors. First, Biestek did not intend them as ethical principles *per se*. Indeed he seems to regard them primarily as principles for effective practice – instrumental to the social worker's purpose of 'helping the client achieve a better adjustment between himself and his environment' (Biestek, 1961, p. 12). Second, his emphasis is primarily on the voluntary one-to-one casework relationship, where the user initiates the contact by coming to the agency and relates individually to a social worker. This is somewhat removed from the complexities of modern social work which include compulsory intervention within a statutory framework and work with families, groups and communities. However, since the principles have been so influential, it may be useful to summarise them here (adapted from Biestek, 1961):

1. *Individualisation* is the recognition of each user's unique qualities, based upon the rights of human beings to be treated not just as a human being but as this human being.
2. *Purposeful expression of feelings* is the recognition of users' need to express their feelings (especially negative ones) freely. The

caseworker should listen purposefully without condemnation and provide encouragement when therapeutically useful.

3. *Controlled emotional involvement* is the caseworker's sensitivity to users' feelings, an understanding of their meaning and a purposeful, appropriate response to them.

4. *Acceptance* entails the caseworker perceiving and dealing with users as they really are, including their strengths and weaknesses, congenial and uncongenial qualities, maintaining throughout a sense of their innate dignity and personal worth.

5. *Non-judgemental attitude* entails that it is not part of the casework function to assign guilt or innocence or degrees of user responsibility for causation of problems, although evaluative judgements can be made about the attitudes, standards or actions of users (that is, the caseworker does not judge users themselves, but their behaviour).

6. *User self-determination* is the recognition of the right and need of users to freedom in making their own choices and decisions in the casework process. Caseworkers have a duty to respect that need and help activate users' potential for self-direction. Biestek stresses, however, that users' rights to self-determination are limited by their capacity for positive and constructive decision-making, by civil and moral law and by the function of the agency.

7. *Confidentiality* is the preservation of secret information concerning the user which is disclosed in the professional relationship. Biestek describes confidentiality as based upon a basic right of users and as an ethical obligation for the social worker, as well as being essential for effective casework service. However, users' rights are not absolute and may be limited by a higher duty to self, by rights of other individuals, the social worker, agency or community.

During the 1960s and 1970s many other theorists adopted modified versions of Biestek's list of principles, often with the addition of the ultimate or basic principle of 'respect for persons', as Table 2.1 demonstrates.

A key theme running through all these principles could be identified as the Kantian theme of *respect for the individual person as a self-determining being*. It is significant that the first principle in the list, and one which has also been taken on board by all the other

Table 2.1 *Principles of the social work relationship*

| Principles | Examples of their adoption/modification | | | | | |
	Biestek (1961)	Moffet (1968)	Plant (1970)	CCETSW (1976)	Butrym (1976)	Ragg (1977)
Individualisation	*	*	*	*	*	*
Purposeful expression of feelings	*	*			*	*
Controlled emotional involvement	*				*	
Acceptance	*	*	*	*	*	
Non-judgemental attitude	*				*	
User self-determination	*	*	*	*	*	*
Confidentiality	*	*		*	*	
Respect for persons			*	*	*	*

writers noted in Table 2.1, is 'individualisation' – the recognition of each user's unique qualities based upon the right of human beings to be treated as individuals with personal differences. The other important principle which has also been adopted by all the other writers is 'user self-determination' – recognition of users' rights to freedom in making their own decisions and choices. Many of the subsequent writers have, in fact, included in their lists the basic or ultimate principle of 'respect for persons' and although Biestek himself did not include this principle in his list, his principles are compatible with it. Some of Biestek's principles directly follow from this ultimate principle – not just user self-determination, but also acceptance, non-judgementalism and confidentiality. Accepting a user as she is, rather then stereotyping or categorising, is obviously part of respecting the innate worth and dignity of every human being. Similarly with non-judgementalism – the social worker should not judge the person as unworthy, evil or inadequate. Breaking confidence would violate the principle of respect for persons, because it would entail not respecting the user's wishes, treating her, perhaps, as a means to an end.

Commentators on social work ethics and values in the 1980s, however, tended to move away from the 'list approach' and from the focus solely on the nature of the social worker–user relationship. There are a number of reasons why the kind of list of principles suggested by Biestek and others has been regarded as unsatisfactory. First, such broad general principles can be interpreted variously, and there are confusions both within and between writers using the same terminology. McDermott (1975) indicates, for example, that the term 'self-determination' is, in fact, defined persuasively in social work and that the favourable connotations of freedom from constraint are used to justify what amounts to a recommendation that the social worker should decide what users' real interests are and may be justified in promoting them against their will, a tendency which can be seen in the Biestek formulation. In fact, self-determination can mean all things to all people, from maintaining that each individual should be completely free to do whatever they want (a version of negative freedom which might be associated with a form of Kantian philosophy based on respect for persons), to justifying fairly large-scale intervention from the state to enable individuals to become more self-determining or self-realising (a version of positive freedom which might be associated with Hegelian or Marxist ethics). Within social work, interpretations at the negative end of the spectrum would tend to advocate freedom from restraint unless another's interests are threatened; whereas on a more positive view, a further clause is often added, 'and/or unless the person's own interests are threatened'.

Similar problems regarding meaning arise for the principles of non-judgementalism, acceptance and confidentiality. For example, Stalley (1978) argues that non-judgementalism appears to be about refraining from making moral judgements about a person's character, yet, at the same time, social workers have a responsibility to society to help users, and to maintain their own moral integrity by making moral judgements. This raises the question of where we draw the lines around these principles, which can only be answered in relation to other principles within a more systematic framework of moral beliefs and principles. This is complicated by the second difficulty arising from such lists of principles, namely, that very little

indication is given of the status of the different principles. Some
appear to be methods for effective practice (for example, purposeful
expression of feelings), others might be regarded as professional
standards (for example, confidentiality), others might be classified as
general moral principles (such as self-determination) and one
(respect for persons) has been characterised as the basic presupposi-
tion of any morality.

A third problem is caused by the fact that many writers do not
rank the principles and no indication is given of what to do in cases
of conflicting principles. We may well ask what criteria are to be used
for judging whether to promote a user's self-determination at the
expense of revealing a confidential secret. Some theorists do state,
following Downie and Telfer (1969), that their sets of principles
follow directly from one ultimate principle, respect for persons. If
this were the case, then respect for persons could be referred to in
cases of conflict. However, apart from Plant, and to some extent
CCETSW (1976), little detail is given as to how respect for persons
can actually be used to justify the other principles, or how it can be
used in actual moral decision-making to arbitrate between principles. While Downie and Telfer do articulate a moral system for
social work based on respect for persons, they do not derive from it
the kinds of principles suggested in Table 2.1 as relevant to social
work. This may not be surprising, since these principles, if regarded
as moral principles, are certainly not complete for social work.
Indeed, as Biestek envisaged them they were more a set of principles
for effective casework, focusing on the *content of the relationship* –
how the individual user should be treated by the social worker.
In so far as moral matters were involved for Biestek, these centred
around notions of individual rights/liberties, rather than the questions of social justice and responsibility, which attention to the
context of the agency and society generally would raise for the social
worker.

Promoting welfare and justice in society: utilitarian principles

More recent writers on social work ethics have been critical of the
lists of principles focusing on the individual worker–user relationship within a broadly Kantian ethical framework, pointing out that

other types of moral principles also influence social work practice (Banks, 1990; Clark, 2000; Clark with Asquith, 1985; Horne, 1999; Rhodes, 1986). Social workers are not autonomous professionals whose guiding ethical principles are solely about respecting and promoting the self-determination of service users. They are employed by agencies, work within the constraints of legal and procedural rules and must also work to promote the public good or the well-being of society in general. Other types of ethical principles concerned with utility (promoting the greatest good) and justice (distributing the good(s) as widely and/or fairly as possible) are important. There may be conflicts between the rights or interests of different people – for example a parent and a child, a confused older man and his carer. Within a Kantian framework it is difficult to decide whose right to self-determination has priority. The Kantian approach also advocates always following one's duty no matter what the outcome. For example, lying is always wrong, because it would involve manipulating a person and failing to treat them with proper respect – even if by lying a life could be saved. Such an approach fails to take account of how social workers actually do behave. Very often they have to look to the consequences of their actions and weigh up which action would be least harmful/ most beneficial to a particular user, and which action would benefit most people or use resources most efficiently. This kind of ethical theory has been termed 'utilitarianism' (see Mill, 1972; Shaw, 1999).

The basic idea of utilitarianism is very simple – that the right action is that which produces the greatest balance of good over evil (the principle of utility). However, so many philosophers have added so many qualifications and modifications to enable this doctrine to capture more and more of our ordinary conceptions of morality that any discussion of what is known as utilitarianism becomes very complicated. First, Bentham and some recent philosophers equate the good with happiness (the sum of pleasures) and the bad with unhappiness (the sum of pains), espousing what has been called *hedonistic utilitarianism* (see Plamenatz, 1966; Smart and Williams, 1973), whereas others, notably Mill, claim that the good consists of other things besides happiness (for example, virtue, knowledge, truth, beauty), a view known as *ideal utilitarianism* (Mill, 1972). Second, some philosophers espouse what has been called *act utilitarianism*, which involves deciding the rightness of each action with reference directly to the principle of utility (Smart and Williams, 1973). Others advocate *rule utilitarianism*, claiming that we do in fact use rules to speed up the process of moral reasoning and decision-making, and that the rules themselves are tested and justified with reference to the principle of utility (Downie, 1971). For example, we adhere to the rule of promise-keeping despite the fact that on some occasions it might produce a greater balance of evil over good, because promise-keeping as a whole generally produces good. This has often been regarded as the most plausible account of utilitarianism and not surprisingly tends to result in the articulation of rules and principles (such as promise-keeping, truth-telling, not stealing, respecting autonomy) that would also be prominent in a Kantian system. However, utilitarians would have less tendency to regard these rules as absolute in the way Kant did, they would test their efficacy against the consequences they tend to produce and they might be more willing to admit of exceptions if this resulted in greater utility.

However, the principle of utility on its own tells us nothing about whose good we should promote, that is, about the distribution of the good. If we could choose between an action which produced a large amount of good (let us assume we are talking about happiness) for two people and nothing for eight people, and an action which produced slightly less total happiness, but distributed it equally between ten people, would we choose the former? This led Bentham to introduce his proviso – everyone to count for one and no one for more than one, and to Mill's formulation of the principle of utility as the greatest good of the greatest number. Here we seem to have a principle against which conflicts between derived principles and rules (if we are rule utilitarians) or between particular actions (if we are act utilitarians) can be decided. However, as critics have pointed out, we now have two principles, in effect: utility (urging us to produce as much good as possible) and justice (as equality of treatment, urging us to distribute it as widely as possible), which themselves may conflict. As Raphael (1981) suggests, the most difficult conflicts in life are between these two principles: he gives the example of whether the government should give large grants to engineering students in the national interest (utility) or the same amount to each student for the sake of fairness (justice). This difficulty does not mean utilitarianism cannot be defended as a system of morality, but if we accept it, it does mean that it cannot be regarded as a system which is founded on one ultimate principle which can be used to decide all conflicts between other principles, rules or alternative courses of action.

Approaches to social work ethics that are explicitly and wholly utilitarian have not been well-developed, partly because such approaches do not lend themselves to taking account of the personal relationship element of social work that has always been regarded as so crucial. Although Downie and Telfer (1980) attempt to develop a form of ideal rule utilitarianism for social work and medicine, in so far as they ground this in the principle of respect for persons, I would categorise it more as a combined Kantian–utilitarian approach which we will consider in the next section.

Aspects of utilitarianism can be discerned to some extent in the radical social work movement which gained momentum in the 1970s (see Corrigan and Leonard, 1978) and the anti-oppressive approaches of the 1980s and 1990s (see Dominelli, 1988, 1997; Langan and Lee, 1989; Thompson, 1993). Such approaches would tend to reject the Kantian principles of respect for the individual as a freely acting moral agent and focus on changing society and promoting the good of groups and classes of people. In this sense, if relevant principles were to be identified for the radical and anti-oppressive approaches, they would be variations on the themes of welfare and justice. However, we must be wary of attributing an ethical theory as such to these approaches. Although espousing some values which look to the consequences of action and stress the importance of the collective good, all radical and anti-oppressive approaches do not clearly fall into a utilitarian paradigm. For utilitarianism, like Kantianism, is premised on the notion of the freely acting individual. Radical approaches, in so far as they are based on Marxist theory, do not see the individual as the basic unit in society (an emphasis is placed on humans as social beings) and regard the idea of human freedom as a myth. The radical literature does not discuss ethics *per se*, and indeed Marx himself discussed morality as a 'bourgeois illusion' – part of the prevailing ideology promoted by the ruling classes to control and dominate (Marx and Engels, 1969; Lukes, 1987). Further, a key theme of radical social work (although not always expressed very clearly) is 'praxis' – the notion of 'committed action'. On this view it makes no sense to regard values, theory and practice as separate. These ideas will be expanded upon in the next chapter.

A 'common morality' approach: Kantian–utilitarian principles

The above discussions suggest that neither Kantian nor utilitarian theories of ethics can furnish us with one ultimate principle for determining the rightness and wrongness of actions. Both, being idealised theoretical systems of morality, inevitably fail to take account of certain aspects of our ordinary moral thinking. The Kantian system tends to emphasise the individual person and their rights and duties, particularly the principles of liberty and justice (as desert); utilitarianism stresses the notion of the public good, looking to the consequences of actions with respect to the principles of utility and justice (as equal treatment). Kantian ethical theory has a tendency to advocate rigidly following what is thought to be one's duty for its own sake, whereas utilitarianism focuses on amounts of good and evil in the abstract as opposed to the people who will experience the pleasure or whatever. Taken to its extreme, the Kantian doctrine might entail, for example, that in a particular case it was morally right to keep a promise even if this resulted in many people suffering (because the consequences or general utility would not be taken into account), whereas utilitarianism might entail that it was right to kill an innocent person for the good of society (because individual liberty would not be taken into account).

In so far as Kantians and utilitarians have attempted to modify their views to account for such cases, they become less distinct, at least in practice, even though they may be unwilling to relinquish the basic emphasis of their outlook. Interestingly, in the field of professional ethics, several influential theorists have advocated an approach that combines Kantian and utilitarian principles – recognising that in our ordinary moral thinking we do, in fact, draw on both. Downie and Telfer, in their book *Caring and Curing* (1980), advocate a form of ideal rule utilitarianism based on the ultimate principle of respect for persons. They argue that the principle of utility presupposes the principle of respect for persons. This argument is elaborated in their earlier book, *Respect for Persons* (1969, pp. 38–9). Taking Mill's formulation of the principle of utility (that right actions promote happiness), they claim that the reason we organise action to maximise happiness is because happiness matters; and it is unintelligible to suppose that happiness matters unless the people whose happiness is in question matter; and to say that they matter in this way is to say that they are objects of respect. The logic of Downie and Telfer's argument may be questioned. For example, we might ask whether individual persons are the only beings capable of experiencing happiness (what about groups or animals?) and indeed whether this sense of people mattering (being valued in themselves) is equivalent to being worthy of respect (which Downie and Telfer interpret as an active sympathy towards others as rational and self-determining agents). However, the important point to note is that they develop a framework for moral thinking which combines Kantian and utilitarian principles, such as liberty, equality, utility and fraternity (Downie, 1971), although by retaining respect for persons as the ultimate principle they still seem to be propounding a foundationalist ethical theory (that is, an ethical theory grounded in one ultimate principle).

Beauchamp and Childress (1994), on the other hand, in developing a principle-based approach for bioethics, explicitly eschew such foundationalist aspirations. They advocate what they call a 'common morality' theory which is both pluralistic (based on two or more non-absolute moral principles) and 'takes its premises directly from the morality shared in common by members of a society – that is, unphilosophical common sense and tradition' (Beauchamp and Childress, 1994, p. 100). They advocate four principles which they claim are usually accepted by rival moral theories: autonomy, beneficence, non-maleficence and justice. Although common morality ethics relies on ordinary shared beliefs for its content, Beauchamp and Childress stress that their principles are universal standards. They make use of Rawls's (1973, pp. 46–50) notion of 'considered judgements' as a starting point for ethical theory. These are the moral convictions in which we have the highest confidence and which we believe to have the lowest level of bias. In the context of medicine, Beauchamp and Childress (1994, p. 21) give the following example of a long-standing considered judgement: 'A physician must not exploit patients for the physician's own gain because the patient's interests come first.' However, such judgements are only provisional fixed points and are liable to revision – a process that Rawls terms 'reflective equilibrium'. This involves adjusting considered judgements so that they coincide and are rendered as coherent as possible. Taking the example about putting the patient's interests first, Beauchamp and Childress state that this needs to be made as coherent as possible with other considered judgements about clinical teaching responsibilities and responsibilities to patients' families, for example.

Principles and rules will never be perfectly coherent and will certainly conflict. They also need to be interpreted (what meanings do they have?), specified (when and how do they apply?) and balanced (which should have priority in certain types of cases?). According to Beauchamp and Childress (1994, p. 22) 'moral thinking is analogous to hypotheses in science that are tested, modified, or rejected through experience and experimental thinking'. Following Ross's (1930) account of '*prima facie* duties', they describe their four principles as *prima facie* principles – that is, we have a duty to uphold each of these principles unless it conflicts with or is overborne by another. When we face conflicts, between, say, respecting a person's request for confidentiality (autonomy) and saving that person's life (beneficence) then we have to make a judgement which involves interpreting the principles in the light of this situation, specifying how and why they apply and balancing them against each other. There is no ultimate principle or set of rules that can tell us how to do this in every possible type of case.

A common morality approach as such has not been explicitly developed for social work ethics in the level of detail offered by Beauchamp and Childress for bioethics. However, in so far as a principle-based approach is appropriate for social work ethics, then this would include a range of principles of both Kantian and utilitarian origin, which have the potential for conflict and which must be weighed up in making decisions in particular cases. Clark (2000, p. 143), in his recent book on social work ethics, identifies what he calls 'four stocks of ethical practice', also described as 'a set of definitive principles for ethically sound social work'. These are: respect (in the Kantian sense of respect for persons); justice (a comprehensive account including procedural, needs- and desert-based conceptions); citizenship (as rights to welfare); and discipline (as professional knowledge and expertise). His inclusion of 'discipline' marks his list out as different from some of the others in the academic literature, although it reflects preoccupations often found in professional codes of ethics. Other configurations of principles of varying levels of generality and specificity can be found in the literature. Horne (1999), for example, stays at a general level with the two traditional Kantian values of respect for persons and self-determination. Thompson (2000, pp. 106–23) is all-inclusive, presenting a list of 'traditional values' which includes Biestek's complete list along with 'Rogerian' principles of respect for persons, congruence, empathy and unconditional positive regard, in addition to a list of what he calls 'emancipatory values', namely: deindividualisation, equality, social justice, partnership, citizenship, empowerment and authenticity. Values and principles identifiable in codes of ethics vary in how they are expressed, but in the BASW code I identified five general principles: respect for persons; self-determination; promotion of human welfare; social justice; and professional integrity (Banks, 1998a).

Although there is not one commonly agreed and coherent set of principles for social work, by looking at the literature and at the actual practice of social work, I think it is possible to determine four basic or first-order principles which are relevant to social work:

1. Respect for and promotion of individuals' rights to self-determination.
2. Promotion of welfare or well-being.
3. Equality.
4. Distributive justice.

I do not present these as a 'definitive list' (especially bearing in mind the shortcomings of the 'list' approach as discussed earlier), but rather as a synthesis and reconfiguration of existing sets of principles. 'Respect for persons' has not been included as a separate principle, since it is subsumed within the right to self-determination and has often been characterised as the precondition of any morality at all, rather than as a principle alongside others. The principle of equality has been included as separate from justice, because although it can be subsumed within a conception of justice (social justice), in social work issues of equality, particularly in the context of anti-discriminatory and anti-oppressive practice, have been highlighted as particularly important. None of these principles is straightforward in meaning or implications for practice. I will briefly discuss each one.

1. *Self-determination* – various meanings of 'self-determination' have already identified, including:

   • *negative* – allowing someone to do as they choose;
   • *positive* – creating the conditions which enable someone to become more self-determining.

   Recent emphasis on user participation (allowing users to have a say) and empowerment (developing users' skills and self-confidence so they can participate more) are manifestations of negative and positive self-determination. Self-determination in both senses has been for a long time one of the fundamental principles stated for social work practice, often phrased as 'client self-determination'. Yet while the social worker may sometimes be able to focus largely on one individual user and take on the role of advocate for the user's rights, often the social worker has to take into account the rights of significant others in a situation. In the interests of justice, it may not always be morally right to promote the user's rights at the expense of those of others.

2. *Welfare* – promoting someone's 'good' or welfare is also open to interpretation depending upon what our view is of what counts as human welfare, and whether we adopt our own view of what a person's welfare is or the person's own conception of their welfare. It is dependent on cultural views about what are the basic human needs and what is a good quality of life. Much of modern social work is explicitly about ensuring that the best interests of particular user groups are served (for example, children in child protection work). Codes of ethics generally stress the social worker's duty to work in the user's interests. Often it is the social worker's view of what the user's interests are that is regarded as important. However, as with self-determination, whilst in some cases it may be clear-cut that it is the user's interests the social worker should be protecting, in other cases the social worker has to consider the interests of significant others and the 'public interest' (for example, through preventing reoffending in work with young offenders). These various interests may conflict.

3. *Equality* – according to Spicker (1988, p. 125), equality means 'the removal of disadvantage'. This can be interpreted in many ways including:

   - *Equal treatment* – preventing disadvantage in access to services, including treatment without prejudice or favour. For example, it should not be the case that a middle-class white man seeking resources for his elderly mother is dealt with more quickly than a black woman seeking similar support.
   - *Equal opportunity* – the removal of disadvantage in competition with others, giving people the means to achieve socially desired ends. For example, a social worker may arrange for an interpreter for a Bengali-speaking woman so that she can express her needs in detail and have the same opportunity as an English-speaking user to receive the services she requires.
   - *Equality of result* – in which disadvantages are removed altogether. For example, the residential home that would provide the best-quality care for two older users with similar needs is very expensive. The user with a rich son who is prepared to pay is able to go to this home; the user who is poor is not. To achieve equality of result might entail the social services department paying the full fee for the poorer user, or, to avoid stigmatisation, the state providing free high-quality care for all people with similar needs.

   Social workers are concerned to promote all three forms of equality, although equality of treatment is much easier to achieve than equality of opportunity or result. Equality of treatment would follow logically from the principle of respect for persons. Equality of opportunity and of result require some more positive action to redress existing disadvantages, and may require additional resources or changes in government policy. To aim for equality of result may require structural changes in society – challenging certain people's existing rights to wealth, property and power. It is this type of principle that underpins some of the more radical and anti-oppressive approaches to social work.

4. *Distributive justice* – is about distributing goods according to certain rules and criteria. The criteria for distribution may be selected:

- according to people's already existing rights (for example, property rights);
- according to desert;
- according to need.

Although justice and equality are linked, and some commentators would argue that equality is subsumed within justice, this depends upon which concept of justice is being used. A concept of justice based on property rights or desert may result in inequality. Rawls's (1973) concept of justice, for example, is based on two principles: equality in the assignment of basic needs and resources; and social and economic inequalities only in so far as there are compensating benefits for everyone, especially the least advantaged. Although distributive justice *per se* is generally not listed amongst the social work principles, it is perhaps one of the most fundamental principles in the work (in so far as it is in the public sector) in that social workers are responsible for distributing public resources (whether they be counselling, care or money) according to certain criteria based variously on rights, desert and need. I would argue that this principle is in operation in much social work decision-making and is becoming more central in the present climate as resource allocation becomes a more common role for social workers.

Conclusions

In this chapter we have explored some of the philosophical foundations of approaches to social work ethics. We have argued that principle-based approaches have tended to dominate professional ethics, that the stated principles of the profession have been broadly 'Kantian', resting on the doctrine of respecting the individual as a rational and self-determining human being and focusing on the *content* of the social worker–user relationship. However, the *context* in which social work is practised, as part of a welfare bureaucracy with a social control and resource-rationing function (based on more utilitarian values), also places ethical duties upon the social worker which may conflict with her duties to the user as an individual. These conflicts reflect the tensions and contradictions of the welfare state discussed in Chapter 1. It was argued that a combined Kantian–utilitarian approach might better encapsulate our ordinary moral thinking and that a set of key principles for social work might comprise promoting the self-determination of the service user, welfare, equality and distributive justice.

3

Character and Relationship-based Approaches to Social Work Ethics

There have been many critiques of 'principlism' in professional ethics, particularly the version developed by Beauchamp and Childress (1994), and indeed of Kantian and utilitarian approaches to morality. These critiques have come from several directions, arguing that a principle-based approach to ethics (including professional ethics) places too much stress on actions (as opposed to the person doing the action), the rational and impartial nature of ethical decision-making and the universality of principles. This ignores important features of the moral life and moral judgements, including the character, motives and feelings of the moral agent, the particular contexts in which judgements are made and the particular relationships and commitments people have to each other. We will now consider two alternatives to this impartialist and action-based approach to ethics, 'virtue ethics' and the 'ethic of care'. These have not been well-developed for social work, but we will discuss the extent to which they may be applicable.

The importance of character in the professional role: virtue-based approaches

In recent years in the field of philosophical ethics there has been a revival of virtue ethics (Crisp, 1996; Crisp and Slote, 1997; MacIntyre, 1985; Slote, 1992; Statman, 1997). Whilst there are many versions, including that stemming from Aristotle, what they have in common is a focus on the character or dispositions of moral agents as opposed to abstract obligations, duties or principles for action.

One of the reasons suggested for the growing popularity of virtue ethics is the failure of the attempts of Kantians and utilitarians to articulate sets of principles for right action. As Statman (1997, p. 6) comments:

> principles are just too abstract to provide helpful guidance in the complicated situations met in everyday ethics. These situations typically involve conflicting considerations, to which principle-ethics either offers no solution, or formulates higher order principles of preference, which, again, are too abstract and vague to offer any real help.

Virtue ethics is an approach 'according to which the basic judgements in ethics are judgements about character' (Statman, 1997, p. 7). In Hursthouse's version of virtue ethics, an action is right if it is what a virtuous agent would do in the circumstances; a virtue is 'a character trait a human being needs to flourish or live well' (Hursthouse, 1997, p. 229). What counts as 'living well' or 'flourishing' then becomes an important question in deciding what characteristics count as virtues. Some virtue theorists argue that these vary according to different time periods and cultures (for example, the kinds of characteristics cultivated as virtues in ancient Greece may not all be applicable in twenty-first-century Europe); others claim that there are universal virtues. Nevertheless, the kinds of dispositions usually regarded as virtues include courage, integrity, honesty, truthfulness, loyalty, wisdom and kindness, for example. A virtuous person will tell the truth, it would be argued, not because of some abstract principle stating 'you shall not lie', or because on this occasion telling the truth will produce a good result, but because they do not want to be the sort of person who tells lies. Virtue ethics also tends to emphasise the particular relationships people have with each other. It could be argued that it makes more sense to see my kindness towards my best friend as arising out of the fact that I have a relationship of friendship with her, I like her and care about her, rather than from some abstract moral principle about promoting the welfare of others.

If we are to develop a virtue-based ethics for social work, we need to consider what are the virtues of the social worker. In one sense, they should reflect the virtues recognised in society at large. According to MacIntyre, the virtues are relative to culture and role; they are qualities 'the possession and exercise of which tends to enable us to achieve those goods which are internal to practices' (MacIntyre, 1985, p. 191). While not all virtue theorists adopt this kind of view, the importance of roles and the idea of virtues as relative to 'practices' or communities of practitioners are useful if we are to attempt to articulate a virtue-based theory for professional ethics. We would have to ask ourselves what it means to be a 'good social worker'. 'Good' would be internal to the role of social worker and would be defined by the community of practitioners who do social work.

There have been few attempts to develop a virtue-based approach in the context of professional ethics, although Solomon (1992, 1997) does so for business ethics. However, Rhodes (1986, p. 42) claims:

> a virtue-based ethics seems particularly appropriate to professions, because the ethical issues so often focus in the nature of the relationships and our responsibilties in those relationships – to the client, other colleagues, our supervisors, the agency itself. What sort of person ought a 'professional' social worker to be? What is human excellence in that context?

In her book on ethical dilemmas in social work, Rhodes (1986, p. 44) claims to have 'adopted the questions appropriate to a virtue-based ethics'. This involves, she says, considering what our relationships ought to be to our service users, the agency, the profession, colleagues and society; what sort of human excellence we are striving for; and in what social and political context. Whilst Rhodes does give consideration to these questions, she does not explicitly or in any depth develop a virtue-based theory for social work ethics. She only briefly touches on the kinds of virtues that might be appropriate for social work, identifying from textbooks on social workers' responsibilities virtues such as compassion, detached caring, warmth and honesty. She also suggests some additional virtues that might seem appropriate: a certain kind of moral courage, hopefulness and humility (Rhodes, 1986, pp. 42–3). Beauchamp and Childress (1994, p. 463), when considering the virtues in bioethics (which they acknowledge are an important complement to principles), identify compassion, discernment, trustworthiness and integrity as important, along with others which they think correspond to their key principles: respectfulness, non-malevolence, benevolence, justice, truthfulness and faithfulness.

Clark (2000, pp. 49ff.), whilst not mentioning virtue ethics or explicitly proposing a set of qualities or character traits, in expounding a set of eight rules of ethical practice for social work nevertheless frames some of them in terms of the qualities of the social worker. Four of these 'rules' state that social workers should be: knowledgeable and skilful; careful and diligent; effective and helpful; legitimate and authorised. Others are framed as qualities of social work practice ('ethical practice is respectful'); social work services (services should be offered in a manner that is honest and truthful); and of professionals and agencies (as reputable and creditable). The final 'rule' is 'collaborative and accountable' which is referred to as a principle ('the principle of collaborative working') as well as a quality of professionals. Although not clearly elaborated as a set of virtues, this list demonstrates the way in which qualities or character traits are regarded as important components of social work ethics and are frequently undifferentiated conceptually from principles and rules of action.

There is no doubt, therefore, that developing certain traits of character, being a certain sort of person, is important in professional ethics, even if academic writing on professional ethics has tended to focus more attention on the articulation of general ethical principles and their use in rational moral decision-making. Indeed, many codes of ethics stress the kind of person a professional should be, as well as listing principles of ethical action, although interestingly few of the current codes in the caring professions contain reference to character traits (see Banks, 1999, pp. 15–16), which is probably a reflection of the recent shift of attention towards principles and actions. Actions are more concrete and measurable than traits of character. However, CCETSW (1995), when discussing the values of social work, in addition to producing a list of principles states that it is essential that social workers are honest, trustworthy, reliable, self-aware and critically reflective. This kind of statement relates to certain views about what it means to be a professional. A virtue ethicist would argue that it is less important that professionals claim to abide by explicit sets of rules stating that they will not discriminate on grounds of religion and gender, for example, or that they will not exploit service users, than that they are particular types of people who have a disposition to act justly and in a trustworthy fashion. They are trustworthy, and therefore act in a trustworthy fashion, not because of a rule devised by their professional association, but because being trustworthy is part of what it means to be a good professional. However, this still leaves terms like 'trustworthy', 'just', 'honest', 'competent' to be explored.

Lists of virtues can be criticised in the same way as lists of values or ethical principles as being abstract and unhelpful in making everyday ethical decisions. It could also be argued that virtue ethics can be subsumed within principle-based ethics; that being a just person simply consists in a disposition to act justly. Therefore our moral judgements must be grounded in judgements about people's actions rather than their characters. This is an area that warrants much more discussion in the context of professional ethics. But it is interesting to note that even Beauchamp and Childress (1994, p. 462), often held up as the major exponents of principlism in professional ethics, devote a whole chapter in the fourth edition of their textbook on biomedical ethics to virtues in professional life and acknowledge that:

> Principles require judgement, which in turn depends on character, moral discernment, and a person's sense of responsibility and accountability . . . Often what counts most in the moral life is not consistent adherence to principles and rules, but reliable character, moral good sense, and emotional responsiveness.

The caring relationship between professional and service user: an 'ethic of care'

The theme of emotional responsiveness is a key element in what has been termed 'an ethic of care'. Okin (1994) points out that virtue ethicists, following Aristotle, have tended to focus on virtues such as justice, courage, honesty and generosity, while paying little attention to the kinds of virtues needed in order to help others. It is not surprising that the virtues put forward by Aristotle should be those appropriate to 'upper-status males', since in ancient Greece women and slaves were not regarded as citizens. Yet this tendency is also reflected in much recent work on virtue ethics where the kinds of virtues that might be displayed principally by women, for example, in nurturing and caring for their families, are largely ignored. Okin suggests that such virtues might include the capacity to nurture, patience, the ability to listen carefully and to teach well, and the readiness to give up one's own projects in order to pay attention to the needs or projects of others (Okin, 1994, p. 228). Since Okin wrote this article, MacIntyre (1999) has taken some account of the importance of the virtues in relation to human vulnerability and disability and dependence on others, but he does not focus on care as such.

Such qualities of caring and particular attention are the focus of an 'ethic of care', which has been particularly associated with feminist approaches to ethics. The majority of the proponents of care ethics have not located themselves within the virtue ethics tradition, although they do share the rejection of impartialist principle-based approaches to ethics and a concern with particularities and relationships. Recent developments of an ethic of care owe much to the empirical work of the psychologist Gilligan (1982), who identified two 'moral voices' in her interviews with people about how they conceptualised and spoke about moral dilemmas. She contrasts the 'ethic of care' with what she calls the 'ethic of justice'. The ethic of justice refers to principle-based approaches to ethics, including Kantian and utilitarian moralities, which are based on a system of individualised rights and duties, emphasising abstract moral principles, impartiality and rationality. Gilligan argues that this is a very male-oriented system of morality which does not take account of approaches to ethics which tend to be adopted by women. This would emphasise responsibility rather than duty and relationships rather than principles – an 'ethic of care'. Gilligan herself is equivocal about the extent to which an ethic of care should be regarded as a 'female' or 'feminine' ethics, although others in this tradition (such as Noddings, 1984) explicitly adopt this kind of view.

Many feminists, however, have argued that it is both dangerous and misleading to attribute what has been termed an 'ethic of care' simply to women (Farley, 1993; Okin, 1994; Tronto, 1993). It may tend to reinforce essentialist views of women as 'merely' carers and leave unquestioned whether the caring role itself can have a negative and damaging effect on carers. Furthermore, research has shown that Afro-Americans, for example, adopt a view of the self which stresses a sense of cooperation, interdependence and collective responsibility, as opposed to the ethic of justice (Tronto, 1993, p. 84). This is echoed in Graham's (1999) account of an African-centred paradigm for social work which emphasises values relating to the importance of interpersonal relationships, a holistic view of the interconnnectedness of all things and the collective nature of identity. Tronto argues that an ethic of justice represents the dominant mode of moral thinking which reflects the power structure in society and tends to marginalise and exclude the experience of women, black people and working-class and other oppressed groups. The distinction between an ethic of care and an ethic of justice is summarised in Table 3.1 which is based on material from Farley (1993).

It may seem surprising, given social work's caring role, that little work has been done so far to examine the relevance of an ethic of care to social work. Some work has been done, however, in the field of nursing and there is a growing literature in this area (for example, Allmark, 1995; Bowden, 1997; Bradshaw, 1996; Hanford, 1994; Kuhse, 1997). The philosophical work of Noddings (1984), who argues that the caring relationship is ethically basic, has been particularly influential in nursing where it has been used both as a basis for the nurse–patient relationship and to provide a theoretical basis for nursing ethics. According to Noddings (1984, p. 30), caring involves 'feeling with' the other, which she explicitly distinguishes from empathy (putting oneself in the other's shoes). She describes caring as 'receiving the other into myself' or what she calls 'engrossment' (p. 33). She talks of this as the 'subjective–receptive' mode in which we see clearly what we have received from the other. She distinguishes this from instrumental thinking – the use of reasoning to work out what to do once we have committed ourselves to doing something – but claims that rationality 'does not of necessity mark either the initial impulse or the action that is undertaken' (p. 36). Noddings develops her thinking in some depth to show how her approach applies to caring for strangers and for people for whom we do not naturally care; she also applies it particularly to the

Table 3.1   *Ethics of justice and care*

	Justice	*Care*
Key value	Justice – reinforces separation of persons	Care – represents connectedness
Appeal to	Principles	Relationships
Focus on	Social contracts, ranked order of values, duty, individual freedom	Cooperation, communication, caring, relationship between persons

teacher–pupil relationship. Noddings is sceptical of the value of principles and rules *per se* and focuses on the concrete features of particular situations and our relationships to other people. She gives as an example Abraham's willingness to sacrifice his son Isaac: 'under the gaze of an abstract and untouchable God, he would destroy *this* touchable child whose real eyes were turned upon him in trust, love and fear' (p. 43).

While Noddings and other care ethicists have drawn our attention to important aspects of morality often lacking in traditional ethical theories, many critics question whether the ethic of care is sufficient to offer a complete account of either ethics in general or nursing ethics in particular. Kuhse (1997, p. 45) suggests that 'dispositional care' (an emotional response, a concern for the other, attentiveness and responsiveness to the needs of the other) is a necessary but not sufficient condition for nursing ethics, arguing that an adequate ethics needs impartiality or justice as well as care. It is very important that we are attentive to the nature of situations and sensitive to people's feelings, needs and the potential for hurt or harm. Kuhse gives an example taken from Blum (1988) where two adults are watching children playing in a park. One adult does not see that one of the children is being too rough and is in danger of harming the other child. The other adult, being more attentive and sensitive does, and hence sees the need to intervene. This enables the second adult to act on the principle 'protect children from harm'.

Care alone, therefore, is not enough for an adequate ethics. As Kuhse also points out, caring can sometimes be harmful (overbearing or stifling for the person on the receiving end), it can be narrow and parochial (as with the mother who only cares for her own child) and its focus only on the maintenance of the caring relationship means it can result in us failing to challenge racism or lying (if, as in an example given by Noddings, my father is racist and I put my care for him above all else). A care ethics, in focusing on the one-to-one relationship, does not help us in deciding how to allocate scarce resources between different patients or service users, or in judging matters of policy. Issues of fairness, justice and equality are an equally important aspect of a professional's role – a feature which is perhaps even more evident in social work than in nursing.

We may conclude that an ethic of care that can take into account the particularity of each situation, people's relationships with each other, cooperation, communication and caring is important and complementary to an ethic of justice which stresses universal principles, individual freedom, social contracts and duty. An overemphasis in professional ethics on the latter may result in over-regulation, a damaging impartiality and neutrality and a mindless following of rules for their own sake. As Baier (1995, p. 48) comments, justice is found to be too 'cold' and 'it is 'warmer' more communitarian virtues and social ideals that are being called in to supplement it'. Yet, at the same time, in the delivery of publicly funded and organised services, universally applicable rules are an important part of what defines the work of the professional delivering these services. It is not expected that professional workers will give preferential treatment to their neighbour's daughter over and above a stranger, for example, although they might in everyday life. An ethic of care and an ethic of justice are not mutually exclusive, but are, as Mendus argues, 'complementary facets of any realistic account of morality' (Mendus, 1993, p. 18).

The fragmentation of value: moral pluralism

Each of these different approaches to ethics, including the principle-based approaches discussed in the previous chapter, seems to have something to offer, but none offers a complete account of morality. There is no doubt that principles and rules play an important role in professional ethics and that one of the important features of a professional is that she should act impartially, without favouritism, treating people in similar circumstances in similar ways and giving a reasoned account of why she acted as she did. Both Kantian and utilitarian principles are frequently invoked in professional decision-making. Yet it seems equally important that professionals are educated to develop attitudes and dispositions which make them the kinds of people who are honest, trustworthy, caring, sensitive and discerning and that they pay attention to the context of each situation and the special relationships they have with people. Surely all these are features of any comprehensive picture of what it is to be moral and to act morally?

Nagel (1979), noting the conflicts that often occur in moral decision-making, suggests that these arise because there are several fundamentally different types of value which cannot be ranked or weighed against each other on a single scale. Although he does not explicitly relate the types of values to particular theories of ethics, I think it is possible to make some connections which I have included in brackets:

1. *General rights* that everyone has that function as constraints on action, such as rights to liberty or freedom from coercion (related to Kantian principles);
2. *Utility*, which takes into account the effects of what one does on everyone's welfare (a utilitarian focus on the ends of human action);
3. *Perfectionist ends* or values, that is, the instrinsic value of certain achievements or creations apart from their value to individuals (a non-utilitarian focus on the ends of human action, which may allow for religious values);
4. *Specific obligations* to other people or institutions which arise out of deliberate undertakings or special relationships (virtue and care approaches);
5. *Commitments to one's own projects* and undertakings (personal commitments which may link with the virtue ethicist's idea of desiring to be a certain sort of person or pursuing excellence. This is different from self-interest).

Sometimes there is only one significant factor in a moral decision – for example, personal obligation – and this makes things easier. On other occasions decision-making may be insulated against the influence of more than one type of factor – for example, in the judicial system which tries to limit itself to claims of right. But on many occasions several different types of value are pertinent and according to Nagel (p. 134) there can be no system for ranking these values because they are fundamentally incommensurable:

> Human beings are subject to moral and other motivational claims of very different kinds. This is because they are complex creatures who can view the world from many perspectives – individual, relational, impersonal, ideal, etc. – and each perspective presents a different set of claims.

However, we nevertheless do have to make decisions when faced with conflicting and incommensurable claims. This requires good judgement – what Aristotle (1954) called practical wisdom, which Nagel

(p. 135) claims reveals itself over time in individual decisions rather than in the enunciation of general principles. 'Good judgement' is a characteristic of the professional that will be explored further later in this book. It can be linked with the notion of the reflective practitioner and requires among other things the ability to learn from and reflect on experience, a sensitivity to people's feelings and situations, attentiveness to features of situations and an ability to reason.

Nagel's argument for what Norman (1998, p. 200) calls 'moral pluralism' seems very plausible in relation to ethics in general. But how does it fit with professional ethics? Could professional ethics fall into a category like the judicial system which by its very nature is artificially insulated from certain types of value? Although there has tended to be an emphasis on principles in the form of general rights based on Kantian principles, we have seen how utilitarian principles are also important, and character traits and specific obligations, whilst underplayed, do not seem irrelevant considerations in professional ethics. Indeed, Beauchamp and Childress (1994, p. 111) while adopting 'principlism' in relation to bioethics, nevertheless reject the assumption that one must defend a single type of moral theory that is solely principle-based, virtue-based, and so forth:

> In moral reasoning we often blend appeals to principles, rules, rights, virtues, passions, analogies, paradigms, parables, and interpretations. To assign priority to one of these factors as the key ingredient is a dubious project.

So why do they adopt a principle-based approach in their book? The answer may be because principles provide a useful framework for discussing and analysing ethical issues in professional practice. When a professional actually makes a decision in real life, then a whole range of factors will influence the decision-making process (see O'Sullivan, 1999), including the emotional response of the practitioner, the quality of the relationships she has with people involved, her appraisal of the particular circumstances of the situation (including the feelings and attitudes of others involved) as well as consideration of her general obligations as a professional, the rights of the service users involved and many other aspects. However, in writing and teaching about ethical decision-making, we are not in the real-life situation and cannot actually see the people concerned or feel the emotions generated. So the focus inevitably tends to be on the general principles involved in cases like this – on the rights and duties that pertain and how they might apply in such a case (a principle-based common morality approach). To examine the principle of respect for the self-determination of the service user, for example, to look at what it means or how it might apply in practice and what exceptions there might be is one way of developing critical thinking about ethical decision-making. What is important is to acknowledge that ethical principles are only one aspect of what is involved in decision-making.

What if we wanted to adopt a virtue-based approach to teaching professional ethics? If we want social workers in training to develop the virtues of honesty, respectfulness, trustworthiness or compassion, how is this to be done? It might involve examination of these characteristics and asking questions like what does it mean to say someone is honest or how would an honest person act in this situation. We might ask whether this would be very different from exploring what is meant by the principle of honesty and how we can implement it in practice. The difference would be in the focus on the character and motivation of the moral agent, which might encourage the social worker to question issues about her own identity and dispositions. But looking to what principles she espouses and when she might make exceptions to them might have a similar effect.

Surely there is something more to a virtue ethics approach than this? Virtue ethics is about developing good character and good judgement in professionals – what we might call moral education. An important part of this is having role models – teachers in both academic institutions and practice settings. According to Statman (1997, p. 13):

> Becoming a good person is not a matter of learning or 'applying' principles, but of imitating some models. We learn to be virtuous in the same way we learn to dance, to cook, and to play football – by watching people who are competent in these areas and trying to do the same.

This probably helps to explain why textbooks on practical ethics do not tend to adopt a virtue-based approach, that is, because the virtues are largely developed in other ways. But I think it is possible to acknowledge the importance of developing the virtues through moral exemplars and imitating role models, whilst at the same time acknowledging the role of ethical principles and rules. Following Statman's analogy, if we want to improve our skills in football, apart from being coached and watching people playing, we may also read books on the principles of good football and indeed we certainly need to study the rules of the game. The two approaches are surely complementary.

The real danger of the principle-based approach would be if it degenerated into a focus on rules, which are more specific and determined. And this then turns professional ethics into a matter of learning the rules and how to implement them, rather than a process of critical and responsible reflection. But principles are not the same as rules, and it requires a lot of work to examine what they mean and how and when they apply. It also requires the development of the faculty of good judgement. In this sense both virtue-based approaches and principle-based approaches require the development of skilled, critical and reflective practitioners. A virtue-based approach is a good corrective to the tendency to adopt a rule-based approach to professional ethics. For we do want professionals to become more than simply rule-following automata. We do want to develop people who respect confidentiality because they are the kind of people who are trustworthy and respectful in all aspects of life, not just because their agency or professional association has laid down a rule to this effect. Yet not everyone is virtuous, and it is not as easy to change or develop people's characters as it is for people to be required to follow a rule. Rules are action-oriented and take account of the fact that people in professional roles should behave in certain kinds of ways, even if they do this out of duty rather than because they have a disposition to act in such ways. Specific rules are needed precisely because people are not always virtuous and because they may not always have the capacity (or be trusted) to make good judgements. But the growth of more and more rules and the emphasis on the specific competencies of social workers to act in certain ways should not lure us away from the need to develop workers of integrity and trustworthiness. This is why consideration of virtue ethics is important, because it emphasises the moral education and development of the professional, as opposed to simply training in competencies for work.

Conclusions

Although not well-developed as yet for social work, we discussed the merits and importance of character and relationship-based approaches as a counterbalance to the detached rationality and impartiality of principle-based ethics. The development of good character, good judgement, the capacity to care and to be morally sensitive to situations are equally important aspects of ethical decision-making. Hugman (1998, p. 95) distinguishes between caring as work (concerned with doing and action) and caring as commitment (to do with being and attitude). He argues that the tendency to focus on quantifiable aspects of welfare practice precludes caring as attitude/commitment, because caring comes to be seen solely in terms of 'the tasks performed'. Further exploration of an ethic of care in social work is important as a challenge to this tendency to separate attitude and action. As Edwards (1996, p. 155) points out in relation to nursing, there is a difference between a cool detached application of principles and the implementation of principles 'in a manner which is infused with care'. Edwards nevertheless argues for the primacy of principle-based ethics, whilst acknowledging an important role for the kinds of consideration which are of concern to care-based theorists. This book will also inevitably tend to focus more on principles and their role in ethical decision-making, since most of the professional ethics literature is couched in terms of ethical principles, and, as has already been argued, principle-based approaches are a valuable way of teaching and thinking about ethics. But this is not to deny the role of emotion, the capacity for sympathy and care and the importance of the specific commitments, relationships and responsibilities we have to particular others.

4

Ethics and Values in Relation to Social Work Practice and Theories

The first part of this chapter will look briefly at how aspects of some of the philosophical theories and principles covered in the previous chapters relate to recent developments in social work practice, including the challenges to traditional thinking posed by radical and anti-oppressive approaches and by consumerist and postmodern trends. In the second part of the chapter we will explore how social work values relate to the theoretical knowledge base of social work.

Challenges to social work values: the growing awareness of structural oppression

As noted in Chapter 2, in the 1960s and 1970s the literature on social work values tended to focus on issues related to the rights and interests of the individual user. The emphasis was very much on the nature of the relationship between the social worker and user, and in particular on how the social worker should treat the user. At the heart of this set of values are the notions of *individualism* and *freedom*. Both these notions are, of course, at the core of the prevailing ideology of western capitalist societies, and hence it is not surprising to find them predominant in the social work literature. However, during the past few decades there have been a number of challenges to this position, from both progressive and reactionary sources.

During the 1970s there was a growing awareness amongst social workers that treating each user as an individual, and seeing the problems faced by that user (such as poverty, homelessness, mental illness) as personal problems was, in effect, 'blaming the victims' for the structural inequalities in society. A range of literature was published advocating 'radical social work', which acknowledged social workers' role as agents of social control on behalf of an oppressive state, and called on them to raise the consciousness of the people they worked with, to encourage collective action for social change and build alliances with working-class and trade union organisations (Bailey and Brake, 1975; Brake and Bailey, 1980; Corrigan and Leonard, 1978). Although the radical social work literature of the 1970s and early 1980s did not itself seem to influence the literature on social work values and ethics of the same period, the broadening of the understanding of oppression created by the feminist and anti-racist movements of the 1980s has now found its way into the lists of social work values. While the contributions from feminist and anti-racist theorists are often highly critical of the Marxist inspired radical social work (Ahmad, 1990; Day, 1992; Dominelli and McLeod, 1989; Dominelli, 1997; Shah, 1989), they can nevertheless be seen to have grown out of, and alongside, the radical social work movement of the 1970s, and the collections of articles on radical work in the 1980s included substantial contributions from feminist and black perspectives (Brake and Bailey, 1980; Langan and Lee, 1989). A concern for anti-oppressive practice was reflected in the list of values produced in the late 1980s by the Central Council for Education and Training in Social Work (CCETSW, 1989), an extract of which is shown in Table 4.1.

Jordan (1991) points out the contradictions between the traditional or Kantian values contained in the first part of the list (which includes variations on respect for persons, user self-determination and confidentiality) and the statements about structural oppression in the second part of the list. The individual freedom which social workers have a commitment to promote is, he claims, dependent on the structural inequalities in society which they also have a duty to challenge. He argues that the liberal values on which the first set of principles is based (including property rights and traditional personal morality based on notions of freedom of choice) are amongst the strongest intellectual defences of the privileges of wealth, whiteness, and maleness upon which structural oppression is based (Jordan, 1991, p. 8). This reasserts the point that social workers in the radical tradition had been making earlier: that the agenda of structural change conflicts with the individualist premises upon which social work is based.

Table 4.1   *The values of social work (1989)*

1. Qualifying social workers should have a commitment to:
   - the value and dignity of individuals;
   - the right to respect, privacy and confidentiality;
   - the right of individuals and families to choose;
   - the strengths and skills embodied in local communities;
   - the right to protection of those at risk of abuse and exploitation and violence to themselves and others.

2. Qualifying social workers must be able to:
   - develop an awareness of the inter-relationship of the processes of structural oppression, race, class and gender;
   - understand and counteract the impact of stigma and discrimination on grounds of poverty, age, disability and sectarianism;
   - demonstrate an awareness of both individual and institutional racism and ways to combat both through anti-racist practice;
   - develop an understanding of gender issues and demonstrate anti-sexism in social work practice;
   - recognise the need for and seek to promote policies and practices which are non-discriminatory and anti-oppressive.

Source: CCETSW (1989), pp. 15–16.

While the 'respect for persons' doctrine would entail that a user who was black,[1] for example, should be treated as an individual with rights, choices and desires, with no prejudgements or prejudice based on irrelevant factors like skin colour, it would, in effect, be a 'colour-blind' approach. For being black would be regarded as irrelevant, whereas the position adopted by anti-racist social workers would be to regard being black as relevant, to see the user as a member of an oppressed group and to take this into account in the social work relationship. It is in the former colour-blind sense that many institutions, agencies and individuals may adopt and implement equal opportunities policies and claim to be 'non-racist'. The brief statements saying everyone will be treated equally 'irrespective of race, gender, religion, etc.' are good examples of this in that they do not recognise institutional or structural discrimination and therefore do not recognise the need for positive action to promote change.

The profession of social work in Britain, on paper at least, has moved beyond the colour-blind approach, and most literature and policy statements recognise institutional discrimination and express a commitment to challenge it. They recognise, for example, that black people are underrepresented in senior and professional posts, that social services departments are not meeting many of the needs of black users, and that action needs to be taken to redress this imbalance. An essentially reformist position can be adopted which seeks to make changes to the law, to policies and their implementation to improve the situation. This would entail focusing not just on the individual, but on the individual's position in society, and working towards greater fairness and procedural justice in the distribution of rewards and punishments – basically a utilitarian outlook. However, the recognition and challenging of structural oppression – the recognition that the very rules and structures within which society operates reflect basic inequalities in power and that therefore fundamental and revolutionary change is required – is at odds with the emphasis on individual freedom of both Kantianism and utilitarianism; it calls for a more radical analysis and approach. Figure 4.1 summarises the differences between what I have called the Kantian, utilitarian and radical frameworks of moral thinking. The 'radical' category is very broad, and could include Marxist and anti-oppressive approaches and the more recent development of 'critical social work' – a term which is being used to embrace 'practice models that incorporate an emancipatory social change orientation' (Healy, 2000, p. 3).

Challenges to social work values: markets, consumers and postmodernity

Simultaneous with the growing concern with structural oppression in the 1980s was the growing influence of the ideologies of the new right in legislation and policies relating to the public sector. This has been reflected in the development of a 'mixed economy of welfare' with a growth in the contracting out of services to the private and voluntary sectors; reduction in the power of professional groups and of the role of the welfare state; an emphasis on individuals' rights to choose as the consumers of services; and a focus on individuals' rights and responsibilities as citizens to complain, or to care for their children or relatives. Despite the initial association of such policies with right-wing governments (particularly the Conservative governments in Britain from 1979 to 1997), they have been pursued also by centre and socialist governments in other countries and continued with variations by 'New Labour' in Britain in the late 1990s.

60

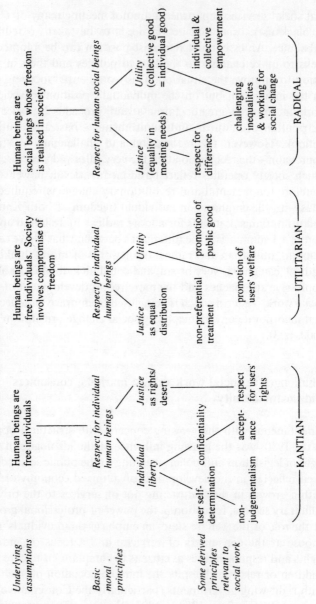

Figure 4.1 Kantian, utilitarian and radical frameworks of moral thinking

At first these developments did not result in changes to the value statements of the profession. This is probably partly because these value statements have tended to be somewhat divorced from the reality of social work practice, and also because aspects of the new approaches to welfare are superficially congruent with the key principles of the profession. Individuals' rights to choose and to complain can be seen as part of the notion of respect for persons. The rights of users to information about their case, to be able to see their social work files, to know their rights to services and how to complain if they are not satisfied all fit in with the principle of treating users as rational, self-determining agents and can serve to protect them against the exercise of excessive parentalism or illegitimate power by social workers or social work agencies.

However, the focus of the new approaches to welfare tends not to be on the user as a whole person, but just on one narrow part of being a person: namely in the role of 'consumer'. 'Consumer rights' are not the same as 'users' rights to self-determination', for the former are limited to the person in the role of a consumer of services, and the rights are to a certain predefined standard of service, a certain type of treatment, and a certain standard of goods. What is meant, in theory at least, by users' rights to self-determination relates to users as whole people – their rights to make choices, to take decisions, and to develop potential in a much broader sense than that of consumer.

Calling the user a consumer also serves to hide the fact of social worker as controller. It implies an active role and the possibility to exercise choice. It covers up the role of welfare as control – what Foucault (1999, p. 93) called 'surveillance-correction', and others have termed the 'new authoritarianism', which is based on the notion of the user as dangerous, as a risk to be assessed, as deviant and as outsider (Jeffs and Smith, 1994; Parton, 1999). This is another aspect of the policies and ideologies of both the new right and the new left which is contrary to the traditional social work values of respect for persons – the reemergence of the Victorian distinction between the deserving and undeserving poor; the determination to punish and control those on the margins of society, the 'outcasts' or the 'underclass'. Some of these trends are reflected in the implementation of legislation in the 1990s relating to child protection, community care and criminal justice. While aspects of this legislation could be regarded as progressive in the promotion of children's rights and user participation in service delivery, other aspects are about treatment and control – the user as a problem to be technically assessed, clinically managed and processed through a proceduralised system. These policies and procedures are now based much more explicitly than in the past on the utilitarian values of procedural justice and the promotion of public welfare.

The statement of values produced by CCETSW (see Table 4.2) in the mid-1990s reflects some of these changes, giving less emphasis to individual rights than the 1989 statement, recognising that people may have competing rights and demands and explicitly acknowledging that control of behaviour may be required at times. In addition to reflecting trends towards more explicit control of behaviour, the statement is also interesting in that it has a much less certain tone than the earlier one, it shows an awareness of the complexities and contradictions in the work, and it also calls on the social worker to respect not only uniqueness, but also 'diversity'. The 'old' values of respect for persons and self-determination are still there ('respect and value uniqueness'; 'promote people's rights to choice, privacy') as are the new anti-oppressive values, although reworded ('take action to counter discrimination'). But the values of individual welfare and the

***Table* 4.2**   *The values of social work (1995)*

In order to achieve the award of Diploma in Social Work, students must demonstrate that they:

- Identify and question their own values and prejudices, and their implications for practice;
- Respect and value uniqueness and diversity, and recognise and build on strengths;
- Promote people's rights to choice, privacy, confidentiality and protection, while recognising and addressing the complexities of competing rights and demands;
- Assist people to increase control of and improve the quality of their lives, while recognising that control of behaviour will be required at times in order to protect children and adults from harm;
- Identify, analyse and take action to counter discrimination, racism, disadvantage, inequality and injustice, using strategies appropriate to role and context; and,
- Practise in a manner that does not stigmatise or disadvantage either individuals, groups or communities.

Source: CCETSW (1995), p. 4.

public good ('assist people to increase control and improve the quality of their lives'; 'recognising that control of behaviour will be required at times') are much more evident. The recognition of complexity and diversity, including the suggestion that strategies used should be appropriate to context, hints at some of the 'postmodern' trends towards a rejection of grand or all-embracing theories, an acknowledgement of the fragmentation of value and attention to local and particular situations which will be further discussed in the next section of this chapter.

We will now consider how the values of social work relate to social work knowledge and the theories identified for social work, highlighting the tension between Kantian, utilitarian and radical values discussed earlier.

Social work knowledge as value-laden

'How do we know the world?' 'What do we know?' 'What is the status of that knowledge?' These are all questions that have long puzzled philosophers, so it is perhaps not surprising if they have also given social work theorists some food for thought. In considering knowledge for social work and its relationship to the values of the occupation, there are a number of concepts and ideas that need to be taken into account. Knowledge is sometimes divided into two kinds: knowing that and why (theoretical knowledge) and knowing how (practical knowledge). 'Knowing that' might be knowledge of 'facts' about the world, such as 'there is a service user in the reception area', which could be said to be known through experience and could be verified by going and looking in reception. 'Knowing why' might be a more theoretical kind of knowledge, such as 'this service user is hiding in the corner because she is suffering from phobic anxiety', which might be verified with reference to various generalisations in psychoanalytic theory. 'Knowing how' is about how to do things like 'writing a pre-sentence report', or 'assessing the needs of a person with disabilities'. Obviously in social work all these kinds of knowledge are important, although the practical knowledge is often described as 'skills' or 'techniques' rather than 'knowledge'.

It is often assumed that knowing that, or 'factual' knowledge, is value-free. To say we know that there is a service user in reception surely does not entail commitments to any particular value position? In one sense this is true. In another sense, if we consider more carefully, we realise that just seeing the person in the waiting room as a 'service user' is already constituting the situation in a particular way. We are already categorising the person in terms of our relationship to her, which may have connotations of the service user as needing to be helped, or as part of the bureaucratic social work system which involves people sitting in reception areas in a subservient fashion. We have already evaluated the situation according to our own perspective as a social worker. This is not the same as making a straightforward value statement like 'this service user ought to be helped', but it does have value connotations. The second statement about the service user hiding in a corner because she is suffering from phobic anxiety might more readily be regarded as having value overtones, as it more obviously rests on theoretical knowledge about how humans think and act, which in turn is based on some fundamental presuppositions about the nature of human beings.

The situation is similar with knowing how, or practical knowledge. Skills such as writing pre-sentence reports or assessing service users' needs already presuppose a lot of factual and theoretical knowledge about the nature of the legal system, or what criteria are to be used in the assessment, for example, which in turn is based on views about what is a need, or who ought to get help. These are fundamentally evaluative presuppositions. This is not to say that in order for a social worker to be able to do an assessment of a user's needs she has to know what concept of need the assessment is based upon, just that any assessment of need presupposes some concept of what need is, and this will be an evaluative concept. The doing of the assessment is not 'value-neutral', even if the social worker is simply filling in a form designed by someone else.

Further, it could be argued that the 'good' social worker – the reflective practitioner (Schön, 1987) – needs to be aware of the societal and professional values underlying her work and her own values, and should adopt a critical stance to her practice. Some commentators have argued that the social worker should be not only a reflective practitioner, but also a committed practitioner, working for change in society through her action (Ronnby, 1992). This fusion of reflection and action has been called 'praxis' – a concept that can be found in Aristotle and is developed in Marxist thinking and through the works of Paulo Freire. This moves beyond simply stating that values, knowledge and skill are inseparable to a normative statement about what the role of the social worker ought to be. If the social worker compartmentalises reflection (values and knowledge) from action (use of skill), she is, in fact, deceiving herself. She is in 'bad faith', as Sartre (1969, pp. 47–70) would say, because she is pretending that her action can be value-free and purely 'technical'. She is denying her own responsibility as a moral agent for that action. For Freire, reflection without action results in 'mentalism', and action without reflection in 'activism'; and both are empty (Freire, 1972).

So, we have argued that there is no such thing as value-free knowledge, and that values, knowledge and skills are inseparably related. Obviously there are degrees of value-ladenness, which is reflected in the fact that we do tend to talk as if knowledge and values are separate entities in our everyday discussions, and sometimes it can be useful to separate them analytically.

Theories, models and techniques in social work

In looking at the values underpinning social work knowledge, we will briefly explore some of the theories, models and techniques that have been developed for social work to consider what value assumptions underlie them. Before we do this, it will be helpful to clarify some of the terminology that will be used, as this can be confusing. Texts on social work knowledge tend to include discussion of a whole range of entities including ideologies, perspectives, approaches, theories, models, techniques and skills. Sometimes terms are used interchangeably, like ideology or perspective, theory or model, for example. In this book, the following definitions will be used:

- *Ideology* – a system of belief about the nature of human beings which is held by some group of people as giving rise to their way of life.
- *Perspective* – a particular way of looking at the world. It may be from a particular ideological or theoretical viewpoint, or some other standpoint.
- *Theory* – strictly speaking, a general rule or law which seeks to offer an explanation or understanding of some aspect of the world. Very often, however, the term is used to mean 'theoretical system' which is a coherent set of explanatory generalisations. It will be used in this way here.

- *Model* – a descriptive classification of part of the world; a model has less explanatory power than a theory.
- *Technique or skill* – the practical ability to do something.

There is often confusion in the social work literature regarding what is being talked about. Obviously all these concepts are interconnected – models and techniques may form part of a theoretical system, which in turn may be based upon certain ideological beliefs about the nature of human society. The use of a term like 'perspective' or 'approach' avoids having to specify exactly what is being talked about – which can be useful, but also misleading. In social work it is useful because knowledge for social work tends to be 'eclectic' – that is, it is drawn from a range of theories and models from various academic disciplines and other professions. In the gathering together and modification of these pieces of theories and models it is not always clear what they are being made into; to say they constitute an approach or a perspective is fairly all-encompassing and vague and is therefore an easy option. It also reflects the fact that research into social work practitioners' use of theory suggests that many rarely consciously use a particular identifiable theory, rather they use 'practice wisdom' based on an amalgam of learning from experience and bits of theories and techniques that have been read about or learnt on the job (Curnock and Hardicker, 1979; Roberts, 1990; Thompson, 1991).

The social work knowledge base: unitary or fragmented?

Knowledge in a social work context has been defined as the 'acquaintance with or theoretical or practical understanding of some branch of science, art, learning, or other area involving study, research or practice, and the acquisition of skills' (Morales and Sheafor, 1986, p. 173). In the past many people judged that it was a failing of social work that it had not yet developed its own unified body of specialised knowledge. This stemmed partly from the quest to establish social work as a profession, since one of the commonly stated features of a profession was that it should be underpinned by a specialist body of knowledge. However, despite much discussion and many attempts particularly in the 1970s to define a unique body of knowledge and all-embracing theory for social work, most commentators would tend to agree that these attempts have failed (Howe, 1987; Roberts, 1990). There are many reasons why. The most significant is probably that the roles and tasks undertaken by social workers are so varied and the contexts so diverse that it has been difficult to agree a common aim or purpose for social work. Without this it seems almost impossible to develop a unifying body of knowledge. The kinds of statements about the purpose of social work which have emerged, such as 'assisting people in their problems of social functioning' (Butrym, 1976, p. 13) or 'enabl[ing] children, adults, families, groups and communities to function, participate and develop in society' (CCETSW, 1995, p. 16) have hardly been sufficiently specific to define a distinctive area of knowledge. What has happened in social work is that theories from various other academic and professional disciplines have been imported and modified, and a plethora of models or approaches have been developed alongside specialist techniques to apply to particular types of situation or problem. So, although it is true to say that it is possible to define a knowledge base for social work, it is not unified or distinctive.

In the last couple of decades this search for a unified theory has tended to diminish. As Chris Payne (1994, p. 9) comments in relation to a discussion of systems theory and the unitary approach, 'social work has to a large extent lost its taste for "grand theory"'. We can see this as simply giving up a lost cause, as well as part of a broader trend in society involving what Lyotard calls an 'incredulity toward metanarratives' (1984, p. xxiv). Instead there is a focus on locally relevant 'theories' that work in specific fields or circumstances and a preoccupation with discrete and measurable competencies to perform particular tasks. Some commentators have called these trends 'postmodern' (Bauman, 1992; Harvey, 1990; Irving, 1994; Jameson, 1991; Leonard, 1997). Regardless of how they are labelled, there is no doubt that a shift in perspective can be detected in social work proponents of what were once presented as totalising explanatory theories. So, for example, we find Chris Payne (1994, p. 9) in his exposition of systems theory emphasising that it is not a comprehensive 'grand theory' on a par with Marxism, but rather that it is about 'help[ing] social workers organize and integrate different perspectives and methods for achieving relatively small-scale personal and social changes'. This echoes recent accounts of radical social work, which have shifted from explicitly Marxist-inspired aspirations for large-scale social change towards a focus on 'micropolitics'. This entails 'making small practical changes in methods of day-to-day working that might have significant consequences both for relationships with clients and for developing more effective modes of participative practice' (Langan and Lee, 1989, p. 8).

Some social work commentators have gone further and developed an explicitly 'postmodernist' view of social work knowledge and practice which involves accepting the fragmentation and specialisation of the work and the accompanying specialisation and fragmentation of knowledge. McBeath and Webb (1991) note the multiplicity of discourses and practices that make up social work theory and criticise social work for mixing various models of intervention and technical practice and failing to pay attention to the 'cold logical contradictions between the models' (p. 749). They call this the 'Esperanto Principle' and suggest that, like the composite language Esperanto, social work esperanto 'is learnt only by a few and remains esoteric'. They suggest that a more positive picture of social work could emerge if this dispersal of social work discourses occurred not by accident but by design. They suggest that the various elements of social work (such as child care or work with offenders) would follow their own laws or criteria of construction but could nevertheless be deliberately united under the name of social work. They paint a picture of postmodern social work as 'a set of irreducible sub-disciplines emerging as a response to the self-evident needs of the community' (p. 755).

McBeath and Webb develop their version of postmodern social work from Lyotard's view of knowledge as a set of irreducible language games. According to Lyotard (1984, p. xxiv):

> There are many different language games – a heterogeneity of elements. They only give rise to institutions in patches – local determinism.

McBeath and Webb argue, therefore, that what they call 'postmodern' social work is characterised by consumer-responsiveness and decentralised social care packages (p. 759). It serves the public immediately, aiming for efficiency and 'performativity'. 'Performativity' is a term used by Lyotard (1984, p. 46) as 'the best possible input/output equation' and links with a stress on usefulness, value for money and technology (as opposed to a search for universal truth, justice and the promotion of the good of humanity through the welfare state).

The postmodernist account of the theory and practice of social work leaves some of the traditional comprehensive theories and perspectives (such as psychodynamic, systems or radical theories) as presented in the social work textbooks looking somewhat old-fashioned. However, since it now seems fashionable, and indeed respectable, to acknowledge the theoretical heterogeneity of social work, the competing discourses can be presented as part of a supermarket 'pick and mix' approach. According to Malcolm Payne (1997, p. 57), the purpose of his book on modern social work theory is to facilitate 'thoughtful rather than casual eclecticism' by offering information about the various theories to see 'how they may be selected and combined'. However, Chambon (1994, p. 71) gives the following warning:

> given the loss of a credible metanarrative and the proliferation of fragments of knowledge, we need to reconsider the limitations of adopting a strictly combinatory model or tool-kit approach (Swidler, 1986) in fostering the ongoing development of our knowledge base. In importing multiple frames of reference, we need to recognize the orientations that such discourses encourage and, conversely, those that they stifle.

While aspects of McBeath and Webb's account do reflect recent trends in social work, there is a danger in taking the fragmentation of knowledge too far and in accepting the managerialist and technocratic approaches that accompany it. As Ife (1999, p. 215) comments:

> For the left to be spending its energies on analysing and deconstructing discourses of power, praising relativism and claiming that the era of unified visions of social justice is past, often in extremely inaccessible language, is very convenient for those who wish to pursue an ideology of greed, selfishness, increased inequality and a denial of human rights in the interests of free markets and private profit.

Chambon (1994, p. 64) also points out that the multiplication of social work theories and perspectives leads to many fragmented narratives of expertise (she gives the example of 'feminist ethics in psychiatry') and leaves little room for examining the sources and commonalities of social problems. This is why it is important to consider values in relation to the knowledge base of social work. There has been a tendency in the social work literature to separate knowledge and values. The texts that cover various theoretical approaches to social.work tend to look at the explanatory theories and models, the aims and methods of each approach, but rarely explicitly look at the underlying values (for example, Davies, 1997, pp. 167–254; Hanvey and Philpot, 1994; Howe, 1987; Payne, 1997). One text on social work models, which does explicitly cover values, includes this in a separate section and does not relate the values of social work to the section on models (Butrym, 1976).

Theories and perspectives for social work practice

There are many texts which list and compare different theories and models, all identifying slightly different configurations (for example, Adams *et al.*, 1998; Butrym, 1976; Hanvey and Philpot, 1994; Howe, 1987; Lishman, 1991; Payne, 1997). One of the problems is that they tend to include a whole range of theories, models and techniques, some of which are more comprehensive, and therefore more value-laden, than others. Payne (1997, pp. 35, 290), following Clark (1995), makes a useful distinction between:

- *perspectives* – expressions of values or views of the world which allow participants to order their minds sufficiently to be able to manage themselves while participating (for example, psycho-dynamic, humanistic, radical, social development and systems perspectives);
- *explanatory theories* – accounts of why an action results in particular consequences and the circumstances in which it does this (for example, communication, anti-oppressive and cognitive behavioural theories); and
- *models* – descriptions of what happens during practice in a general way, applying to a wide range of situations, in a structured form, so that they extract certain principles and patterns of activity which give the practice consistency (for example, crisis intervention, task-centred models and empowerment models).

Payne uses the term 'theory' in a loose sense to include perspectives, explanatory theories and models. He suggests that many of the 'theories' put forward for social work may be stronger in one or two of these aspects than others. For example, radical theories of social work have tended to focus on offering perspectives and have been weaker in developing explicit models for action, whereas task-centred theories are primarily models (Payne, 1997, pp. 36–7). Nevertheless, he argues (1997, p. 290) that in a practical activity like social work, all 'valid practice theories' must contain a perspective, a theory and a model.

I would argue that it is only possible to identify value assumptions in perspectives and some of the explanatory theories. This is not to say that advocates of models do not do so from an explicit or implicit value position; just that a particular value position is not inherent in the model itself, and will depend upon the broader theoretical or ideological perspective adopted. For example, an empowerment approach could be advocated by a radical feminist as part of the route towards revolutionary change. The key value position might be a belief in equality of result, viewing empowerment as a collective taking of power by members of an oppressed group. A reformist might use it to work towards changing policies and laws, based on a principle of distributive justice entailing power-sharing between service users and officials. A conservative might adopt a citizen's rights approach to empowerment with the aim of giving individuals more power and reducing the role of the welfare state. The key under-pinning principle might be individual self-determination, giving users the right to complain if certain standards of service are not met.

Using Payne's (1997) categorisation and account of social work theories, we will now examine the value implications of four of those he describes as perspective theories which are: psychodynamic; systems/ecological; humanist/existential; and radical/Marxist. Payne also includes social/community development as a perspective theory, partly because he thinks it is important to offer an alternative frame-work that may be relevant outside the 'developed' world. However, because of the multiplicity of different types of social/community development approaches, theories and models (see Popple, 1995), it is hard in the context of the present discussion to use this as a per-spective theory. I will also include behaviourist theories, which Payne includes in the category of explanatory theories rather than per-spectives. I have included behaviourism because, whilst agreeing with

Payne that it does not tend to be used as an overarching theory encompassing the whole of social work practice, it is based on a set of explicit theoretical assumptions about the nature of human beings and how they operate.

In assessing the extent to which the stated values of social work are reflected in these theories, it is important to remember that a basic assumption of both Kantian and utilitarian theories is that human beings are viewed as individuals who are free to make decisions and choices. These assumptions of individuality and freedom can be regarded as the fundamental basis of western, liberal conceptions of morality. Freedom (as the opposite of determinism) is certainly presupposed in our whole way of thinking and speaking about morality, which assumes people are capable of making choices and are responsible for their behaviour, which it is therefore appropriate to praise or blame. While it may be acknowledged that on some occasions people are not capable of making choices (their mental capacities may be permanently or temporarily impaired, for example) and sometimes people's behaviour may be regarded as determined by forces outside their control, these are regarded as exceptions. If determinism was the norm – that is, if people's decisions and choices were predictable on the basis of knowledge about physical, psychological or social causation – then it would make no sense to praise or blame people for their actions.

Psychodynamic theories

There is no doubt that psychoanalytic theories derived from Freud have been very influential in social work. However, social work has not adopted psychoanalytic theory, or its associated therapeutic techniques, *per se*. Various theories, models and approaches have been developed for social work which are derivative of psychoanalytic theory. According to Payne (1997, p. 72), there are two important ideas underpinning the theory which are:

> *determinism* – the principle that actions or behaviour arise from people's thought processes rather than just happen;
>
> *the unconscious* – the idea that some thinking and mental activity is hidden from our knowledge.

Although different variations of psychodynamic theory for social work have different emphases (such as problem-solving, psychosocial functioning, or ego psychology), it could be argued that they all rest to some degree on the principle of psychic determinism, they focus on the individual, and they tend to adopt a scientific approach which puts the social worker in the role of expert, using a medical model which uses language like 'diagnosis' and 'treatment'. This is not to say that the user is not seen as the main agent of change, since the ways in which psychoanalytic theories have been adapted for social work tend to take account of the important values of social work, including user self-determination, and incorporate a social dimension. Nevertheless, their roots in psychoanalytic theory mean that the primary focus for the explanation of people's behaviour is deterministic. This kind of view is in conflict with the principle of respect for persons as rational, self-determining human beings with the ability to make free choices.

Behaviourist theories

Again, theories from another discipline, behavioural psychology, have been adapted for use in social work. In contrast to psychodynamic theory, behavioural social work concentrates on observable behaviour and uses learning theories to analyse and modify behaviour. Unlike psychodynamic theory, there is a focus on the present rather than the past, and on the external and observable, rather than the internal and reported. It also sees itself as scientific, based on principles 'derived from empirical research about how behaviour is learned, maintained and unlearned' (Hudson and Macdonald, 1986, p. 2) with a focus on changing the individual. It is also a deterministic theory, although this time it is a materialistic determinism, rather than psychological. Behavioural theories have been sharply criticised in social work for being excessively mechanistic and even for being unethical, in that some of the techniques they use (such as token-economy or aversion therapy) are incompatible with respecting individuals as human beings with free will and dignity (Butrym, 1976, p. 30). They also tend to focus on the ends (the change to be brought about) at the expense of the means (the methods used). This can be, and has been, counteracted, and as with psychodynamic theory many versions of behavioural social work have been modified and adapted to take into account such issues (see Sheldon, 1995). The important point to note is that the fundamental view of human nature on which behavioural approaches are primarily based is deterministic.

Systems theories

The development of systems theories for social work gained momentum in the 1960s and 1970s as part of the movement to unify the occupation. Payne (1997, pp. 137–56) categorises systems theories along with ecological theories which emphasise the adaptiveness of people to their environments. Systems approaches in social work have their origins in von Bertalanffy's (1971) biological theory which states that all organisms are systems, composed of sub-systems, and are in turn part of super-systems. This can be applied to social systems like families and societies. There have been several variations of systems theory developed for social work, one of the most well-known of which is that of Pincus and Minahan (1973). They argue that people depend on systems in their immediate social environment for a satisfactory life, so social work must focus on the interventions and linkages between people and social systems. They distinguish the 'client system' (the people who engage in working with the social work or 'change agent' system) from the 'target system' (the people whom the change agent is trying to change to achieve its aims). As Payne comments, such theories are among the few comprehensive sociologically-based theories of social work, very different from the traditional focus on individualisation and psychology.

However, as Chris Payne (1994, p. 9) points out, with the demise of social work's ambitions for unification, little of substance has been written on it recently. Systems theories were criticised as being over-inclusive (Butrym, 1976; Payne, 1997; Roberts, 1990); they cannot explain why things happen, they just offer ways of seeing what is happening. The technical terminology of 'change agents' and 'target systems' does not fit in easily with the traditional social work values, and the emphasis on technological strategies for change again tends to put the social worker in the role of expert and emphasises the ends to be achieved (the change). It is difficult to reconcile the value of respect for users as persons with the 'client as system'.

Radical perspectives

'Radical' approaches to social work have been influenced by Marxism and shift the focus of the work away from the individual and on to the structures of society. We have already discussed the development of Marxist-inspired radical social work in the 1970s, noting how this paved the way for the anti-oppressive approaches of the 1980s and the incorporation of these traditions more recently within 'critical social work'. While there is a variety of radical approaches, what they have in common is a critique of traditional social work theories and methods as tending to focus on changing individuals rather than changing the social structures that cause problems like poverty, poor housing, patriarchy or racism (Brake and Bailey, 1980; Corrigan and Leonard, 1978; Fook, 1993; Healy, 2000; Ife, 1997; Langan and Lee, 1989). Feminist, anti-racist and other anti-oppressive approaches which focus on the structural causes of social problems would tend to fall into this category – although it should be noted that not all 'feminist' or 'anti-racist' approaches are radical; some may be liberal or reformist. Although radical social work would want to hold on to the idea of respecting the user as a person, the view of 'person' is not that of a free individual in the Kantian sense. It is more a vision of a 'social being' – which leads to a recommendation for social work practice which involves raising the consciousness of individuals to recognise the nature of their oppression and developing their capacities to work collectively for social change. Traditional morality (linked to the Kantian notion of individuals following their duty for its own sake) would be regarded as a system of rules and principles reflecting the interests and values of powerful and dominant groups in society. Radical perspectives, therefore, would reject the traditional social work values in so far as these focus on promoting the freedom of the individual, but would include a commitment to positive freedom – that is, the social worker should work towards creating the conditions under which users can exercise more choice and develop their potential as human beings in a socialist/non-oppressive society (a radical form of 'social justice').

From the point of view of traditional social work, radical approaches have been criticised for focusing less on the here and now, the immediate and pressing problems facing individuals, and more on the creation of a better society in the future. This might involve treating individual users as a means to an end, and not respecting their own current expressions of needs and wants. In the short term, Marxist approaches could be interpreted as recommending a utilitarian approach – using people as a means to an end, for the greater good of humanity as a whole. Yet, as with all the other perspectives and theories described above, there are many versions of 'radical' social work which have different emphases. Many feminist and anti-racist approaches are concerned with individual empowerment and working for small, 'prefigurative' changes within their own agencies, rather than massive structural changes in society (Langan and Lee, 1989, p. 14). Recent developments of critical social work have also taken into account some of the postmodernist challenges of valuing difference and relativism, while maintaining a commitment to social justice and human rights (Leonard, 1997; Ife, 1999).

Humanist/existential perspectives

Payne (1997, p. 749) groups together a number of models of social work practice which have in common the idea that:

> human beings are trying to make sense of the world that they experience. Also social workers are trying to help people gain the skills to explore themselves and the personal meaning that they attach to the world they perceive and which affects them. Humanist models propose that people's interpretations of their own selves are valid and worthwhile.

One of the strongest influences on the development of 'humanist' ideas in social work is the work of Carl Rogers (1951, 1961) in the field of counselling, where he focuses on the importance of the relationship between the counsellor and user and stresses that the approach should be non-directive, non-judgemental and empathic and that the counsellor/worker should have 'unconditional positive regard' for the user. There is a focus on the uniqueness of each individual and the importance of the self seeking personal growth. There are many variations on these themes, including the work of Brandon (1976) who develops an approach based on Zen philosophy, England (1986) who develops the idea of social work as 'art', Wilkes (1981) who advocates a strongly Kantian approach to the rights of users to freedom from social work interference and speaks of the user as 'a mystery to be apprehended' and Thompson (1992) who develops an existentialist perspective. Butrym groups such approaches under the heading of 'ministration in love' and sees their foundations as largely derived from the Judaeo-Christian tradition and the existentialism of philosophers such as Buber and Kierkegaard (Butrym, 1976, p. 26). Howe (1987) categorises them as 'client-centred approaches', all of which are based on the view that people are subjects to be understood in terms of the meanings they attach to their own lives, and not objects to be explained, controlled, acted upon or changed according to external mechanistic or scientific laws.

Such a humanistic perspective is entirely congruent with the stated values of social work founded on the principle of respect for persons. The focus on the importance of relationships and the one-to-one encounter could also be compatible with an 'ethic of care' (Noddings, 1984) or an 'ethic of proximity' (Bauman, 1993). It seems strange, therefore, that such approaches are not more widespread, and that comprehensive theories with associated methods and techniques have not been more widely developed and accepted in social work. Payne (1997, pp. 196–7) suggests that the location of social work in bureaucratic agencies with social control functions is not conducive to the approach of humanist therapies where users are in control of the exploration and the worker has a non-directive role.

Incompatible values?

This brief discussion of some of the theories and perspectives that have been promoted for social work practice suggests that the values underlying many of the theories do not appear compatible with stated values of social work. Most of the theories and approaches – particularly the one that has been most dominant in social work, psychodynamic theory – are based on determinist assumptions about human thought and action and have a tendency to adopt a 'scientific' approach, which entails regarding the user as an object to be changed rather than a person to be respected. The perspective that is closest to the traditional social work values – the humanist/existential – is underdeveloped as a comprehensive theory for social work practice. It is easy to explain why this might be the case, as suggested above, because the conditions within which social work is actually practised do not lend themselves to the use of approaches and techniques based on humanist values or assumptions about users as rational agents. Service users are usually people who are in difficulty, facing crisis or in need of help and who are therefore less capable of rational decision-making than they or others might be in different circumstances. Social workers are often acting within the constraints of the law, agency policy, limited time and resources, and bureaucratic procedures which are more conducive to treating the user as a 'case' than as a person. A concern to establish social work as a profession based on a sound and 'scientific' knowledge base (including the concern in the last few years with 'evidence-based' practice) also encourages the use of approaches and techniques that have their origins in positivistic conceptions of natural science (technical and objective) rather than humanistic views of social science (intentional and subjective). The idea of social work as an 'art' may not appeal to a profession trying to establish itself and gain respect amongst the doctors and lawyers, and looking for specific techniques which will work, the results of which can be measured. What is puzzling is less why the theories for social work do not reflect the stated values of the profession, and more why the stated values are not in tune with the actual theories and day-to-day practice.

There are a number of explanations for the persistence of the 'respect for persons' approach in the stated values of social work. First, the separation of knowledge and values in the literature and much of social work education has discouraged discussion and analysis of their interrelationships. Second, it may be precisely because of the contexts in which social workers work and the predominance of technicist values in these institutions that it is important that the profession holds on to an alternative vision of the human being as a free agent to be respected. Since service users are usually powerless, lacking real options for choice and needing to be dealt with quickly, it is tempting to treat them all in a mechanistic way. The doctrine of respect for persons is a reminder of another way of looking at people and treating them. A third related reason may be the desire to hold on to a unity within social work, which is more readily achieved through retaining a common set of values than through the very diverse sets of knowledge and practices. As McBeath and Webb (1991, p. 754) comment:

The desire of social workers to believe that their activity is broadly unified under an ethical teleology of personhood and helpful interventions on behalf of self-realising persons conceals social work's theoretical heterogeneity.

They view the competing discourses or theories as presenting contradictory views of the human subject and argue that attempts to portray social work as homogeneous reduce the possibilities for 'multiplicity, flexibility and difference' (ibid.), which, following Lyotard, they see as a positive feature of the postmodern condition.

Accepting and valuing fragmentation and localised and specialist discourses is one way of coping with the *bricolage* of social work theories. Another slightly more modernist approach would be to suggest that the different ways of looking at service users (or human beings in general) are not as incompatible as we might have thought. They may be contradictory, in that it is difficult to see a user as both free and determined simultaneously, but perhaps they are compatible in that they are two ways of looking at the world, both of which are valid. Strawson (1959) argued that the language of determinism is compatible with the language of free will in so far as they may be regarded as complementary attitudes towards particular actions. The reactive attitude characterises the interpersonal behaviour of 'normal' adults, assuming free, purposive behaviour (free will); while the objective attitude is applied in cases where reactive attitudes are suspended. An objective attitude might be applied to a particular person because of illness, insanity, or when she wants to escape the strain of involvement (Downie and Telfer, 1969, p. 108). This kind of view is developed further by Hollis, who suggests that purposive explanation of behaviour is primary and is generally used until this type of explanation breaks down; and what is left, the incompletely explained part of a person's behaviour, is explained causally (Hollis, 1977).

This would suggest that there is no incompatibility in social workers regarding some people as incapable of rational, self-determined action and as needing treatment, while at the same time respecting others as rational, self-determining agents. The problem with behaviourist or psychoanalytic theories is that they focus excessively on the objective causal mode of explanation. However, we would be looking for a theory which took account of the con-traditions – the fact that all human beings, including users of social work services, are both free and unfree, both objects and subjects, and action can be explained in terms of both external causes and internal reasons or purposes. Determinism could be regarded as a framework of social norms and rules of behaviour (including morality) and of modes of explanation and thought (including scientific thought) which sets limits to people's action and thinking, outside of which it is very difficult to think or act. Within this framework human beings do have choices and do act according to their own purposes and desires. What is important about this framework, however, is that it is a *social* framework, and society is made up not of unique individuals, but of social beings who relate to each other in the context of publicly understood rules and norms. If we hold this kind of view, however, it does become very difficult to sustain the first basic premise of traditional morality – that of individualism, which sees the individual as the primary mode of being. The notion of an individual person only makes sense in the context of a world of other people; individuals have no identity in themselves, except in relation to others. That is, I can have no concept of myself as a separate being without defining myself as not other people. Or, as Sartre puts it, 'I need the other in order to realise fully all the structures of my being' (Sartre, 1969, p. 222).

Generally, much of the social work literature on ethics and values states the social context of people's behaviour. Indeed, social work is claimed to be concerned with social functioning (the interaction between people and their environment). However, the distinctness of individuals from their social context is nevertheless maintained, and the emphasis is still on the abstract individual as the primary unit of being, to whom certain rights attach to protect them from outside intrusions. This is why the Kantian–utilitarian liberal morality has been criticised as 'alienated' morality, for the social and moral laws come from outside the person, rather than being regarded as an internal part of their very being.

Wittgenstein's ideas about understanding people's actions within a public context of rule-governed behaviour (Wittgenstein, 1967) have been applied in the social sciences by Winch (1958) and have been expounded in social work literature, particularly by Ragg (1977). On this type of view, to understand a rule is to know how to act in certain situations and to be able to give reasons for action, which presupposes a public, social context. On this interpretation of human beings as rational in a social context, the principle of respect for persons would become respect for social beings (rather than individuals). This is close to Marx's idea of the dignity of people as social beings whose natures are fully realised in a truly collective society: 'man is not an abstract being squatting outside the world. He is the human world, the state, the society' (Marx, 1963, p. 43).

At a theoretical level there is a need to go beyond the dualisms of the individual and society, free will and determinism, means and ends, knowledge and values. At the level of practice this means acknowledging that the context within which social work takes place is based on values which are about public welfare, social control, and encouraging the individual to fit into society, and that the kinds of theories that tend to fit this role are deterministic and mechanistic; but within this framework, at the micro-level of the one-to-one relationship with the user, if we can 'bracket off' the societal and agency constraints, we can try to treat the user as a person to be respected. 'Bracketing off' should not mean pretending that the context of constraints and utilitarian values does not exist. That would be self-deception. The social worker must acknowledge that she is in the role of social worker, a publicly paid helper or controller, and the laws of the land and the rules of the agency form part of that relationship with the user. That is not to say that the social worker cannot or should not relate to service users as a fellow human being – feel for their pains, empathise with their suffering – but that both the user and the worker must be aware that the relationship is governed by additional and different rules to those in a purely personal relationship. Figure 4.2 illustrates this situation.

For example, a social worker making an assessment of the needs of a person with a disability is doing so within a framework prescribed by her agency – probably using a standard form – and is only able to offer a certain level of resources to this person. Yet within this framework the service user can be spoken to and treated with respect and honesty. Similarly, a decision may have been made by a case conference that a child should be removed from her parents because the parents are not capable of giving adequate care. This may have been the outcome of a utilitarian process of moral decision-making involving the weighing up of risks and working out what would be the best outcome for the child. It may have been influenced by psychodynamic theories about families and the causes of abuse. Yet within this process the parents may be given a chance to

Figure 4.2 *The constraints on the social worker–user relationship*

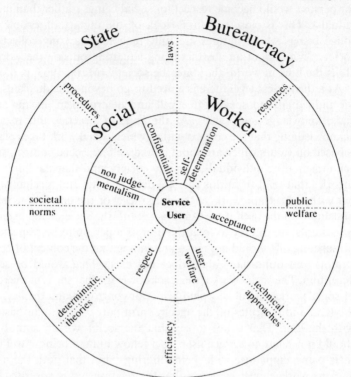

state their views, told honestly what the role of the social services department is, and given the opportunity to get legal advice – that is, treated with respect.

Conclusions

In this chapter we gave an overview of the changing nature of social work values which, whilst still dominated by Kantian principles relating to the respect and self-determination of individual service users, are now taking more account of radical or anti-oppressive principles around social justice and utilitarian principles relating to the promotion of the public good. We have also argued that it is impossible to have value-free knowledge. We have suggested that the knowledge – the theories, models and techniques – proposed for social work in the literature tends to presuppose a view of human thought and behaviour as causally determined – by unconscious psychological factors, natural instincts, the social environment or social and economic structures. This view of human nature fits uneasily with the values of social work as traditionally stated in the literature, which are based on the notion of the service user as a person who is free to make choices and to determine their action according to purposes and goals. We suggest that both the theories for social work and the values of social work need to be modified and interconnected. The predominant theories tend to lay too much stress on scientific and technical approaches and to objectify the user, whereas the values focus on the individual in the abstract and assume freedom and choice which plays down societal and agency constraints. The reflective practitioner needs to be aware of these tensions and contradictions, in order to understand her role in relation to users and to realise that she is both a publicly paid professional with some 'expert' knowledge whose aim is to change and control behaviour, and a fellow human being whose aim is to relate to and empathise with the user. Neither role is 'pure', and the praxis of social work, that is, the unity of practice informed by and informing theory and values, reflects this.

Exercise 2

Aims of the exercise – to encourage the reader to reflect critically on the stated values of the profession in the light of his/her own value commitments.

1. List what you think are the important values *you* hold as a social worker.
2. How do they compare with the list in Table 4.2?
3. Can you suggest any modifications/additions to Table 4.2?

Note 1: The term 'black' is used to refer to people of African, Caribbean and Asian origin with a common experience of racism on grounds of skin colour. While it is recognised that the use of the term in this way may be regarded as essentialist, it reflects the common usage in social work in the UK (see Ahmad, 1990).

5

Professional Codes
of Ethics

This chapter looks at the meaning of 'professionalism' and the role
of professional codes of ethics in social work. The discussion is illus-
trated through examination of codes of ethics from twenty different
countries.

Professionalism and codes of ethics

In most western countries the occupation of social work has a code
of ethics. This is often said to be one of the defining features of a
profession. In the 1960s and 1970s there was much debate about
whether social work was a profession (Etzioni, 1969; Toren, 1972).
The 'trait' theory of professionalism tended to be used, which maintained that, to be a profession, an occupation must possess certain
characteristics. One of the most commonly quoted lists of ideal
attributes of a profession was that of Greenwood (1957) which
includes the following:

1. a basis of systematic theory;
2. authority recognised by the clientele of the professional group;
3. broader community sanction and approval of this authority;
4. a code of ethics regulating relationships of professionals with
   users and colleagues;
5. a professional culture sustained by formal professional
   associations.

Social work has often been termed a 'semi-profession' because
while it meets some of these criteria (it has a code of ethics and professional associations), it does not meet them all fully. First, as was

suggested in Chapter 4, it does not rest on a firm theoretical knowledge base. Second, members cannot claim a monopoly of exclusive skills – many people not qualified as social workers may be performing the same or comparable tasks, and the authority of social workers is often contested. Third, in Britain, unlike most other European countries, the title of 'social worker' has not been protected by law and unqualified people or volunteers may be called 'social workers', although this situation is now changing. Fourth, as was suggested in Chapter 1, there is a public ambivalence regarding the authority of social workers. Finally, social workers' special area of competence (their function) is less well-defined compared with the so-called 'fully fledged' professions, and their period of training is relatively short (Toren, 1972, p. 52).

There has, however, been considerable criticism of the 'trait theory' (see, for example, Abbott and Meerabeau, 1998; Hugman, 1991; Johnson, 1972; Koehn, 1994). First, there is disagreement over what the essential characteristics of a profession are. Some commentators speak of 'state licensing' rather than 'community sanction'; 'esoteric knowledge' rather than 'systematic theory'; and a 'public pledge' as opposed to a 'code of ethics' (see Koehn, 1994, p. 40). Others add additional criteria such as professional education and qualification (Millerson, 1964). According to Koehn (1994), the most defensible trait of professionalism is the public pledge that professionals make to render asistance to those in need. This often takes the form of a code of ethics which new entrants to a profession pledge to uphold. Koehn argues that the other traits are neither necessary nor sufficient to define a professional.

Another criticism of the trait theory is that it is modelled on the old-established professions, such as medicine and the law, defining any occupation that does not share the same characteristics as less than a profession (Abbott and Meerabeau, 1998; Hugman, 1991). Commentators have pointed out how the 'caring professions' such as social work, nursing and occupational therapy have tended traditionally to be women's occupations and have been denied full professional status partly for this reason. Caring work (meaning caring for others) is thought to be women's work; it has less status and prestige and does not require special knowledge and skills. Medicine is not a 'caring profession' in the same way. Although the profession includes the 'service ideal', this is the idea of commitment to serve patients – caring *about* them, not *for* them. It is the nurses who care for patients in performing the everyday tasks of bathing or feeding (Hugman, 1991, p. 17).

Some have argued that an alternative set of traits is needed for the 'people work' professionals, which takes account of their location in bureaucratic settings and 'their affective knowledge based on intuitive interpersonal understanding' (Holmes, 1981, p. 27). However, this would perpetuate the trait model of professionalism which lacks usefulness in developing our understanding of the nature and role of professions in society. As Johnson (1972, p. 29) points out, professions have developed in different ways depending on historical and cultural factors and variations in the role of governments and academic institutions. There is no one set of traits that uniquely characterises a profession, nor one set of stages which an occupational group passes through to reach this end point of 'professionalism'. There are big differences in these respects in the development of professions between countries, as well as between professions in the same country (see Burrage and Torstendahl, 1990; Siegrist, 1994).

Johnson and others following him (Wilding, 1982; Hugman, 1991) focus instead on power as a factor in the success of an occupation in achieving status in society and see professionalism as a peculiar type of occupational control whereby a community of practitioners defines the relationship between professional and service user. Hugman argues that the language of professionalism often obscures the issue of power. Talk of the service ideal, trust, expertise, colleague control and public accountability appeal to the sentiments embodied in the trait approach, but can be interpreted as 'occupational bids for status and privilege' (Hugman, 1991, p. 6). On this analysis, it would be more useful to explore the reasons behind and the process of the professionalisation of social work than to debate whether it could be regarded as a profession in the terms delineated by the trait theory. Nevertheless, although discredited, trait theory is still influential in that occupations continue to make claims to certain attributes in order to affirm their professional status. As Johnson (1984, p. 19) comments:

> professionalism has become an occupational ideal in a society in which its attainment becomes less and less likely as more and more work is routinized through technological advances and occupational practice increasingly finds its typical setting within bureaucratic organizations of various kinds.

While 'caring professionals' may not be regarded as full professionals in many people's eyes, and are given less status and recognition than, for example, doctors, they do wield considerable power, particularly over users. And this aspect of professionalism – the claim to expert knowledge, the control not just of resources, but also the power to define the terms of the professional–user relationship – has been strongly attacked from many quarters, ranging from right to left. Illich speaks of the 'disabling professions', arguing that power and control over individuals' lives has been taken away by so-called 'experts' such as doctors, teachers or social workers (Illich *et al.*, 1977). Professions can be seen as protective and exclusive groups, seeking to retain power over their own occupations and hence over users (Wilding, 1982). These criticisms may be levelled at social work, regardless of whether one regards it as an aspirant profession, a semi-profession or a profession. In defending professionalism from the critiques of recent decades, Freidson (1994, pp. 9–10) talks of a professionalism reborn, 'stripped of the compromising institutions that assure workers a living, a professionalism expressed purely as dedication to the committed practice of a complex craft that is of value to others'. While this may seem an unrealistic aspiration, this notion relates to Koehn's highlighting of the importance of the 'public pledge' or service ideal of the professional, which is quite commonly expressed through a code of professional ethics.

What is a code of ethics?

It is partly an acknowledgement of the power that professionals have – particularly related to their possession of specialist knowledge and skills, which may not be fully (or even partially) understood by the users – that professions are said to need codes of ethics. The British Association of Social Workers (BASW) code states:

Social work is a professional activity. Implicit in its practice are ethical principles which prescribe the professional responsibility of the social worker. The primary objective of the Code of Ethics is to make these implicit principles explicit *for the protection of clients* and other members of society. (BASW, 1996, para. 1; emphasis added)

The term 'code of ethics' is used to cover quite a broad range of different types of codes of conduct or behaviour. Millerson sees professional ethics as a part of what is entailed by 'professional conduct', dividing professional conduct into professional practice and professional ethics. This is a useful distinction which links to a distinction that will be developed later between codes of practice and codes of ethics. Thus, according to Millerson (1964, p. 149), professional conduct consists of:

1. *Professional practice*, which relates to the adoption of schedules of uniform professional fees and charges, standard forms of contract, regulation of competition for projects;
2. *Professional ethics*, which are concerned with moral directives guiding the relationship between the professional and others; they are designed to distinguish right from wrong action. A professional ethic may be a formal code, or an informal understanding.

It is professional ethics, in the form of written codes of ethics, which concern us at present. In social work such codes generally include a statement of the fundamental values of the profession – usually recognisable variations on the themes of respect for persons and user self-determination and frequently some statement of commitment to the promotion of social justice and to professional integrity. This is usually followed by short statements of ethical principles, often with a brief commentary attached. Some codes are quite detailed, and offer guidance about how to act in certain types of situation. Others offer general statements of principle with little commentary or specific guidance. They range in size from one to over twenty pages. Whatever the level of detail, however, probably none would claim that they aim to provide detailed guidance to social workers about how to act in particular situations. The United States code, which is also the longest, states quite clearly in its preamble:

> The Code offers a set of values, principles, and standards to guide decision making and conduct when ethical issues arise. It does not provide a set of rules that prescribe how social workers should act in all situations. (NASW, 1996, p. 2)

In attempting to counter criticisms of the code of ethics proposed for BASW, Rice argues that a code of ethics should not attempt detailed guidance, and those who expect this misunderstand the nature of such a code. Those critics who say that the code of ethics will be of no use to a social worker 'confronted by conflicts about Mrs X, with agency Y' are, he claims, seeking a particularity of rules and of guidance 'that would become a substitute for ethical reflection, not a stimulation and illumination of it' (Rice, 1975, p. 381). He continues:

> A code of ethics creates the spirit and standard of ethical reflection in that community [of social workers] of ideals, skills and practical concern. A code, over-precise and detailed, would undervalue the professional community . . . (ibid.)

This point is also echoed by Watson (1985) in his reflection on the purpose of the BASW code of ethics ten years after its introduction and by other commentators on codes of ethics (Banks, 1998a, 1998b; Clarke, 1999; Harris, 1994; Jackson, 1994).

Why have a code of ethics?

Although it is often assumed that a code of ethics is a key hallmark of a profession (if one follows the 'trait theory'), Millerson argues that the presence or absence of a code of conduct does not signify professional or non-professional status:

> Some occupations require greater control than others, due to the nature of the work involved. Some need a severe, comprehensive code, others do not. Need for a code depends upon the professional situation. (Millerson, 1964, p. 9)

Millerson (pp. 151–3) identifies the factors determining the need for introducing a code of ethics as follows:

1. *Type of practice* – a professional working alone in a non-institutional practice would need the guidance of an ethical code much more than an individual in an institutional setting.
2. *Nature of the practice* – if it is based on a so-called 'fiduciary' relationship between the professional and the user, especially trust involving life and property, there is more need for a code.
3. *Technique involved* – if the technique is complex, a code may be

necessary to remind the professional to provide the best possible service.

4. *Technical comprehension by users* – where the user cannot be expected to understand the professional's work, a code is required for the protection of the user.

5. *Contact with the user* – if contact is distinct, direct and personal, then it is open to possible abuse, owing to its intimacy. A code therefore protects both professionals and users.

6. *Duty towards the user* – when there is a single user, the duty needs to be clearly defined by a code. With multiple users there is less chance of hiding responsibility (for example, as with the teacher's responsibility to the child, parents, school authorities, the community, in different ways and for different reasons all at once).

Factors which particularly apply in the case of social work relate to its fiduciary nature (2); the level of comprehension of the user (4) – although this may be less to do with the complexities of the techniques than users' lack of knowledge of social workers' powers and legal duties; and the fact that it involves direct, personal contact with the user, often involving the user giving confidential information (5). The other factors – a non-institutional setting, working with single users and using complex techniques – *may* apply in social work practice, particularly in non-statutory work in private practice, or in specialisms such as family therapy. However, in public sector, generic social work they tend not to apply.

Millerson then goes on to look at the elements that determine the possibility of actually introducing an ethical code. He concludes that it is easier to introduce a code where there is a single form of training leading to qualification, where the professionals concerned are mainly involved in one type of work, and where they work for many employers in a strongly organised and registered profession. Given these factors, it may seem surprising that social work, particularly in Britain where hitherto it has not been a registered profession and social workers are involved in many different types of activity, actually has a code of ethics. However, apart from the factors mentioned above in connection with determining the need for a code of ethics, there are perhaps several other reasons why social work has developed a code of ethics which relate to our earlier discussion of professional status and power:

1. It is aspiring to be a 'full profession' with comparable status to, say, medicine and the law. Therefore it is felt to be important to have this feature of professionalism to demonstrate professional status and integrity to the public. It can be seen as part of a move towards becoming recognised as a profession. As Wilding (1982, p. 77) suggests: 'codes of ethics are political counters constructed as much to serve as public evidence of professional intentions and ideals as to provide actual behavioural guidelines for practitioners'.

2. Equally important, a code of ethics may help to generate a sense of common identity and shared values amongst the occupational group. It may be as much about internal recognition as external. Given that social workers are quite fragmented in terms of the variety of types of work they do and the settings in which they operate, the code of ethics and the values upon which it is based may be the one feature that is held in common.

Comparison of codes of ethics for social work from different countries

In order to study in more depth the nature of codes of ethics in social work, all the professional associations in the 73 countries in the membership of the International Federation of Social Workers (IFSW) were sent a letter in August 1999 requesting a copy of their codes of ethics. Associations from 25 countries replied, three of which said they did not have a code of their own. The Portuguese and Sri Lankan Associations said they were currently using the code of the International Federation of Social Workers and the Belarussian Association reported that it was not responsible for codes. The Bolivian Association reported that its code was currently being revised and Iceland that a code had recently been developed but a translation was not yet available.

Copies of codes of ethics were received from the associations in the 20 countries listed in Table 5.1 (p. 96). Codes were received from two of the unions representing social workers in Sweden. Only one code was translated and used for the purpose of this research, that of the SSR (Swedish Union of Social Workers, Personnel and Public Administrators). It is possible that a significant proportion of those countries not responding did not reply because they did not possess a code of ethics. However, the letter requesting information was written in English, and a much higher proportion of English-speaking countries and those where English is a common second language replied. So the information from the codes that were obtained cannot be said to be representative of social work worldwide. It simply serves to illustrate our discussion of the nature and purpose of codes of ethics.

General features of the codes

Of the 20 professional bodies included in Table 5.1, several sent codes of ethics which were versions of the current or past versions of the code of the International Federation of Social Workers (1994) modified slightly to refer to their own countries, for example Denmark (Dansk Socialrågiverforening, 1997), or included the IFSW principles and standards as part of their own code, for example, Norway (FO, 1998) and New Zealand (NZASW, 1993). The codes of the other associations were all different, though some were obviously derivatives of the IFSW or other codes – for example, the Hong Kong code has some similarities of wording to the United States code, and the Luxembourg code is very similar to the 1981 version of the French code. Many have been recently revised or created in the 1990s. These two factors – that some countries have used codes developed elsewhere and slightly modified or adapted them, and that some versions of codes are much more recent than others – means that differences in the form and content of the codes do not necessarily reflect current differences in social work practice, its legal basis or cultural norms in the various countries.

In some cases the codes of ethics have remained virtually the same with minor revisions and slight changes of wording and format over several decades. The BASW code, first published in 1975, is one such case (see Banks, 1998a). Others have changed significantly in style and content. For example, the SSR (1997) code for Sweden is a completely different document from that of 1991. The majority of the document now comprises a background discussion of ethical issues and potential conflicts, with a very short set of ethical guidelines at the end. The Irish code (IASW, 1995) has also changed its style and is more succint and general (a double-sided A5 sheet) than its earlier version. These, however, are exceptional, with the overall trend being for codes to become gradually longer and more detailed over the years (the NASW code for the USA is a very good example of this, having expanded from a nine-page booklet in 1990 to a 27-page booklet in the 1996 version).

The codes are predominantly principle-based as opposed to character-based, with a greater emphasis on Kantian-type rights and duties than on utilitarian principles. However, several codes do make reference to characteristics or qualities of workers ('virtues' in the ethical terminology). For example, the USA code states that the principles and standards must be applied by 'individuals of good character' (NASW, 1996, p. 4) and the Slovakian code mentions 'honesty' as important (ASPS, 1997, para. 1. D). The Hong Kong code has one statement referring to the characteristics of workers as follows: 'The social worker should maintain honesty, integrity and responsibility in professional practice' (Hong Kong Social Workers Association, 1998, p. 6). The South African code talks of serving the profession with 'dignity, honour, diligence and faith' and being 'conscientious, sincere and unselfish' (SABSWA, n.d.). However, this code is very different in style, format and tone to all the others, explicitly taking the form of a one-page oath, rather like the Hippocratic oath in medicine. The Swedish document, in its discussion of ethics in social work (not in its brief 'guidelines in professional ethics'), refers on occasion to character traits. For example, a meeting between people in a public setting is described in terms of 'empathy, respect, responsibility, commitment, trust, prudence, equality, modesty and sincerity' (SSR, 1997, p. 4) and later 'moral maturity' is defined in terms of 'compassion, respect, veracity, attention to detail, humility, bravery and generosity' (p. 5). As noted earlier, the Swedish document is unusual in that it largely comprises discussion about ethical issues with only a very short set of guidelines, in the form of principles, at the end. It makes the only reference in any of the codes to 'love' as a 'central theme within ethics' (p. 2):

> Morals lack a deeper personal basis without experience of values and love. Ethics purely under subjects such as rational egoism, obedience, group pressure or care of one's own conscience is not sufficient, as they have not been touched by love and seriously discovered the other individual and the value of one's own life.

As this brief discussion indicates, there are some interesting differences between codes, which may arise for many reasons, including national law, culture and attitudes towards the welfare state and the role of social work, as well as the composition of the commit-tees responsible for drafting the codes. Yet there are also some very striking similarities. The majority of codes start with an initial 'statement of principles' (Britain), 'general principles' (Netherlands), 'basic values and beliefs' (Hong Kong), 'guiding principles' (Singapore) or 'philosophy' (Canada) which tend to include state-ments about respecting the unique value and dignity of every human being, promoting user self-determination, working for social justice and maintaining professional integrity. We will now discuss each of these broad sets of principles in turn, before looking at the extent to which codes separate out the duties or responsibilities of social workers to various parties (such as users, employers, colleagues) and whether they cover professional practice issues such as advertising and setting fees.

Respect for persons

There is a remarkable consistency in the wording of the principle relating to respecting human value and dignity, which usually comes first. For example:

> The social worker holds that: Every human being has a unique dignity irrespective of nationality, ethnicity, social and economic status, gender, sexual preference, age, beliefs, or contribution to society. (Australian Association of Social Workers, 1994, p. 2)

> Professionals in the social field respect the individuality and dignity of each human being. (Association suisse des profession-nels de l'action sociale, 1999, p. 5)

> Every human being should be respected as an irreplaceable individual regardless of origin, race ... (Japanese Association of Social Workers, 1992)

> I believe in the worth of every person and their relative capacity for development worthy of a human being. (SABSWA, South Africa, n.d.)

As can be seen from Table 5.1, all codes, except that of the Slovakian Association, contain some variation of this basic principle of respect for persons. It is implicit in the Slovakian code, which starts with the statement that: 'social work is a profession based on democratic and human rights values' (ASPS, 1997). This illustrates the general tenor of most codes, which place an emphasis on individualism and tend to include the kinds of general statements about human dignity, worth and rights found in documents like the UN Declaration of Human Rights.

User self-determination

Most codes also make reference to the promotion of user self-determination in their statements of general principles (although the term 'client' rather than 'user' is found in many codes). The codes vary, however, in the extent to which this principle is developed in the further guidance or principles of practice through, for example, advocating participation of users in ensuring and defining appropriate services (BASW, 1996, para. 10.iv), or making efforts to build cooperation (SSR, 1997, para. 7). In some codes, most notably the very lengthy code for the United States Association, such explicit statements about user participation and control are not included over and above the general statement about social workers fostering maximum self-determination on the part of users. There is little evidence of positive commitment to empower users, more a concern that their rights should be protected (negative freedom). However, at the end of the code, under the heading of 'social and political action', a statement is made about the social worker acting to expand choice and opportunity for all persons (NASW, 1996, para. 6.04(b)).

While the general emphasis of most codes is, as Briskman and Noble (1999, p. 57) point out, on 'individual choice, minimising structural disadvantage and diversity', there is nevertheless some subtle variation in the way 'self-determination' is presented. Many talk simply in terms of respecting and promoting service users' rights to make their own choices (negative and positive self-determination, as discussed in Chapter 2). However, the Dutch code speaks in terms of recognising 'clients' responsibility to decide on their own actions' (NVMW, 1999, p. 10) and the code of the Association of Social Workers in the Czech Republic states: 'The social worker leads his clients to the consciousness of self-responsibility' (SSPCR, 1995,

***Table* 5.1** *Comparison of codes of ethics from different countries*

Country	Date	Principle 1	2	3	4	Range of duties	Professional practice issues
Australia	1994	yes	yes	yes	yes	no	yes
Britain	1996	yes	yes	yes	yes	no	no
Canada	1994	yes	yes	yes	yes	yes	yes
Czech Rep.	1995	yes	yes	yes	yes	yes	no
Denmark	1997	yes	yes	yes	yes	no	no
France	1994	yes	yes	no	yes	no	pt (records)
Hong Kong	1998	yes	yes	yes	yes	yes	pt (fees)
Ireland	1995	yes	yes	yes	yes	no	no
Italy	1998	yes	yes	yes	yes	yes	pt (fees)
Japan	1992	yes	yes	yes	yes	yes	no
Luxembourg	n.d.	yes	yes	no	yes	yes	pt (research)
Netherlands	1999	yes	yes	no	yes	yes	pt (records)
New Zealand	1993	yes	yes	yes	yes	yes	yes
Norway	1998	yes	yes	yes	yes	yes	no
Singapore	n.d.	yes	yes	yes	yes	yes	yes
Slovakia	1997	no	yes	no	yes	yes	pt (fees)
South Africa	n.d.	yes	yes	yes	yes	no	no
Sweden	1997	yes	yes	yes	?	yes	no
Switzerland	1999	yes	yes	yes	yes	yes	pt (research, records)
USA	1996	yes	yes	yes	yes	yes	yes

Notes
General principles: does the code include the following principles – yes, no or partly (pt)?
  (1) Respect for the unique value of the inividual person
  (2) User self-determination
  (3) Social justice
  (4) Professional integrity
Range of duties: does the code divide the responsibilities of the social worker into at least three of the following – those to users, agency, colleagues, society, profession?
Professional practice issues: does the code cover some professional practice issues such as guidance or rules on advertising, charging fees, user access to records, using clients in research, etc.?

para. 2.1.1). The use of the term 'responsibility' moves the emphasis away from enabling people to exercise their rights and more towards encouraging them to recognise their responsibilities, for themselves and for others in society. The South African code has another interesting twist in talking about people's rights to 'make their own decisions in conducting their lives within the framework of the standards of behaviour accepted by society' (SABSW, n.d., para. 4). Although this probably reflects the reality of social work practice in most countries, it is generally not stated in this explicit way in most codes, which tend to be idealistic and dwell little on the constraints of the social and economic context within which social work is practised.

Social justice

Another feature of the majority of codes is a statement that the social worker should have a commitment to social justice, although these exact words may not be used. For example, the British code states:

> The worker has the right and duty to bring to the attention of those in power, and of the general public, ways in which the activities of government, society or agencies create or contribute to hardship and suffering or militate against their relief. (BASW, 1996, para. 7)

Many codes include statements such as that found in the Swiss code about 'denouncing and reducing injustices' (ASPAS, 1999, p. 5) or as in the Norwegian code, that social workers are expected to:

> reveal structures and systems which contribute to inequalities, social injustice and oppression and to work to modify and change such structures and systems. (Fellesorganisasjonen for Barnvernpedagoger, Socionomer og Vernpleire (FO), 1998, p. 17, para. 2.2)

This statement from the Norwegian code, which featured in previous versions of the International Federation of Social Workers code, is found in many codes which either adopt with minor modifications, or are loosely based on, the IFSW code.

One of the codes that stands out in its emphasis on the social worker's proactive commitment to social justice is that of the Australian Association, which states as its first principle that the social worker should:

advocate changes in policy, service delivery and social conditions
which enhance the opportunities for those most vulnerable in the
community. (AASW, 1994, p. 2)

The achievement of social justice is said to be 'co-equal with the
attainment of fulfilment for the individual' (AASW, 1994, p. 1). The
New Zealand Code discusses this 'dual focus' of social work and
affirms that its members are fully committed to both enabling users
to find solutions to their problems and changing the structures of
society (NZASW, 1993, p. 1). This may well be the intention in some
of the other codes, but it is certainly not stated so clearly in any of
the others, where statements such as 'a social worker shall maintain
the best interest of the client as the primary obligation' (Canadian
Association of Social Workers, 1994, p. 9) imply that the social
worker's first responsibility is to the welfare of the individual
users.

The New Zealand code is also distinctive in that it contains a
separate 'Bicultural Code of Practice' which affirms the right of the
Maori people to independence. The code of ethics is in three parts:
'Principles' (based on the IFSW principles, with minor modifications); 'The Social Worker's Ethical Responsibilities' (which give
more detail about specific responsibilities to clients, agencies, society
and so on); and the 'Bicultural Code of Practice' (which is based on
the same IFSW principles as the first part of the code, but with significant changes). The bicultural code calls on social work organisations and workers to 'acknowledge and support the whanau [the
extended family] as the primary source of care and nurturing of its
members' and 'recognises the rights of Maori clients to have a Maori
worker' (NZASW, 1993, p. 17). Social workers are called upon
'actively and constructively [to] promote change in those organisations that operate from a monocultural base' and it is suggested that
'monocultural control over power and resources needs to be relin-
quished so that Maori can achieve liberation' (p. 18). Briskman
and Noble (1999) regard the New Zealand code as a good example
of a code that attempts to accommodate difference and diversity
and offers some direction for change. They see this a possible
model for reformulating codes in the light of diversity and otherness,
unlike most other codes with their 'global assumptions' and
tendency to discuss all social workers and service users as having

the same concerns and occupying the same political positions in society.

There is no doubt that the Maori people have a very significant position in New Zealand society, recognised in the Treaty of Waitangi, which explains why the New Zealand Association felt concerned to acknowledge this in its code of ethics. Yet this does not explain the decision to have a separate 'bicultural code' relating specifically to Maori people, rather than integrating those principles into the first part of the code. If we pursue the recognition of 'diversity and otherness' as suggested by Briskman and Noble, there seems no reason why there should not be a proliferation of separate codes for social work with different groups. Their starting point, a 'critical postmodernist' approach, would more logically lead to the abandonment of codes of ethics as such, since however specifically they are targeted, their format is inevitably prescriptive and general (relating to 'all Maori people' for example).

Professional integrity

All codes also lay great stress on what is often termed 'professional integrity'. Indeed, this could be said to be the whole purpose of a code of ethics – to affirm publicly the commitment of members of the profession to act in a manner befitting their knowledge and status in society. In most codes this is framed in terms of actions, which include professionals taking responsibility for their actions and ensuring they are in line with the code, a commitment to the continuing development of their knowledge and skills, not using their special knowledge and skills for inhuman purposes, not abusing the relative powerlessness of the user through having sexual relationships, not bringing into disrepute the good name of the profession through malpractice, and monitoring and challenging agency policies and practices which may be contrary to the ethical code.

However, the codes vary in the extent to which they clearly and unequivocally state that the professional code must take priority over agency rules and procedures. For example, the Canadian code states: 'If a conflict arises in professional practice, the standards declared in this code take precedence' (CASW, 1994, p. 7), whereas the British code simply calls upon social workers to work for 'the creation and maintenance in employing agencies of conditions which will support and facilitate social workers' acceptance of the obligations of the code' (BASW, 1996, para. 10, xii).

Range of duties

Some codes are also much clearer than others about the potential for conflict between different principles and duties (for example, duties to the agency or to society as opposed to the promotion of the user's interests). The International Federation of Social Workers code (1994) includes a separate section entitled 'problem areas' which itemises areas of potential conflicting interests, and also mentions the problems of the dual function of social worker as carer and controller. This is perhaps the clearest statement about the potential for conflict of all the codes. However, the IFSW code, partly no doubt because it is intended to apply universally, does not give any guidance regarding how to solve such conflicts. Some codes, although not the IFSW one, probably for the reasons just mentioned, are actually laid out in a format which itemises in turn the social worker's responsibility to users, colleagues, employers and employing organisations, the profession and society (see Table 5.1). The USA code is a good example of this, and many others are also laid out in this way, although some do not separately itemise responsibility to society. This does seem a very helpful format, because it acknowledges that the social worker has a range of duties to a variety of interest groups. The British code, for example, while acknowledging in one sentence in its foreword that members of a profession have 'obligations to their clients, to their employers, to each other, to colleagues in other disciplines and to society' (BASW, 1996, para. 3) does not go on to specify clearly what these different obligations are and what to do when they conflict.

Professional practice issues

Some codes are very lengthy and go into a lot of detail on issues such as advertising, fees or the use of videos. The most detailed is the USA

code, where in the section on 'Ethical Standards' statements of the
following specificity can be found:

Social workers should not discuss confidential information in
public or semipublic areas such as hallways, waiting rooms, eleva-
tors, and restaurants. (NASW, 1996, p. 11)

As was noted earlier, the USA code has gradually grown over the
years. For example, the section on confidentiality and privacy
consists of five relatively short statements in the 1990 version of the
code. By 1996, the equivalent section comprises 18 statements, some
of which are of paragraph length. The Netherlands code of 1999
explicitly itemises the revisions made since the first 1990 code, which
include new rules relating to confidentiality, in particular dealing
with service users' records and providing information about service
users to other organisations. In explaining these additions, comments
are made that: 'Society is becoming ever more complex' and 'The
privacy of clients has been placed under increasing pressure'. A separate chapter is also included in the latest version of the Netherlands
code to take into account 'partnership agreements, where all participants contribute their own objectives, codes of conduct and
methodologies' (NVMW, 1999, p. 7).

The Canadian code is also relatively detailed, giving some very specific guidance including, for example, a detailed specification of the
knowledge and skills it is the social worker's duty to possess, when
educational degrees can be cited, what to do when disclosure of confidential information is required by order of a court, and how the
self-employed social worker should disclose charges at the beginning
of a relationship. It is at this point that codes of ethics, or statements
of general principles and general guidance, begin to merge into what
we earlier called 'codes of practice'. Some codes state nothing about
matters such as advertising of qualifications or setting reasonable
levels of fees (see Table 5.1 under the heading of 'professional practice issues'); others make some general statements, but not at the level
of detail of the some of the items in the Canadian and USA codes.

Obviously issues about fees and advertising are pertinent in countries where private practice is commonplace. Elsewhere, as in Britain,
it may not be thought necessary to include these matters in a code
of ethics. The extent to which such detailed codes of practice are
appropriate and enforceable will also depend upon whether the profession of social work is legally recognised in a country and whether

the professional association (or some other regulatory body) has established committees and procedures for hearing complaints, making investigations into breaches of the code, and disciplining members through fines, suspension or termination of membership. For example, the Swiss code includes a section on the 'application of the code', outlining procedures in cases of infringements of the code and the measures and sanctions that can be taken by the Association's commission on professional ethics. Attached in a pocket at the back of the Netherlands Association code is an eight-page booklet of 'Regulations for Disciplinary Procedures'. It is reported that the Netherlands Association set up a professional register of social workers in 1990 'as part of the professionalisation of social work' (NVMW, 1999, p. 4). This suggests that the disciplinary procedures can be used to strike people off the register. This appears to be the role of the professional associations in those countries where the title of qualified social worker is legally protected. In fact, in all European Community countries except Ireland, Italy and Britain, the title of social worker is protected by law (IFSW, 1989). The proposed new General Councils in Britain will take on the function of registration and regulation of the profession, and will no doubt develop codes of ethics and practice of a more detailed nature than the current British Association of Social Workers code (membership of BASW is voluntary and it does not hold a register).

'Professional autonomy' and codes of ethics in bureaucracies

'Professional autonomy', that is, the power of professionals to make their own considered decisions and judgements based on their expertise and ethical values, is a feature traditionally associated with professionalism. Several codes explicitly refer to this, including the Netherlands code which stresses that 'social workers have to shape and guard their own professional autonomy' (NVMW, 1999, p. 8). This point is made also in the Italian code:

> The profession is based on technical–professional autonomy, on independent judgement, on personal knowledge of the profession and on personal consciousness of the social worker. The social worker has the duty to defend his/her autonomy from pressure and conditioning. (Ordine Nazionale Assistenti Sociali, 1998, para 1.6)

Similar sentiments are expressed in the codes from Luxembourg (Association Nationale des Assistantes d'Hygiéne Sociale, n.d., art. 24) and France, with a specific stress on the fact that social workers should not agree to practise in 'conditions that compromise the quality of their interventions' (Association Nationale des Assistantes de Service Social, 1994, art. 7) and should assume 'responsibility for the choice and application of techniques concerning their professional relationships with people' (ibid., art. 22). However, the majority of codes are not so explicit, perhaps because it has long been acknowledged that professional autonomy for social workers is less than that of some other professions and is declining along with that of all professions.

Social work is frequently practised in bureaucratic organisations, and there is a tension between the ideal of professional autonomy and the reality of a rule-governed, hierarchical structure. As Toren states:

> One of the main features of a bureaucratic organisation is that the work of its members is directed by a set of universalistic rules and procedures. These can be maintained only if the work done is specific and routine; the helping professions, and in particular social work, are neither. (Toren, 1972, p. 57)

She argues that the approach of social workers to users (which would be in accordance with the codes of ethics as well as their education and training) is to treat them as whole people, taking account of all of their needs; and also to see them as unique – in which case there will always be special circumstances, or exceptions to the rule. So the primacy of the ethical code, which professionals are supposed to apply according to their own judgement, is challenged by the clearly defined organisational rules and supervision or line management of a bureaucracy.

While there is obviously some truth in this, it may be questioned whether the distinction is as clear and straightforward as has been made out. We might question whether doctors working in a state-funded hospital, or a lawyer employed by a large law firm, are really completely autonomous or free from control from their superiors (Toren, 1972, p. 53). Talcott Parsons (1959) outlined a system of dual authority which could be applied to a hospital: the administrative system which is concerned with the organisation as a whole – patient numbers, financial matters, recruitment of staff; and the operative system, which is concerned with implementing the organisation's goals, that is, treating patients. A hospital could be characterised as what Mintzberg calls a 'professional bureaucracy'. Mintzberg makes quite a useful distinction between what he calls 'machine bureaucracies' which rely on authority of a hierarchical nature, and 'professional bureaucracies' which allow for participative decision-making by the 'frontline' staff with less hierarchy imposed over them (Mintzberg, 1979). In professional bureaucracies standardisation or quality of output is not controlled by direct supervision, but by 'professional' standards, learnt through training and experience, and regulated by professional bodies and peer pressure from outside any one organisation. Individual staff work largely autonomously with little need for direct supervision. Examples might be universities, hospitals, social work and other human service agencies (Bloxham, 1993).

However, while it may be appropriate to describe many of the organisational settings in which social work is practised as professional bureaucracies, arguably social workers do not have as much control over their own work or as much professional respect and status as doctors or university lecturers; also the local authority structures in which many social workers still work in Britain are traditionally quite hierarchical and rule-bound. While it may be argued that the concept and practice of 'supervision' in social work is as much about personal development and support in an emotionally demanding job as it is about management, close supervision is nevertheless enshrined in social work and it is largely carried out by people in a managerial role (although usually qualified social workers). Traditional local authority procedures often demand, for example, that individual social workers cannot even sign their own letters, which must all go out under the signature of the area manager or divisional director. It could still be argued that there is less scope for social workers employed in bureaucratic organisations to retain as large a degree of professional autonomy as other professionals such as doctors who also work in bureaucracies, or as social workers working in less bureaucratic structures in small independent or private agencies. This would seem to imply that there might be less scope for retaining professional identity and upholding the code of ethics as a primary obligation to the profession. There are changes taking place in the management and structure of social work in Britain and in other countries which are resulting not only in more responsibility being devolved to social workers (for example, by managing budgets) but also in the centralising and proceduralising of more of the tasks undertaken by social workers. The implications of this will be discussed later.

It may be more useful to explore which aspects of a professional's practice are controlled, by whom and how, than to try to categorise professions in terms of which are autonomous and which are not. Toren argues that the encounter between the social worker and user is usually not observable and is therefore not directly controllable, which allows the social worker a great degree of autonomy in relation to contacts with users. Yet many other aspects of the job are much more controlled, such as the distribution of resources and services to users. It is these aspects of the job that are subject to bureaucratic procedures as opposed to professional standards. This is reflected in the fact that most codes of ethics are more concerned with how the social worker should treat the individual user than they are with prescribing how resources should be allocated between users, which might seem to be an agency or governmental matter.

Yet while in theory it may be possible to separate the pure encounter with the user from the bureaucratic controls and procedures of the agency, in practice it is the rules of the agency which define who is to be regarded as a user and provide the context in which the social worker operates. They already define the *person* who approaches the social work agency for help, or who is approached by the agency offering help, surveillance or control, as a *service user* and the kind of help that can be given or control required. Within this context the social worker has some freedom to treat the user in the way she thinks fit. Yet this is limited, and is being even further limited in Britain as the government and social work agencies develop many more sets of procedures and rules regarding how to carry out the work. This trend is happening not only in social work, but also in the older established professions of medicine and the law, as part of a challenge to the autonomy and power of professionals. There is also a trend towards the fragmentation of social work into specialisms and multidisciplinary work, which again tends to result in a loss of professional identity. This is happening across Europe and was noted by Thérèse Rossel at a seminar in 1990 when she commented on:

the movement towards the administrative decentralisation of social services on the one hand; and the introduction into work and to projects or programmes of notions such as multi-disciplinary and community development. (IFSW, 1990, p. 27)

She suggested that these changes were responsible for 'the fragmentation of the profession, and the dangers of a loss of identity'. The International Federation of Social Workers recommended therefore:

> that to develop, at an European level, the values on which social work depends in our respective countries constitutes a professional obligation, articulated in the International Code of Ethics. This code is the proper expression of values which must, here and now, guide social work and social action. (IFSW, 1990, p. 29)

The code of ethics is seen to be a unifying factor which may help to hold together the profession at a time of fragmentation. Yet, equally, it could be argued that professional codes of ethics may become increasingly irrelevant if this trend continues and the occupational identity of 'social worker' begins to crumble. We noted earlier Millerson's view that it is difficult to introduce a code of ethics if there is not one main dominating kind of work. If there are many different specialisms (child protection, community care, mental health, family therapy, welfare rights, case management) in different agency settings (public, private, independent, voluntary) this may mean there is an even greater need for a code of ethics to hold the profession together, while at the same time it becomes more difficult to maintain the code as important, relevant and a primary source of moral guidance. Certainly there will be very different codes of practice, and arguably the agency rules and procedures will be more influential than a set of general moral principles published by the professional association.

How useful are codes of ethics?

Some commentators are sceptical about the value of codes of ethics. This is not just because of their link with the evolution of an occupation towards professional exclusivity and elitism (Wilding, 1982). Downie and Calman (1994), when examining codes of ethics in health care, identify a number of limitations:

1. The codes tend to imply that professionals are given their ethics, whereas it is at least as true that professionals bring with them their own individual values.
2. Many aspects of welfare and caring work are not expressible in terms of rules or duties – for example, the cultivation of certain attitudes such as compassion.
3. Codes tend to be exclusive to one profession, whereas welfare and caring work are now increasingly provided by multidisciplinary teams.
4. Codes assume an exclusive professional–user relationship, with the professionals doing the best they can for the individual users; this ignores the pressing economic considerations in welfare and caring work.
5. Codes assume a consensus on values both within the professions and their public. But it is doubtful whether this still exists, as professions are fragmented and users are increasingly demanding that services are delivered in terms of their own values rather than those of the professions.

As Downie and Calman (1994, p. 268) comment:

> To the extent, then, that professions are now expected to work *through* the community rather than *on* it, the position of codes of ethics has shifted from the centre of professional life to the margins.

Indeed, many social workers are also rather sceptical about the value of a code of ethics. How useful a code of ethics is depends upon what one wants to use it for. While many of Downie and Calman's criticisms are very valid, we need to recognise that a professional code performs a number of different functions, one of which may be an attempt to maintain professional power and identity at a time when these are threatened. We have already noted that there are a number of reasons why a profession may have a code of ethics, including:

1. to contribute to the 'professional status' of an occupation;
2. to establish and maintain professional identity;
3. to guide practitioners about how to act;
4. to protect users from malpractice or abuse.

The first two reasons relate to the occupation of social work as a whole, and are about perceptions and identity rather than directly about practice. They are about how the outside world sees social work, and how social workers view themselves. Of course, if it is effectively to fulfil the first two aims, the code must relate to social work practice and be known about by members of the profession. But such a code can be quite general in nature; indeed, it is probably helpful if it is general – consisting of statements of values or general moral principles that can be accepted by all members of the occupation. It is this kind of function that the International Federation of Social Workers sees for its code at a time of change and fragmentation within the occupation. Arguably this is also the main role played by many of the more general codes, such as the British, Irish, or Swedish. In countries where social work and professional associations are just being established, with new codes (for example, the Czech Republic, Slovakia), these codes also tend to be short and general – more akin to mission statements.

However, most of the codes include other aims or purposes, particularly (3) guiding social workers and (4) protecting users. How effectively can they do this? If social workers are looking for detailed guidance on how to act in particular situations, then they will usually be disappointed. As was stated earlier, this would both be impossible, given the complexity of social work practice, and would also contradict a key feature of what it means to be a professional – namely that education and a commitment to a set of values enable professionals to make their own (autonomous) informed and considered judgements on professional matters. If the code of ethics was to be turned into a detailed rulebook, then the social worker would merely have to follow it unthinkingly, and there would be no room for discretion and judgement.

On the other hand, while recognising that ethical codes cannot and should not be detailed rulebooks, it could be argued that they frequently consist of a set of principles of such a general nature as to be open to wide interpretation and are therefore useless in guiding practice. We suggested in Chapter 2 that user self-determination, for example, could be interpreted as meaning anything from leaving the user completely alone to justifying parentalist intervention to increase the user's capacities for self-determined action. The codes, to be successful in their aims of guiding practitioners even in a general way, probably need to be related more clearly to practice than many in fact are. One way of doing this is to ensure that the general value statements are discussed and analysed during the course of social work training and related to the daily practice of social work. Otherwise the codes of ethics are left hanging in a vacuum, or sitting in a drawer, unused and unusable. Another way in which they can be related to practice is by including codes of practice alongside the codes of ethics (as is the case in the Canadian code). The problem with the development of more detailed codes of practice at a national level by the professional association alongside the codes of ethics is that they can be overprescriptive and do not allow for variations in work contexts and user groups in which some of the 'rules' or guidance may not apply. While it may be appropriate for the Law Society in Britain to devise detailed codes of conduct relating to the minutiae of fees or advertising, in social work such a project seems much more problematic.

What is happening, however, is that most agencies are developing their own codes of practice for dealing with specific issues, especially relating to the user's rights – such as confidentiality, access to records, or making complaints. These vary from agency to agency, but such codes of practice seem much more clearly designed to protect and clarify users' rights and to clarify the roles of the social worker and the agency. What is important is that these codes of practice are related clearly to the more general value statements in the codes of ethics and can be seen to be a development from them. The most appropriate statement that might be made about confidentiality, for example, in a national code of ethics might be that social workers should ensure that their agencies have policies and codes of practice clearly stating the extent to which information given by the user to a social worker will and will not be kept confidential. Obviously the extent to which information can be kept confidential may be very different in an independent counselling agency, compared with a statutory child protection agency. Therefore the role of the code of ethics in guiding practice seems to be to outline the broad principles of the profession and the potential areas where ethical issues will arise.

Regarding the role of a code of ethics in protecting the user, this can only be fulfilled in a very general way in laying down broad principles relating to respect, non-exploitation or abuse. Yet these should be obvious anyway, and it is the more subtle and detailed use of power and knowledge from which the user may need some protection. Perhaps this can also be better served (though still very imperfectly) through well-publicised and clear agency codes of practice regarding such issues as making contracts with users, procedures for access to records, or rights to complaint. The next chapter will explore further the concept of codes of practice and their relationship to codes of ethics.

Conclusions

In this chapter we have examined the nature and function of codes of ethics in social work. We noted that the existence of codes of ethics for social work is intimately related to the notion of professionalism and one of their main functions is to maintain professional status and identity. In looking at codes of ethics developed by professional associations in different countries, many common features were noted, particularly a congruence around the stated values or principles underpinning social work including: respect for the individual person, promotion of user self-determination, promotion of social justice and working for the interests of users. The extent to which the codes acknowledge that the societal and agency contexts in which social work is practised may also place demands on social workers varies, as does the level of detail regarding practical guidance on matters such as charging fees, advertising qualifications or user access to records.

The extent to which social workers regard such codes as useful will depend upon what they want to use them for. For practical guidance on how to act in certain types of situations and as a means of safeguarding users' rights, agency codes of practice may be more useful. However, as a means of defending the profession from outside attack, of maintaining professional identity and of setting some general benchmarks against which to judge agency policies and practice, they do have a role to play. The codes emphasise that social workers have a responsibility over and above just doing the job and following the agency's rules. This may be useful at a time when resources for social work are being reduced and standards of work and the quality of service may be threatened. The codes of ethics remind social workers that because they possess particular knowledge and skills, and work on a daily basis with people living in poverty and suffering crises and problems, they have a duty to inform governments and agencies of inequities, lack of resources or the need for policy changes. Yet, because of the changes in the management and delivery of social services, codes of ethics are also becoming increasingly irrelevant, with their emphasis on professionally defined values (as opposed to those defined by the users), their assumption of a professional consensus (when much work is specialised and multidisciplinary) and their focus on service to users (in a climate where economy and efficiency are also of prime importance). In such a climate, codes of practice developed by social work agencies are more important ways of safeguarding user rights. Social workers still need to be prepared to challenge agency policies and practices and to view themselves as more than just employees doing a job. The professional code of ethics, along with education and training, obviously has a role to play in this.

6

Users' Rights: Codes of Practice and the New Consumerism

In the last chapter we argued that the main role of codes of ethics is to establish and maintain professional identity. Although they claim to play a role in protecting the interests and rights of users and in guiding social workers, this is an indirect role. The general principles in the codes of ethics cannot immediately and obviously be put into practice. They must be interpreted and translated into some more specific principles or guidance. In this chapter we will look at what is meant by 'rights', the difference between regarding the user as a person, a citizen or a consumer, the growing trend towards developing procedures and codes of practice which state and protect users' rights, and the approaches that need to be adopted by social workers to enable users to exercise these rights.

Rights

There are many different political and philosophical theories regarding the nature of rights (as claims, benefits, choices or entitlements), where rights come from (God, nature or a social contract) and whether they are regarded as the basic category of morality (see Jones, 1994). I will suggest a view which I think makes sense in the context of this book and reflects how rights tend to be regarded in western society in general and social work in particular. Rights are generally regarded as belonging to individuals, although this view does not necessarily make sense in societies where the individual person is not the prime focus of cultural norms and ways of life.

Rights are an important part of the western liberal tradition in politics and moral philosophy, which we have already linked to the Kantian notion of respect for persons. If respect for persons is regarded as the ultimate principle of morality, or indeed a precondition for any morality whatsoever, then it follows that persons have certain rights which should be respected.

According to Feinberg (1973, p. 64) a right is a valid claim. By 'valid' he means justified according to a system of rules. If someone has a right, then at least one other person must have duties towards that person. He elucidates the concept of a right with reference to a claim, arguing that a right is more than just a claim. Whereas claims may differ in degree (some may be stronger than others), rights do not. Whereas claims may be invalid, rights cannot be. He gives the example of young orphans throughout the world needing a good upbringing, including a balanced diet. He argues that this is a claim, not a right, because in many places resources are not available and therefore no particular person has a duty to provide goods. This definition of rights obviously has implications for how we regard some of the 'rights' included in the United Nations Universal Declaration of the Rights of the Child: for example, the right of all children to 'adequate nutrition, housing, recreation and medical services' (1959, principle 4). Feinberg regards the use of the term 'human rights' in the UN and other similar declarations as a 'special manifesto sense of right' which identifies basic needs with rights. He argues that such statements should more properly be described as urging on the world community the moral principle that all basic human needs ought to be recognised as 'claims worthy of sympathy and serious consideration now, even though they cannot yet plausibly be treated as valid claims' (Feinberg, 1973, p. 67).

Having defined rights as valid claims, we should now explore different types of rights. The distinction is often made between negative and positive rights as follows:

- *Negative rights* (or liberties) relate to the freedom to do something without interference (for example, free speech).
- *Positive rights* (claim rights) claim against someone else to do something (for example, medical treatment).

Another distinction is that between legal rights and moral rights, and both of these can be either positive or negative:

- *Legal rights* are valid claims by virtue of the legal code or customary practice (for example, the right to vote).
- *Moral rights* are valid claims bestowed by a moral code (for example, the right to be treated with honesty).

These two categories are not mutually exclusive, as many moral rights are also legal rights (for example, the right to free speech). There are two further important distinctions between types of rights: absolute (or unqualified) rights and conditional (or qualified) rights; and universal rights (applying to everybody without exception) and particular rights (applying to a limited class of people). Clark with Asquith (1985, p. 24) draw up a useful table relating to the four possible combinations of rights in these categories, from which the following list is derived:

1. *Absolute universal rights* – apply unconditionally to everybody. Clark with Asquith argue that there is probably only one right in this category, and that would be the right to be treated as an end and not simply as a means (which logically follows from the concept of respect for persons).
2. *Qualified universal rights* – apply to everybody, except they may be withdrawn from anybody on the basis of the application of criteria which apply to all. This category would include those rights that have often been put forward as 'natural rights' (that is, rights simply deducible from the nature of humankind) and some of what are included as 'human rights', such as the right to liberty, which can be withheld on certain grounds. For example, the right to liberty is suspended for the imprisoned criminal.
3. *Absolute particular rights* – apply without qualification to everybody in a certain category. For example, all parents who are British citizens have an absolute right to claim child benefit.
4. *Qualified particular rights* – apply to certain persons under certain conditions. For example, a British citizen has a right to a state pension if over the prescribed retirement age and having satisfied the necessary contribution conditions.

The question as to whether there are any basic universal human needs and any universal moral rights links to questions of cultural imperialism and moral relativism and is much debated (see Doyal and Gough, 1991; Outka and Reeder, 1993). In relation to social work it is important to note that the International Federation of Social Workers certainly believes in the existence of universal moral rights and endorses as part of its code of ethics the UN Declarations of Human Rights and the Rights of the Child.

Clark with Asquith (1985, p. 27) argue that social workers mainly deal with qualified particular rights on a day-to-day basis and that the 'application of universal rights cannot, without absurdity, be essentially different in social work from any other context'. However, the statements of values and ethics made by the social work profession invariably focus on what appear to be regarded as either absolute or qualified *universal rights*.

Clark with Asquith produce a typical list of users' rights drawn from the social work literature as follows:

1. to be treated as an end;
2. to self-determination;
3. to be accepted for what one is;
4. to be treated as a unique individual;
5. to non-discrimination on irrelevant grounds;
6. to treatment on the principles of honesty, openness and non-deception;
7. to have information given to the worker in the course of social work treatment treated as confidential;
8. to a professionally competent service;
9. to access to resources for which there exists an entitlement ('welfare rights').

The first six rights on the list could be said to be derived from the principle of respect for persons and are very similar to Biestek's list discussed in Chapter 2. The first right is an absolute universal right, and (2) to (5) could be regarded as qualified universal rights. The right to welfare (9) relates to users as citizens of a specific country; the welfare rights may be universal in that country (the right to health care) or, more usually in Britain, particular (the right of parents to child benefit). The right to confidentiality (7) and a professionally competent service (8) refer specifically to someone in the role of a social work user and therefore are particular. Confidentiality is qualified, as there are rules regarding when one is allowed to break confidentiality (for example, when someone else's rights or interests are seriously threatened, or if it is in the user's interests). The right to a professionally competent service is, arguably, an unqualified right. It may be the case that a professionally competent service is not delivered due to lack of qualified staff as a result of resource constraints. However, this should not negate the user's right to that standard of service.

The user as a person

The lists of principles such as those of Biestek and the others high-lighted in Table 2.1 focus more on the universal rights which should apply to all people than on the particular rights applying to the service user *qua* user. The emphasis on the social work user as a *person* with the basic moral rights derived from the principle of respect for persons was the dominant one in the social work literature until perhaps the 1980s. This meant that the kinds of moral principles stated for social work were no different to the kinds of moral principles that would be stated for morality in general, although the context in which they were applied obviously presented specific issues and difficulties for workers. This type of view based on Kantian philosophy and Biestek's list of casework principles has already been discussed in the section on the principles of the social worker–user relationship in Chapter 2.

The user as a citizen

In the late 1970s and early 1980s the notion of 'clients as fellow citizens' began to be stressed (Jordan, 1975; BASW, 1980) as part of the reaction against the view of the social worker as expert giving psychological explanations of users' problems, and as a move towards regarding social workers as allies of users (Payne, 1989, p. 121). Studies had been published (for example, Mayer and Timms, 1970) relating to users' views of social work which contributed to the pressure to alter the power balance between users and social workers. As Phelan commented: 'As social workers we have a responsibility to bear constantly in mind that our clients are equal with us. They have complete citizenship' (BASW, 1980).

This kind of view entails that the rights of users should be seen as rights of citizens not to be treated arbitrarily by state officials, and therefore as having rights of access to information about the purpose of social work, to see personal information held by social work agencies on file, and to participate in planning and decision-making, for example. The principle of respecting the user as a fellow citizen could be regarded as a development of the idea of respect for persons. However, the term 'citizen' is narrower than 'person', in that it focuses on the rights of the person in the role of citizen, rather than respect for the person as a person. Citizenship entails more specific rights, including social rights to the benefits and services of the welfare state, as well as political and civil rights. The 'user as fellow citizen' approach therefore increases the accountability of social workers, although it is reductive in its view of the user.

The term 'citizen' is as contested as many of the others we have been using. The notion of the user as a fellow citizen will be interpreted differently depending on how citizenship is construed – whether in terms of the liberal tradition of individual rights, social citizenship with a stress on reciprocity and common interests (Jordan, 1989), or citizenship based on meeting people's needs (Taylor, 1989). The idea of users as fellow citizens suggests that both social workers and users are members of a common community or society and as such possess certain rights. If we follow T. H. Marshall, these could be described as political (for example, the right to vote), civil (for example, the right to freedom of speech), and social (for example, the right to education). According to Marshall, citizenship is: 'a status bestowed on those who are full members of a community. All those who possess the status are equal with respect to the rights and duties with which the status is endowed' (Marshall, 1963, p. 87).

This implies that these rights and duties apply equally to everyone. Yet as Taylor (1989) has argued, citizenship, with its notions of membership of a community (particularly a nation) is based on a set of practices which excludes certain people from full membership. He gives as an example the Immigration Act 1988 which ruled that the wives of British and Commonwealth men settled in Britain could only be brought into the country if they could be supported themselves and would have no recourse to public funds. There are many other ways in which some people are denied full citizenship rights, particularly women, black people, people with disabilities, people who are lesbian, gay or bisexual, and children (Taylor, 1989; Lister,

1991). It is likely that a significant number of the people who become users of social work services may not have or may not be able to exercise full citizenship rights. While social workers may believe that everyone in society ought to have equal status, and it may be a good principle for the social worker to regard the users as fellow citizens, we cannot pretend that this is the case in our present society. Users are often people who have been excluded from the political process (for example, with no address they cannot vote), and who do not share in the rights and benefits associated with employment. Social workers do not have the power to make people fellow citizens. However, the services and contact offered by social workers can treat people in a way fellow citizens ought to be treated – that is, users should not be stigmatised, or treated as undeserving. This relates to the discussion at the end of Chapter 4 where it was suggested that users could be treated with respect, within a framework of societal and agency constraints.

Social work, as part of social services, is one of the institutions responsible for delivering what Marshall called 'the right to welfare' or social rights. Social rights include the right to education, a state pension, and many other rights, some of which social workers may be regarded as contributing to, ranging from: 'a modicum of economic welfare and security to the right to share to the full in the social heritage and to live the life of a civilised being according to the standards prevailing in society' (Marshall, 1963, p. 74).

Some of these rights are enshrined in law (such as education), others are what might be described as moral rights (such as the right to live the life of a civilised human being). The fact that these are all described as rights of citizenship means that those who receive benefits or services through the welfare state should regard them as theirs of right, that is, they should not be regarded as dependent or stigmatised, and should not be treated arbitrarily by state officials (Campbell, 1978). This obviously poses a challenge for social work. Many of the people seeking social work help, or required to have contact with social workers, may have already been denied full citizenship rights, and/or may find it difficult to exercise their rights due to poverty, lack of confidence or lack of competence, for example. They may feel they do not have a genuine right to services, or they do not have the power or confidence to complain if the services are inadequate. Except in areas of social work which are subject to the law, such as child protection, mental health or probation work, there have not been clear rules or guidelines about who should be offered social work help and what the nature of the help should be. This has made it doubly difficult for users to complain or appeal about the service received from social workers. Campbell suggests that social workers have exercised considerable discretionary powers over users based on their professional judgement of what is in the users' best interests. He suggests that the user's rights to social work help or consideration are discretionary, which makes it very difficult to appeal against the treatment or service received. One of the ways in which users' rights as citizens can be made more real is if they are given more information about the service offered and the right to appeal, and treated more as equals and partners than as needy recipients of welfare handouts and social work advice. As Marshall said: 'the right of appeal helps keep alive the idea that the granting of assistance is not a fact of grace, but the satisfaction of a right' (Marshall, 1963, p. 89).

It should also be noted that there has been a growing trend towards the end of the twentieth century to emphasise not just citizenship rights, but also the duties and responsibilities of citizens to each other. As Lund (1999, p. 447) comments in relation to the welfare reforms of 'New Labour' in Britain, there is a 'fastening of duties to rights' and a stress on the importance of mutual obligations. These kinds of ideas are part of the 'new communitarian' thinking which will be touched on again later in this chapter in connection with the discussion of community involvement.

The user as a consumer

The notion of the service user as a 'consumer' possessing quite specific rights to be treated in a certain kind of way and to receive a certain standard of service is an even further narrowing down, or arguably a move away from, the concept of a person with universal rights. This developed in the 1980s and 1990s as part of the growth of charterised standards and quality assurance indicators. One of the aims, particularly of the Conservative government in Britain, of adopting the terminology of consumers (or 'customers') was to emphasise the notion of *choice*. Although customers are people who receive services, they are able to choose between the services on offer. If they do not like a particular service, they are free to go elsewhere (the power of 'exit'). They exert some power in exercising this choice and are therefore not merely passive recipients. This model is obviously based on the traditional idea of the marketplace, with sellers of goods and services competing with each other to find buyers. The buyers will be looking for services that meet their particular needs, offering the level of quality desired, at the right price. Such a notion has not traditionally been applied to the services provided by the welfare state – largely because there has usually been a monopoly supplier, the state, and although it would make sense to say that people's welfare rights entitled them to a certain standard of service, it was usually difficult for them to 'take their custom elsewhere'.

With the introduction of 'quasi-markets' into many of the key services of the welfare state (Le Grand and Bartlett, 1993; Adams, 1999) some might argue that this notion of the user as consumer is becoming more meaningful. However, the 'consumers' of health and social services are still in a very different position from consumers in the marketplace, and therefore the notion of consumer choice is misleading (Banks, 1998a; Payne, 1995, p. 181). Despite the introduction of internal markets, it is still not the user as such who is the 'purchaser', it is usually the doctor or the social worker (or 'care manager') who actually buys the services on behalf of the patient or user, and it is not just the interests and needs of that user that are taken into account, but also the level of resources available in the budget and the agreements the purchaser may have to contract with certain providers. Indeed, Rea (1998, pp. 203–4) argues that the market in health and social care is best understood as a 'metaphorical device' and comments that 'markets have not been extended to permit consumers to determine expenditure levels, nor to determine any particular type of provision'. Although users may have more choice than previously, it is still restricted. This is one of the reasons why Hugman (1998, p. 149) prefers to use the term 'quasi-consumer'. Of course, the notion that consumers in a marketplace can exercise free choice is also a myth. The extent to which choice can be exercised depends upon the wealth and the power of the consumers. Berry has argued that the perspective which sees consumerism as about offering choice is interpreted as letting market forces have a controlling influence:

This moves away from the idea of universal entitlement to benefit or service towards a perception of the tenant or client as customer.

It is a short step from here to introducing charges for services and basing choice on ability to pay. Since the ability to be perceived as a consumer is limited to those who can pay for the privilege, this analysis can also lead to the targetting of specific (second-class) programmes at those who are too poor to exercise that choice, too poor to be customers, or even to pay indirectly as tax- or rate-payers. (Berry, 1988, pp. 268–9)

Choice for many social service users may, in fact, mean 'the right of exit from services starved of resources and left to wither' (Taylor, 1991/2, p. 88). In fact, many users of social work services cannot be regarded as consumers even in the very tenuous sense we have discussed above. Some people, such as those on a compulsory court order or a parent whose child is suspected of having been abused, do not have the right of exit from the 'service' – or if they do exit, their choice may be imprisonment, a fine, or removal of a child. This does not mean that many of the users' rights promoted under the auspices of the new consumerism do not apply in the case of compulsory statutory social work involvement (such as rights to access to files or to information about legal rights). Indeed, many of them are now enshrined in the law. Rather, the idea of consumer *choice* makes even less sense in this context.

Nevertheless, the notion of the user as a consumer is quite a helpful one, provided it is not linked with the idea of consumer choice. It is more honest about the nature of the social work relationship, which is not a relationship between two free individual persons, or even two fellow citizens, but between representatives of an agency which provides or purchases services on behalf of the state and someone who enters into a relationship with that agency or its representatives for a specific purpose. While this may not be how social workers wish to see the relationship, this may, in effect, be how it is, especially in the context of the statutory and purchasing side of local authority social services.

New professionalism or new consumerism?

The increasing concern with users' rights has been termed both 'the new professionalism' and the 'new consumerism' in the social work literature. While the use of terminology may not always be significant, the two phrases do have different connotations. Significantly it is the professional association, BASW, which particularly uses the term 'new professionalism'. In the introduction to its model complaints procedure in 1989, the following statement is made:

> The new professionalism, of which BASW has been in the vanguard, is committed to shifting the balance of power between the worker and client by consolidating the rights of the client, by securing client participation in decision-making and by opening up services to consumer influence. Complaints procedures, so often seen as a threat by social workers, have a vital part to play in helping to change the organisational culture of social work agencies. They safeguard and secure clients' rights. They provide a foundation for good professional practice based on respect for clients as equal citizens. And they provide a useful mechanism to monitor how agencies are viewed by recipients of their services. (BASW, 1989, p. iii)

BASW states that the new approach to professionalism does not draw upon the traditional models of medicine and law (presumably meaning the model of professional as expert), but incorporates ideas of participation and rights derived from the consumer movement. It is suggested that BASW has taken a leading role in developing this new approach since publishing *Clients Are Fellow Citizens* in 1980. Although the quotation from BASW given above seems to elide the notions of citizen and consumer, as do several other commentators (for example, Bamford, 1990, p. 57) arguably the new professionalism (as opposed to the new consumerism) is about users as fellow citizens.

The new professionalism is about giving more power to users in the context of the professional relationship, but the focus is on the professional as the one giving the power. So although the user may be given more rights and be referred to as a 'partner' or even a 'co-producer' (Øvretveit, 1997, pp. 83–4), it could be argued that it is still the professional that is in control. The new consumerism, on the other hand, is moving away from the idea of the social worker as a professional who exercises professional judgement on the basis of expertise towards the idea of social workers as officials – as distributors of resources according to certain prescribed standards and procedures. The new consumerism has strong strands of anti-professionalism embedded in it, exemplifying a desire on the part of the government as well as the consumer rights movement to challenge the power and exclusiveness of professional groups (in medicine, law and education, as well as social work). The new professionalism, on the other hand, may be trying to retain some of the status and power, or at least the identity, of the professional, while also becoming more responsive to user rights – developing a new model of professionalism which does not have to be elitist and exclusive. As Bamford says: 'The new professionalism does not deny the existence of that [professional] knowledge and skill but seeks to bridge the gap between worker and client, and to widen the range of choices open to the client' (Bamford, 1990, p. 57).

The new professionalism seeks to retain the notion of the social worker as a professional requiring special education and adhering to a professional code of ethics while trying to regard the user as more of an active participant. The traditional values still apply, although the way they are put into practice has changed. For example, promoting user self-determination is now extended to include user participation in decision-making. In practice it is difficult to distinguish the new professionalism and the new consumerism. Developments which began as part of the new professionalism (for example, complaints procedures, advocacy and contracts between worker and user) have become absorbed into the broader changes brought about by government legislation and the new consumerism. The new consumerism tends to see the social worker more as a 'producer' of services (Hugman, 1998, pp. 109–34), which would include assessment and care planning, according to certain standards and criteria. Some of the traditional values still seem relevant. For example, user self-determination means users having the choice whether to accept the service or not, or whether to complain. The social worker has to individualise the service (which relates to treating each person as a unique individual) to take account of individual needs. However, this must be according to the criteria laid down and the type of needs prioritised by the agency, so the social worker becomes more of a rule-follower and the principles of fairness and consistency in allocating resources will be important.

The next half of this chapter will consider some of the recent developments associated with the new consumerism/professionalism relevant to enhancing users' rights. We will consider whether the gap between day-to-day social work practice and the general principles relating to user self-determination in the codes of ethics can be bridged by national or agency codes of practice in matters such as access to records, complaints procedures and user participation.

Access to records, complaints and user participation in case conferences and reviews

Legislation and policy guidance in the late 1980s and early 1990s required social services departments to give users the right to see the information kept in their personal files and to make complaints about standards of services, and encouraged the participation of users in decision-making about their cases. This is obviously a very important way in which users can be given more power in the social work relationship and treated with respect. Newcastle City Council's policy statement on access to information (Newcastle upon Tyne Social Services Department, n.d.) includes the following principle: 'Underlying this policy statement is the principle that it is unethical and ineffective to be working with people without sharing fully objectives, plans and information on which these are based.'

Shared recording and open access to records are said to enhance users' rights and therefore give them more power in the social work process (BASW, 1983). This can be further strengthened by the use of explicit contracts or agreements between users and social workers (Corden and Preston-Shoot, 1987). Some commentators, however, question to what extent this is the case (Payne, 1989; Rojeck and Collins, 1987, 1988). Although shared recordings and contracts do encourage more honesty between the social worker and the user, they do not necessarily enhance the user's freedom in a positive sense, unless they are also accompanied by a commitment on the part of the social workers to supporting users to participate in decision-making. Further, the records are still kept by the social services departments and although users have a right to see them, this is often treated as a concession. According to the organisation PAIN (Parents Against Injustice), parents who believe they have been wrongly accused of child abuse face great difficulties if they ask to see their files (Chamberlain, 1992; Amphlett, 1998). In addition, many of the procedures are time-consuming and cumbersome. A typical procedure for dealing with users' requests to see their files, for example, involves forms being completed, and then a responsible officer tracing the information requested which may be located on computer and in manual files in several different sections. Letters must be sent out to third parties and health professionals and the information will need to be collated and possibly edited. The applicant must be given help by means of explanation and interpretation to understand the information. In some cases preparatory counselling may be needed (for example, where someone looks at the records concerning their adoption) and there must also be procedures for the user to challenge and change the record and to appeal if access is denied.

Similar blocks also occur for users wishing to make complaints. Systems for complaints and appeals have been criticised as inadequate and lacking independence (Amphlett, 1998). Even if leaflets are produced outlining the range of services available, the standards of treatment to be expected and how to make complaints, social work users are very often reluctant to complain. A report on residential homes for older people suggests that older people in care are often afraid to complain because they think it would be useless and dangerous. They have very little access to the outside world and are totally in the control of the people running the home (Counsel and Care, 1992). A report from the National Consumer Council (1993) found that people felt grateful for social services and guilty about complaining. As one person commented, 'the sense that we do not have a right to service raises fears that we will lose what we have got, as a punishment for making a fuss'. This tends to suggest that the publication of a leaflet saying people can complain is not enough to create a climate where users feel they have a right to social services. Some users may need an advocate to speak on their behalf. The kind of climate that would make it easier for people who are regular users of a service to complain might be created if user involvement in service planning and delivery has been encouraged and social workers or others have spent some time working with the users to develop their skills and confidence. This kind of work is only possible if the workers are in regular contact with the users, or if the users are part of a self-help or campaigning group or seek the assistance of an advocacy project.

Procedures have been developed within the community care assessment process for users' own definition of their problems and their needs to be recorded and taken into account. Similarly, within procedures for assessing risk to children and their needs for care, the views of the child should be sought and taken into account, as should those of the parents. Many local authorities, for example, have policies and procedures encouraging parents to attend initial child protection case conferences where decisions about their children are to be made, although this is not a legal right. Similar shortcomings in implementing these procedures exist as for the others discussed above (Bell, 1999). If parents are simply informed that they may attend a case conference, but not given any information about what to expect and no support in making their contribution, then the 'participation' may be nothing more than a token gesture. Recent research on parent participation in case conferences suggests that this is generally welcomed by all participants and most professionals think it improves the quality of the decisions made (Bell, 1999; Katz, 1995). However, Bell and Sinclair (1993, p. 25) conclude as a result of their study of parental involvement in initial case conferences in Leeds that:

> one of the unforeseen and unfortunate consequences of the professional's quite proper preoccupation with getting parental participation at case conferences right is a concentration on procedure and interagency communication at the expense of engagement with the child.

This raises again the issue of the 'proceduralisation' of child protection work and indeed of social work generally. It indicates that while procedures are necessary to ensure that the interests and rights of the child and the parents are all considered and decisions are taken according to relevant evidence in a fair manner, correctly following a mass of complex and time-consuming procedures can become the goal or end of the case conference rather than a means to achieving a fair decision.

The involvement of young people (and their parents) in case reviews raises similar problems. The degree of users' involvement or participation in decisions about their own cases obviously varies not just according to the policies of particular agencies and the commitment of individual social workers, but also according to the social worker's judgement regarding users' abilities to understand the situation and to make an informed statement of their own needs and choice of services or courses of action. However, as Lansdown (1995, p. 29) points out, it is important to distinguish between a service user's capacity for self-determination (the right to make their own decisions), which will be limited by judgements of their competence and their need for protection, and their rights to participate in the process of making decisions about their case. In the context of work with children, he argues that the right to participate and have their views listened to is not contingent on adults' judgements about children's competence or their best interests. However, this depends on what we mean by 'participation'. The term can be used in a number of senses, and is often regarded as a continuum or 'ladder', which may include: (1) informing, listening to or consulting service users; (2) giving service users some involvement in decision-making; and (3) joint decision-making with professionals, or service users having full decision-making powers (see Øvretveit, 1997, pp. 85–8). The terms 'participation', 'involvement' and 'consultation' are often used rather loosely and interchangeably. Whilst the consultation (1) and involvement (2) of service users should no doubt be a right, 'participation' in the strong sense of joint or full decision-making powers (3) will usually depend on the capacity of the service user to make a decision.

The question of how to judge whether someone is capable of understanding what is going on and making a decision has been much more discussed in the context of medicine and the principle of 'informed consent' to treatment than it has in social work. According to Wicclair (1991), decision-making capacity is judged according to whether people have a capacity to understand and communicate, to reason and deliberate, and whether they possess a set of values and goals. Not surprisingly, there is no single, universally accepted standard of decision-making capacity. This is not only because medical professionals' judgements about what constitutes a capacity to understand and reason will vary, but also because the levels of competence required will vary according to what type of decision is being made. Buchanan and Brock (1989) suggest that the relevant criteria should vary according to the risk to the patient's well-being. If the treatment is relatively low-risk, then a weaker standard of decision-making capacity is appropriate. These are debated issues (see Wicclair, 1991; Brock, 1991; Veatch, 1999), but are of relevance to the issue of user choice in social work, particularly in relation to work with children, people with learning disabilities or mental health problems.

This is why it may be appropriate for some users to have independent advocates to support them in speaking for themselves or to speak on their behalf. This is especially important where the social worker's role is to act on behalf of the agency in distributing resources or exercising control. In the community care procedures, the worker (care manager) who assesses the user and purchases and manages the care package is separate from the person or organisation that provides the care. It might therefore be assumed that the care manager would advocate on behalf of the user to gain the best possible package. However, since the resources for purchasing are limited, and the social services department will have set some limits on certain types of services and prioritised the meeting of certain kinds of needs, the care manager will be constrained. The care manager may be working on behalf of the user, but he or she is also working for an agency. The rights and needs of the individual user will often conflict with agency policies for distributing available resources between users; and needs that cannot be met may not be taken into account. Brandon (1991, p. 118) argues that it is always preferable to have an independent advocate working on behalf of psychiatric patients:

> The advocate nurse, social worker or doctor has an inherent and critical conflict of interest. The alleged oppressor pays their salaries.

This discussion of access to records, complaints procedures and participation in decision-making suggests that laws, policies and procedures can lay the ground rules for users' rights, but are meaningless if not developed alongside the commitment of agencies and workers to give support and resources for users to exercise their rights. In the next part of this chapter we will look at various ways of doing this, including the promotion of advocacy, community-based user involvement and empowerment.

Advocacy

In the last decade there has been a growth in advocacy projects in Britain. This trend has been reinforced by the National Health Service and Community Care Act 1990 which requires wide consultation of users in the drafting of community care plans and in the process of assessment, and the concept of advocacy is being taken on board by many social services departments and voluntary sector agencies. In County Durham, for example, an Advocacy Project was established in 1992 (Durham County Advocacy Project, 1993), with the aim of promoting a range of types of advocacy. Different kinds of advocacy include: citizen advocacy which gives training to volunteers to work with service users on a long-term one-to-one basis; professional advocacy which tends to involve a more short-term relationship in which an advocate with special knowledge or skills helps the user with particular decisions; and self-advocacy which involves training users to develop the skills and confidence to speak up for themselves. Advocacy is based on the notion of enabling users to articulate their needs and ensuring that their rights are respected. When users are unable to speak for themselves and do not have the capacity to decide what type of needs they have or how they would like them to be met, then the advocate will have to act in what is judged to be their best interests.

Advice, Advocacy and Representation Services for Children (ASC) is a project set up in 1992 designed to help young people who feel their voices are not being heard (Dalrymple, 1993, 1995; Patel, 1995). The director comments that it has been hard to convince those responsible for caring for young people of the importance of advocacy services. When schemes have been set up for ASC representatives to visit a residential home on a regular basis to offer a confidential and independent service to young people, this can seem threatening to some staff. She reports that: 'Our experience is that staff (both field and residential) who support the service and actively promote it to young people are those who are also committed to respecting young people with whom they are working' (Dalrymple, 1993, p. 13). An evaluation of the scheme showed that a number of social workers disliked its young-person-focused and rights-oriented approach (Dalrymple, 1995, p. 118).

Community-based user involvement

User involvement in planning and delivering services is another important aspect of the community care legislation. The promotion of user involvement became popular in the 1980s and has been partly linked to a general trend in local authorities to 'democratise' their services – which includes bringing them closer to people (decentralising offices), making them more responsive to local needs (through

consulting and perhaps involving local people in local community
councils or neighbourhood forums), and developing systems to
promote the participation of local people and service users in the
planning and delivery of services. In a social services context these
moves were often linked with the development of 'patch'-based
offices and 'community social work' (Hadley and McGrath, 1980,
1984; Beresford, 1984). Bayley sees such locally-based work as
coming about because of the recognition that the community itself
is the main provider of care, and that formal services must be organised to fit in with informal caring networks (Bayley, 1989, p. 45). This
is obviously one very important reason in terms of effectiveness of
services. Other reasons might include concerns around reducing the
distance between the user and the worker (as expert professional),
seeing individual users' problems as problems shared with other local
people, and developing community action as well as community care
systems. It also fits with the recent revival in popularity of communitarian ideas, espoused by both right and left, with an emphasis on
individuals' interconnnectedness and mutual responsibilities to their
families, neighbours and the localities where they live (Etzioni, 1995;
Giddens, 1998; Lund, 1999; Tam, 1998).

There is an important difference between decentralising service
delivery (for example, moving social workers from a city centre office
to neighbourhood-based offices in a small patch) and democratising
services (encouraging participation and sharing power with local
people and users). The former may fit in well with viewing the user
as a relatively passive consumer (with the main concern being to meet
their needs as effectively as possible) and the latter with the user as
an active citizen with a right to have a say in, some control over and
even responsibility for how services are planned and delivered. The
move to genuine participation of local people in service delivery and
policy-making, which would involve politicians and officials sharing
some of their power with local people, is less easy to achieve and less
common than approaches which inform, consult or merely involve
local people or users. As Croft and Beresford (1989, p. 107)
comment, neither of the two best-known patch social services projects (Dinnington and Normanton) were able to indicate any significant transfer of say and control to service users or local people.
Recent evaluations of specific initiatives to make services user-
friendly and participative, such as County Durham's Investing in
Children Initiative (Shenton, 1999), demonstrate some progress,
along with similar difficulties. This is partly because of a reluctance

of managers, professionals and councillors to give up power, but also because of the time and effort needed to support and train users to participate effectively and above all the difficulty of encouraging local people or users to want to participate. Those who do participate may be a few experienced activists, whose opinions may not be assumed to represent those of other local people or users. This type of participation may be no more than a token gesture towards genuine participatory democracy. Walzer speaks of 'the sharing of power amongst the activists . . . the rule of the people with most evenings to spare' (quoted in Gyford, 1991, p. 179).

Bearing this in mind, the skills, approaches and values of those social workers who do attempt to promote more than token user involvement tend to be of the more 'radical' kind, closer to those of community workers, with an emphasis on skills in mobilising and empowering individuals to work together collectively, seeing problems experienced as part of wider social and economic conditions, and working to change the attitudes and policies of agencies, councillors and society in general. The time needed for this kind of developmental work is considerable, and unless a social worker has a brief to work directly with groups or communities, then it is unlikely that she will find the time to develop such approaches. Croft and Beresford (1989, p. 107) quote a comment from a worker on a patch project: 'It is difficult to make space to develop innovatory approaches given continuing statutory responsibilities, particularly when the team is not fully staffed.' It is easier for community workers or group workers who have a specific brief to do this kind of work, and whose skills and values are less oriented to the individual user, to develop styles of working that focus on 'empowering' users, groups and communities. However, strong emphasis in recent government legislation and policies on partnership and participation in service planning and delivery, particularly in areas such as neighbourhood regeneration, community safety and youth crime reduction, is beginning to provoke a more serious concern for user and resident involvement.

Empowerment

'Empowerment' is another contested concept which it is important to mention in this context. Rather like user involvement, it has a range of meanings from giving users some limited choices (the consumerist approach) to power-sharing (the citizenship approach) to supporting and encouraging people or groups to realise their own power and take action for themselves (a 'radical' approach). A 'radical' approach is often advocated through linking empowerment to oppression, and seeing empowerment as part of anti-oppressive practice (see, for example, Ahmad, 1990; Mullender and Ward, 1991; Thompson, 1993). Thompson defines oppression as:

> Inhuman or degrading treatment of individuals or groups; hardship and injustice brought about by the dominance of one group over another; the negative and demeaning exercise of power. Oppression often involves disregarding the rights of an individual or group and thus is a denial of citizenship. (Thompson, 1993, p. 31)

The rhetoric of anti-oppressive practice is generally couched in terms of challenging structural oppression – that is, challenging the systems of beliefs, policies, institutions and culture that systematically discriminate against and demean women, black people, people with disabilities, lesbians and gays, working-class people and other oppressed groups. Yet as this rhetoric is incorporated into mainstream practice, it is questionable sometimes whether 'empowerment' and 'anti-oppressive practice' consist of anything more than enabling individual users to gain confidence and offering 'individually sensitive practice' that takes account of, for example, a user's dietary and religious needs and their personal experience of oppression. This is not to undermine some of the radical and challenging work that has happened and is taking place, but rather to suggest that this does not represent the mainstream of social work practice, despite the lip-service that is paid to anti-oppressive work. As we commented in Chapter 4, the values relating to challenging structural oppression are in fundamental opposition to the individualistic values underpinning traditional social work.

Mullender and Ward, in their book *Self-Directed Groupwork: Users Take Action for Empowerment* (1991), produce a statement of values or practice principles for empowering practice. This is a good example of some of the principles being promoted by the 'new professionalism' regarding non-elitism and the participation of users in defining the agenda to be worked on. Yet it adds to these by adopting a structural approach to the cause of social problems and advocates challenging structural oppression while at the same time maintaining the traditional individualistic values of respect for persons and the right to self-determination. While the examples given in the book are very varied and include some that involve campaigning for change, the title of the book might suggest the focus is on empowerment as an end in itself ('users take action for empowerment') rather than as means to an end (which might be 'users become empowered to take action for change'). Obviously the process is circular and it is impossible to distinguish empowerment from action (see the discussion in Chapter 4 relating to 'praxis' and the work of Freire). But in social work generally the emphasis is more on individual users becoming more confident and personally powerful than on achieving societal change. Thompson's definition tends to reflect this when he states that empowerment 'involves seeking to maximise the power of clients and to give them as much control as possible over their circumstances. It is the opposite of creating dependency and subjecting clients to agency power' (Thompson, 1993, p. 80).

In talking of users gaining control over rather than changing their circumstances, this suggests that the aim is to empower people to live a better quality of life in the world as it is. Of course, other parts of Thompson's book on anti-discriminatory practice do embrace societal change, but the focus in social work generally is on the individual user or family and therefore inevitably the stress is on personal change, even if the broader societal context is acknowledged. This is particularly evident in the literature related to the development of community care and the promotion of the rights of people with disabilities (see Ramon, 1991). Whilst the existence of structural oppression is frequently acknowledged and the role of social workers in challenging it is emphasised, in practice much of the work they do is about helping people with disabilities 'conform' to what is accepted as 'normal' behaviour (for a critique of normalisation theory see Dalley, 1992; Brown and Smith, 1992).

Conclusions

In this chapter we have examined the gradual shift from seeing the user as a person to user as a fellow citizen to user as a consumer. In one sense the move towards a consumer rights approach can be regarded as a development of the principle of respect for persons, in that it is actualising the rights of a person in the specific situation of being a social work user – in particular, rights to information, certain standards of service and to choice. We noted the development of codes of practice and procedures for gaining access to records, shared record-making, shared decision-making and making complaints. Within the predefined boundaries of the social work relationship and the agency context, these procedures aim to give users more power. But the procedures in themselves do not guarantee respect for the user as an equal citizen or a consumer with real choice. The social worker inevitably tends to be more powerful and articulate than the user and there may be constraints in terms of agency resources. These procedures need to be developed alongside a systematic and long-term approach which promotes the participation of users in service delivery, works towards empowerment and offers advocacy for those users who find it difficult to articulate their needs and rights. This is not an easy task, as it is time-consuming and involves social workers and agencies being prepared to give up some of their power and change their ways of working. It also brings into focus the contradictions between individual and structural approaches to change. While social workers may work towards empowering individuals to take control over parts of their personal lives, unless the policies and practices in the welfare state and in society generally which oppress certain individuals and groups are changed, then social work can only go so far towards putting these principles into action.

Exercise 3

Aims of the exercise – to encourage the reader to think practically about what rights are possible and desirable in relation to a context of which he/she has experience.

1. Think of an agency that you are currently working for/have worked for.
2. Draw up a list of what you think should be the users' rights in relation to their contact with this agency.
3. Why do you think these particular rights are important?
4. How would you ensure that they are put into practice?

7

Social Workers' Duties: Policies, Procedures and the New Managerialism

In the last chapter we focused on users' rights. According to our definition of a right, if users have certain rights, then some person or some institution has a corresponding duty to fulfil those rights. In many cases it may be the social worker directly (for example, the duty to treat the user with respect), or it may be the social worker indirectly acting on behalf of an agency (the duty to provide services for children in need). The direct duties could be said to be inherent in the role of professional social worker, and the indirect ones inherent in the particular job the social worker has. In this chapter we will explore the nature of social workers' duties to users in relation to their other duties, including those to the employing agency, the profession and society. The professional codes say more about duties to users and to the profession and tend to argue that these duties have primacy. Employing agencies, on the other hand, tend to require that employees put agency policies and procedures first. This chapter will explore the conflicts that arise between different sets of duties, particularly in the context of the increasing proceduralisation and bureaucratisation of social work ('the new managerialism').

Duties

The types of duties we have been talking about (those to the profession and to the employing agency) are those that people commit themselves to when they take on the job of social worker. In

135

this sense, a duty is a consequence of a contract or undertaking, either implicit or explicit: 'My duty is that which I am engaged or committed to do, and which other people can therefore expect and require me to do. I have a duty to keep a promise, because I have bound myself thereto' (Whitley, 1969, p. 54).

However, we may have conflicting duties, because different commitments may have been undertaken which are incompatible with each other in a particular situation. Therefore, we may have to choose between different duties. For example, I have a duty to keep the information users give me confidential; but I also have a duty to protect users from serious danger. Therefore I might decide to break the confidence of a young person who has said she is planning to commit suicide. The duty of confidentiality may be said to be a *prima facie* duty – that is, it is what I ought to do, other things being equal. This notion of duty is connected also with accountability. If I have made a contract or undertaking to do something (duty) then I am also expected to be able to explain or justify my performance or non-performance of that duty (accountability). In social work this latter aspect of a duty is regarded as important, as social workers must be publicly accountable for what they do.

It is important to distinguish this sense of duty – an obligation or commitment as a consequence of a contract or undertaking – from how the term is sometimes used, particularly in moral philosophy, to mean 'the right action': 'what I ought to do'. We might say in relation to the case of the girl threatening to commit suicide that I decided it was my duty to tell her parents. 'Duty' in this sense is a definitive recommendation regarding what ought to be done taking all the circumstances into account. 'Duty' here means *the* right action, and there is only one action. Therefore it would not make sense to talk of a conflict of duties. I am going to use the term 'duty' in the first sense, where duties are regarded as commitments or obligations which may be in conflict with each other. Therefore a duty is what I am committed to do, other things being equal. Very often, other things are not equal. It may be morally right for me to neglect one particular duty in favour of another. When talking about duty in the sense of the right action, or what I ought to do having taken all circumstances into account, I will use terms like 'making a moral judgement about how to act' or 'deciding on the morally right course of action'.

Social work as a 'role-job'

Social work takes place within an institutional framework of rights and duties defined by the law, the employing agency and the professional code. Chapter 5 discussed the duties of the social worker as laid down in professional codes of ethics. There are other rights and duties which make up the job, such as the legal right (or power) and/or the duty to intervene in people's lives in cases where a child is thought to be at risk, or the procedural duty to follow agency guidelines in assessing risk in child protection cases. For this reason Downie and Loudfoot (1978) describe social work as a 'role-job' – meaning that the job of social work is defined by a set of institutional rights and duties. They argue that it is important for social work to have an institutional framework because social workers intervene in the lives of others and it is in the interests of users that they have a right to intervene. Second, social workers discover many intimate details of people's lives and it is important that there are rules, such as confidentiality, which provide security for the user. Third, social workers themselves can find security from working in an institutional framework – for example, they can fall back on their official position to give guidance on proper procedures with a user in case of legal action.

Downie and Loudfoot list four different types of rights and duties that attach to the role of social worker, to which I have added a fifth:

1. *Legal rights and duties* to users, employers and others.
2. *Professional rights and duties* arising from membership of a profession with its own standards of conduct.
3. *Moral duties* arising from the fact that the social worker is dealing with specific individuals in specific situations.
4. *Social duties* arising from the fact that the social worker is also a citizen who has the opportunity to do more civil good than many; for example, through working towards reforming or changing social policies.
5. *Procedural rights and duties* arising from the fact that the social worker is employed by an agency which has its own rules concerning how the work should be done and how social workers should behave.

When someone takes on the job of a social worker, they are in effect agreeing to work within this framework of rights, duties and rules. In particular, the employing agency will expect them to work within its rules and procedures, since it is this agency that is paying their wages. Usually an employing agency will also expect the worker to work within the framework of the law and indeed if it is a statutory agency many of its policies and procedures will be based on interpretations of Acts of Parliament and Statutory Guidance.

Conflicting duties

In an ideal world it might be assumed that legal, professional, social, moral and procedural rights and duties would complement or coincide with those required by the agency. However, this is not always the case. A social worker may judge that the employing agency's procedures regarding confidentiality are too lax compared with the standards laid down in the professional code, for example, or that the methods it uses entail treating users as objects rather than respecting them as persons. The professional associations usually state that it is the principles laid down in the professional codes that should come first as these codes are designed with the protection of users in mind, whereas the law or agency rules may be designed for the convenience of the majority.

In taking on the role of social worker a person takes on several different layers of duties which may conflict with each other. We can summarise these duties and the main sources of guidance as follows:

1. *Duties to users* – for example, to respect users' rights to make their own decisions, to respect their rights to confidentiality, to safeguard and promote the welfare of children (acting on behalf of the local authority). Sources of guidance include the professional code of ethics; agency policies and codes of practice; the law; public opinion; charters for users' rights.
2. *Duties to the profession* – for example, to uphold the good name of social work by maintaining effective and ethical practice. Sources of guidance include: the professional code of ethics; guidance from the professional association.
3. *Duties to the agency* – for example, following the prescribed rules and procedures, safeguarding the reputation of the agency.

Sources of guidance include: the worker's job description and contract; agency policies and procedures.
4. *Duties to society* – for example, maintaining social order, executing the responsibilities of local authority social services departments as laid down by statute. Sources of guidance include: the law; government guidance; public opinion.

How does the social worker judge between these different duties when they conflict? The professional code aims to cover all these areas and suggests that its guidance should come first in cases of conflict. This implies that first and foremost a social worker is a professional, and it is from this stance that all other duties must be judged. For example, if the agency policies and procedures contravene the ethical principles stated in the code, then the social worker must not collude with this, and must try to change them. Yet there are also cases where different obligations in the code itself conflict – such as the duties to maintain confidentiality and to promote user welfare. How do we resolve these? Surely it is the person in the role of professional who has to decide which duties have priority – not only within the code, but between different sets of duties to the agency and to society. Ultimately it is a person's own personal moral code that will determine what action is morally right.

The relationship between personal, professional and agency values

There is a school of thought in social work (and other caring professions) that social work is a vocation, which suggests a blurring of the distinction between personal and professional life, values and duties. The view taken by Ronnby (1993) seems to imply that someone becomes a social worker as part of their personal identity, and the duties attaching to being a social worker are the same as, or become the same as, personal or private rights and duties. This type of view might be akin to someone taking on a religious calling – becoming a priest – whose whole life should be lived according to the moral duties of the religion, not just parts of it when he or she is performing the role of a priest. This is the kind of view taken by Wilkes (1985, p. 54) who notes Lewis and Maude's three views of professionals: as tradespeople with special skills; as officials using their techniques to modify people's conduct; or as

> guardians of a tradition, humane and Christian, of study and service to their fellows, whether this is based on a confidential and fiduciary relationship with individual clients or on voluntary sacrifice of extra monetary gain in the interests of the community. (Lewis and Maude, quoted in Wilkes, 1985, p. 54)

Wilkes argues for this latter view of the professional social worker. This may seem a strange attitude to have towards state-sponsored social work. However, it may be easier to understand if we look more carefully at the professional codes of ethics and note that the kinds of duties they espouse are those of the liberal individualist ethics that are current in western society generally. The International Code and some of the others explicitly acknowledge that they are based on the United Nations Declaration of Human Rights and the Rights of the Child. They are advocating the kind of moral behaviour that it is thought any morally upright decent human being should follow. This is why Ronnby (1993) asks why social workers feel the need to add in writing to their professional codes that one shall respect every human being's unique worth and integrity: 'Social worker's ethics do not differ from those that characterise others' humanistic ideals.' In effect, he is saying that there should be no need for a code of ethics for social work, because the person who is a social worker should have their own personal ethical code which involves treating others with respect as fellow human beings. According to Ronnby (1993, pp. 5–6):

> The prerequisite of ethically proper actions in social work would be that the social worker cares about, even cares for, the help seeker. The social worker must dare, and be able, to open herself for the client, she must be capable of being herself with open senses, feelings and empathy. Techniques and routines as well as professional self-interest can prevent the social worker from acting humanely.

This seems to amount to an argument against the separation of the personal and the professional. It may not amount to an argument against the notion that social work is a role-job with specific rights and duties attached to it; but it does imply that the specific rights

and duties should not be fundamentally different from or in opposition to the general moral principles by which the social worker
leads her life. Ronnby notes the tendency for the welfare state (of
which social work is a part) to reinforce existing inequalities in
society and to treat those who are the poorest and least powerful as
objects to be pitied or changed. His solution is for social workers to
adhere to their personal humanistic ethics and to come closer to their
users as fellow human beings. A similar view is argued for by Halmos
(1978) and Wilkes (1981). This has resonances with the references
to 'love' in the Swedish code of ethics (SSR, 1997) and to the 'ethics
of proximity' of Levinas (1989) and some Nordic ethicists such as
Løgstrup (1997). Bauman (1993), in his discussion of postmodern
ethics, is also influenced by Levinas, talking of the 'moral impulse'
– a personal capacity to act morally, which is the property of an
individual as opposed to external ethical frameworks (such as
professional ethics). Bauman (1993, p. 19) emphasises the moral
responsibility of the individual over and above the various roles
people play (one of which might be 'social worker'), each with their
ethical rules. Husband (1995, p. 99) applies this to social work,
arguing that the moral impulse is a necessary basis for responsible
social work intervention: 'By its untrammelled innocence and generosity it is the creative core of caring.' This sort of view seems to
entail that the relationship between social worker and user might be
one of unconditional caring, in the same way as a mother cares for
her child, for example. It would involve removing the distinction
between private morality and public ethics. It has resonances with
(although it is distinct from) the 'ethic of care' discussed in Chapter
3, based on relationships of caring between connected individuals as
opposed to the externally imposed ethic of justice based on duty,
universal principles and the notion of separate individuals.

But the view that the social worker should genuinely care about
her users and treat them as she would friends or strangers in her ordinary life seems problematic in the context of current social work
practice. Whilst an ethics of proximity based on the responsibility
I feel in the face-to-face encounter between myself and the 'other'
may be a foundation, precondition or starting point of ethics, there
is a need to go beyond 'the moral party of two' to reach justice –
'the realm of choice, proportion, judgement – and comparison' as
Bauman (1997, p. 222) acknowledges. Bringing the discussion back
to concrete realities, when out shopping on a Saturday I might give
£10 out of my pocket to a man in the street who asked for some

money for food, and take him home for a cup of coffee. But surely I should not give £10 out of my pocket to a social work user in the office who asked for money for food and take him home for a cup of coffee whilst on duty as a social worker on Monday? First, this might leave me open to accusations of favouritism, as I cannot do this with all users. Second, if I did give this level of personal care to all users I would be impoverished and exhausted. Third, this would involve developing a personal relationship with a user which might leave him and me open to abuse. These reasons echo those given by Downie and Loudfoot as to why it is important that social work operates within an institutional framework of rights and duties, to protect both the social worker and the user.

It is doubtful if Halmos, Wilkes, Ronnby or Husband are actually arguing that social workers should treat users as friends, rather that we should treat them as fellow human beings for whom we feel empathy and respect, and that we should regard ourselves as people first and social workers second, applying the same fundamental ethical principles to the situations we encounter in social work as we would to other situations in other parts of our lives. However, as social workers we are employed by organisations which operate by certain rules and procedures and we are constrained by societal mores and the legal system. Within this framework we should treat users with as much honesty and respect as possible, but it is not part of the job to care for our users unconditionally. It is arguably more important that the social worker holds on to her own personal values not in order to give unconditional love to users, but in order to challenge laws, policies and practices regarded as unjust, including 'blowing the whistle' on institutionalised malpractice.

At the other extreme, Leighton argues for the separation of personal, professional and agency values. He suggests that social work aims to manipulate and change people; social workers act not as ordinary human beings as they would in their personal lives, but take on a separate role, which requires them to appear to care, but not in the genuine way in which one would care for a friend. He gives the example of a social worker who needs to get certain intimate information from a young person in residential care (presumably for a report):

> The social worker is therefore obliged to try to draw the child into a relationship for no other purpose than to satisfy the social

worker's job requirements. It is exceptional if the worker offers important parts of himself or herself to the child's personal social world. The relationship is part of a statutory and financial transaction from which only the social worker benefits financially. (Leighton, 1985, p. 78)

He argues that we must separate the personal and the professional, so that we do not feel guilty about manipulating people and using relationships as we would if we treated someone in the same way in ordinary life. According to Leighton, the social worker is required to:

manipulate people and their relationships, and must learn the art of appearing to care when his natural feeling is not to care. To survive as a private person and to do his work well he must sometimes operate within a mode of 'bad faith', a lack of absolute honesty in the relationship. (Leighton, 1985, p. 79)

Leighton's view seems rather extreme. It could ultimately lead to the social worker simply taking on a job and following all the procedures and practices required by the agency regardless of whether they appeared to be morally wrong according to the ethical principles of the profession or her own personal moral code. Taken to its limit, such a view could imply that the social worker working in a residential home where children were regularly tied to chairs and left without food could justify her actions by saying 'I was only doing my duty in accordance with the agency procedures' as if it was nothing to do with her if the agency procedures were immoral or cruel. It would leave little room for whistleblowing as a moral duty in cases of insitutionalised malpractice.

This type of view seems to entail that there is no person over and above a series of social roles of which the private/personal is just one. Leighton gives an example of a social worker, Mr Anthony, and argues that certain values from his personal life, such as converting people to Catholicism and believing abortion to be morally wrong, conflict with professional values such as user self-determination and non-judgementalism, both of which conflict with the employer's values such as assisting with birth control techniques and encouraging conformity to social norms. His conclusion seems to be that being a social worker is a totally different and separate thing from being a private individual. But is it? Surely the private individual or person decided to accept the job of social worker with its particular values

Figure 7.1 *Relationship between the personal, agency, professional and societal moral codes*

PERSON with own moral code	takes on the role of	PROFESSIONAL WORKER with professional code of ethics	who takes	JOB OF SOCIAL WORKER in particular agency with specific responsibilities and duties

influenced and circumscribed by

SOCIETAL NORMS, PUBLIC OPINION, THE LAW

and duties. If he was the kind of person who was such a strong Catholic that he went around trying to convert neighbours, friends and people in the street and he strongly opposed birth control, then arguably he would not have chosen to become a social worker. Most Catholics do not try to convert people in the street or to dissuade strangers from having abortions. Surely the same moral standards Mr Anthony has for relating in his private life to strangers and acquaintances may apply also in social work. Or, rather, social work may be regarded as a particular setting in which certain ways of behaving are appropriate and to which particular duties apply. When Mr Anthony goes to a concert or visits the bank, certain rules of behaviour apply which do not usually involve trying to convert the bank clerk or handing out anti-abortion leaflets in the concert hall. Leighton is right that the social worker should refrain from trying to persuade users not to have abortions and that social workers do not and cannot treat users as friends. However, he is mistaken in arguing that this means that personal, professional and agency values should be treated as totally separate. Where they conflict, the social worker as a person has a moral responsibility to decide which have primacy and to justify this decision. He may decide that he cannot work in an agency that involves so much work promoting birth control, or that he will request not to deal with certain cases where he would feel compromised. Figure 7.1 illustrates the relationship between the personal, agency, professional and societal moral codes.

Professional, technical–bureaucratic and committed/radical models of practice

Table 7.1 outlines three broad models of social work practice which I have called the professional, the technical–bureaucratic and the

Table 7.1   *Models of social work practice*

	Professional	*Technical–bureaucratic*	*(1) Committed/ (2) Radical*
Social worker as:	Professional	Technician/ official	Equal/ally
Power from:	Professional expertise	Organisational role	Competence to deal with situation
Service user as:	Client	Consumer	Equal/ally
Focus on	Individual worker – user relationship	Service provision	(1) Individual empowerment (2) Societal change
Guidance from:	Professional code of ethics	Agency rules and procedures	Personal commitment/ ideology
Key principles:	Users' rights to self-determination, acceptance, confidentiality, etc.	Agency duties to distribute resources fairly and to promote public good	(1) Empathy, genuineness (2) Raising consciousness, collective action
Organisational setting that would best facilitate this:	Private practice or large degree of autonomy in agency	Bureaucratic agency in voluntary, statutory or private sector	Independent voluntary agency or campaigning group

committed/radical. As with all attempts at categorisation, this is obviously artificial, but it is a way of exploring the different emphases that social workers may adopt in their practice according to their ethical stance and their particular work settings. The professional model focuses on the social worker as an autonomous professional with expertise gained through education and guidance coming from the professional code of ethics. Her first priority would be the rights and interests of users, and her identity as a social worker would be as a member of the profession first, and as a private individual or worker in an agency second. The technical–bureaucratic model regards the social worker first and foremost as a worker in an agency with a duty to carry out the prescribed tasks and roles of that agency. Guidance comes from agency rules and procedures. The committed/radical practitioner model sees the social worker as a person who has chosen to take on the job out of a personal or ideological commitment to work for change and who puts this first. This model encompasses many different types of approach ranging from the individual 'ministration in love' model to the more collectivist approaches espoused by Marxists, feminists and anti-racists. Although the same heading has been used to encompass all these approaches, there are obvious differences in focus ranging from individual empowerment to societal change.

All three strands are evident in the social work literature and social work practice. The professional codes contain elements of all three, but the emphasis is more on the professional model, tempered with duties to the employing agency (technical–bureaucratic) and personal commitment to work for societal change (committed/radical). Social work has never comfortably fitted into the role of 'professional expert' for reasons which include its ideological tendency to identify with oppressed users and its location in state-sponsored agencies. As Howe comments: 'I remain impressed with analyses which reveal social work to be largely a state-sponsored, agency-based, organisationally-tethered activity. It is not wise to tackle any examination of social work without taking note of this formidable context' (1991, p. 204). This is why attempts to make social work fit into either the professional or the committed models are very difficult, given the organisational context.

Arguably, the technical–bureaucratic model is becoming more dominant, at least in the local authority sector and large voluntary organisations. Many commentators are expressing increasing concern about the 'deprofessionalisation' of social work, which relates to the increasing specification of tasks and procedures, attempts to reduce indeterminacy in decision-making and to reduce reliance on or trust in autonomous professional judgement and the adoption of competency-based approaches to education and training (Dominelli, 1996). The growth of interest in 'evidence-based practice' could be seen to be part of this trend. Although only just beginning in social work, in medicine it is already well-developed and has been described as a 'process of systematically finding, appraising and using contemporaneous research findings as a basis for clinical decisions' (Long and Harrison, 1996, p. 11, quoted in Malin, 2000, p. 21). This has led to the development of an increasing number of clinical guidelines as a way of 'ensuring the avoidance of mistakes and/or sub-optimal treatments' (Dent, 1999, p. 161). This inevitably results in a standardisation of practice and a reduction in the individual autonomy of professional practitioners. However, Malin (2000, p. 21) sees the evidence-based approach as offering opportunities for greater professionalisation in the social care field and a way of advancing claims to professionalism. The reasons for this, of course, are that it is an approach based on scientific rationality which appears to give more credibility to the effectiveness of professional interventions, hence enhancing the notion of professional expertise in dealing with increasingly technical and complex tasks. In the context of medicine, Dent (1999, p. 161) argues quite categorically that these practices 'cannot be seen as the start of any process of deprofessionalisation, McDonaldisation, de-skilling or proletarianisation'. However, they do amount to a process of rationalisation which the organised profession is willing to countenance as a way of medical practitioners enhancing their collective autonomy (in defining the clinical guidelines) while giving up some of their individual autonomy (in each practitioner having leeway to make different judgements in similar cases). This could be seen as another feature of the 'new professionalism', whereby professions and professionals have absorbed aspects of the managerialist, technical–bureaucratic approaches, while still retaining the notion of professional expertise.

With the increasing fragmentation of social work, and with services previously provided by social services departments being shifted to the private and voluntary sector, there is also an increasing opportunity in some areas of work for workers to operate within more traditional professional or committed models of practice. For example, specialist advocacy or counselling projects can be established with an unequivocal focus on the individual user–worker relationship, where it is very clear that the advocate or counsellor is primarily concerned with the rights or interests of the user. As it is increasingly recognised that people in powerless positions or who find it difficult to speak for themselves should have independent advocates to support them, then this is separating out the advocacy role from the general social work role. This means that the local authority social worker may be concerned with allocating and rationing resources between many users, whereas the advocate will push for the wishes, needs and rights of this particular user. Similarly, there is a growth of a range of 'detached', outreach or street-work posts with specific user groups (often defined as 'hard to reach') which recognises the importance of workers having personal and life experiences close to the experiences of those with whom they are working. Deverell's research with HIV prevention outreach workers demonstrates that many do the job because as gay men they have 'a keen interest in seeing HIV prevention done amongst gay men . . . and because politically I wanted to be involved in a job that had something to say to me personally' (worker quoted in Deverell and Sharma, 2000, p. 29). Deverell found that at times they felt 'more like a peer than a professional' (p. 30), with workers using the terms 'vocation' (p. 35) and 'way of life' (p. 31). Yet whilst recounting many instances when they were 'off duty' but still responded to requests for advice, many were also very aware of the importance of setting certain professional boundaries and standards in the work, which could otherwise be very fluid and open-ended, with potential for exploitation (of users by workers and vice versa).

So while it may often be the case that a social worker will find herself working within all three models (and hence experience conflicts of duties), the emphasis will vary not only according to the individual worker's view of her role, but also according to the particular piece of work being undertaken and the type of work setting. A social worker employed as a counsellor by an independent voluntary organisation to work in complete confidence with people with HIV/AIDS will find the organisational and work setting much more conducive to operating within a professional model of practice than a local authority-employed practitioner working in an Area Office as part of an Elderly Team, a large part of whose job is to assess and plan care packages for older service users. A community worker employed by a Tenants' Federation with a campaigning brief will find it easier to work within a radical model. If we look briefly at some of the key ethical principles for social work we can see how the organisational and work setting changes the interpretation and implementation of these principles.

1. Confidentiality

- *HIV/AIDS counsellor* – can assure complete confidentiality (privacy) between counsellor and user except in circumstances where it is legally permitted or required that the counsellor disclose information (for example, where another is likely to be seriously harmed, or where a court requires information) (see Thomas *et al.*, 1993; Bond, 2000).

- *Social worker/care manager for the elderly* – the limits of confidentiality are much broader and may include other members of the team and other health care professionals and service providers. If this particular social worker is unavailable or sick, then it would be expected that another social worker would consult the user's file and continue with the work. The relationship between user and worker is not a private one.

- *Community worker* – while acknowledging the need to respect the confidentiality of certain personal information relating to individual tenants, confidentiality might be regarded as relatively unimportant in the context of tenants working together collectively to achieve change.

2. *The primacy of user self-determination and the user's interests*

- *HIV/AIDS counsellor* – while the counsellor may need to ration time between one user and another, and in exceptional cases consider the interests of others (for example, if a user has not disclosed their HIV status to a partner), within these limits the counsellor can focus on the needs and interests of the user. It will depend on the style of the particular counsellor and the nature of the user's needs as to whether the counsellor respects the user's own choices and decisions or adopts a more parentalist or directive style.

- *Social worker/care manager for the elderly* – this worker will need to keep in mind the needs and interests of other people as well as the user – for example, any family carers, neighbours, service providers and other current and potential users who will need resources. While the user's own choices and interests may be respected as far as possible, there are many limitations on this.

- *Community worker* – would see the promotion of individual self-determination or empowerment as part of the process of collective empowerment to achieve change.

3. Distributive justice

- *HIV/AIDS counsellor* – except, as we have mentioned, for the rationing of time between users, this worker does not have a direct role in distributing resources between individual users. The worker may choose to campaign and draw to the attention of service providers and policy-makers the inadequacy of resources for this user group in particular and the discrimination they face in society; indeed the social work codes include this as a principle. It is interesting to note that this principle is not prominent in the code of ethics for counselling (British Association for Counselling, 1997), which highlights a general difference in the roles of a counsellor (whose focus is primarily on helping the individual user) and the social worker (whose focus is the user in the context of a family, community or society).
- *Social worker/care manager for the elderly* – this worker does have a duty to distribute the resources of the department fairly between individual users and to manage them efficiently. In making a decision about what course of action to take, resourcing issues will be as important as user choices and needs.
- *Community worker* – will be concerned to achieve redistribution of resources (power, wealth, good housing) to tenants as a group according to need, linked to a striving for equality of result, and may use campaigning and community action approaches.

These examples suggest how the work setting – the type of agency and the role defined for the social worker – influence the extent to which a social worker may work more within one model than another. At the present time, as we have suggested, there is an increasing shift towards the bureaucratic model within statutory social work, which we will now explore.

The 'new managerialism' and the 'new authoritarianism'

Since the late 1980's there has been a growth in the production of quality standards, procedural manuals and assessment schedules in local authority social work. This is particularly noticeable in the field of child protection, although it is a trend throughout social work, and indeed the public, independent and private sector generally. This trend is related to the 'new consumerism' and a concern to offer a consistent standard of service, linked to users' rights and quality assurance; the 'new managerialism' which seeks greater control over the work of employees; the 'new authoritarianism' which emphasises the social control function of practitioners; and a deprofessionalising trend which seeks to see social workers as officials carrying out agency policy. In child protection, these trends have been given added impetus by the series of public inquiries in the 1980s into child abuse cases where either children died in their homes, or they were taken away from home unnecessarily and it was said that social workers should have acted differently. This has led to a vast quantity of guidance and advice from central government about how to assess children thought to be at risk, how to monitor them and their families, how to conduct inter-agency case conferences, how to investigate suspected cases of child abuse and how to prepare evidence for court (for example, Department of Health, 1988, 1999).

Most statutory agencies now have child protection manuals which contain this kind of information and give detailed guidance on the procedures that social workers should follow. Harris (1987) notes the tendency that this encourages towards defensive social work, whereby social workers 'go by the book' and are as concerned about protecting themselves and the agency as they are about the interests of the user. Howe (1992) talks of the 'bureaucratisation' of child care work, and McBeath and Webb (1990–1) note the technicist language of one of the first key books of guidelines produced by the Department of Health (*Protecting Children*, 1988). Cooper (1993, p. 45) warns that: 'Social workers who are simply agents of protection agencies may find it more difficult to operate beyond official procedures and guidelines arising from legislation, more difficult to use professional discretion in taking risks.' Lengthy recording schedules following a checklist approach have also been developed in relation to assessing and monitoring children in the looked-after system (Department of Health, 1995), which some have argued 'enhance the bureaucratic nature of being in public care' (Knight and Caveney, 1998, p. 29).

If we take the example of child protection work, it could be argued that a new perspective is emerging. As Howe comments:

injury and neglect suffered by some children results in the demand
that children should be protected; that protection is achieved by
improving, standardising and prescribing full and proper methods
of investigation and assessment; and that bureaucratic forms of
organisation appear to be the best way of handling the ever more
detailed and complex requirements of this new perspective.
(Howe, 1992, pp. 496–7)

King and Trowell (1992, p. 7) comment that social workers from both
statutory and voluntary agencies 'find themselves spending less
time working to support and advise parents, and offering services
to help needy children, and more time investigating allegations of
child abuse, collecting evidence and helping bring cases before
the courts'.

Parton argues that in a time of increasing public concern about
child abuse and limited resources for social work, the aim of social
work is to predict which families are 'dangerous' and therefore to
protect children from abuse in these families by removing them
(Parton, 1989, 1991, 1997, 1998; Parton and Small, 1989; Parton,
Thorpe and Wattam, 1997). The rest of the families who are not
regarded as dangerous should be left alone. The assumption is that
there is a scientific method which can predict with relative accuracy
the levels of risk that children may be subject to in their families and
home environments. As Alaszewski (1998, p. 142) comments, 'risk
offers an alternative to need'. Most of the child protection manuals
work on the basis of a checklist of predictors (for example, is there
evidence of sustained, stable and sound family relationships; are
there supportive networks; is the child generally well cared for?).
However, the manuals do not suggest how each factor should be
weighed against another, nor do they offer any statistical methods
for calculating risk. This is because it would be a fairly meaningless
exercise. Although it would be possible to ask social workers to place
a numerical score against each predictor, and then to calculate an
overall level of risk, would this actually help in predicting which children were most likely to be at risk of abuse? Parton (1989) quotes
research using a checklist of predictors applied to the maternity
notes of women discharged from a maternity unit. Of the families
screened, 18 per cent (511 out of 2802) were predicted as being 'at
risk' of child abuse. Subsequently, 19 out of the 28 recognised cases
were in this predicted high-risk group. So only nine cases were missed

(false negatives). However, 492 were included in the original high-risk group that did not subsequently abuse (false positives). Parton (1989, p. 68) concludes that: 'We do not have the predictive tools to identify correctly all actual and potential cases of abuse – nor are we likely to have them.' Resolving the question of the balance between missing some (false negative) and falsely accusing others (false positive) 'is essentially a political and ethical question – in the same way as how child abuse is itself defined is essentially a political and ethical question' (ibid.).

To regard child protection purely as a technical exercise is misguided and ignores the ethical questions which are really about how much 'abuse' society is prepared to tolerate, balanced against how much interference in family life is thought to be justified. As was argued in Chapter 1, social workers are faced with trying to balance these contradictory, ambivalent and changing societal values. Their major role becomes one of surveillance and collecting evidence, rather than therapy with the families, and their function is more to do with social control than with care and therapy (Howe, 1992).

Major changes in approach are also taking place in the field of community care in Britain, following the implementation of the National Health Service and Community Care Act in 1993 with its stress on assessment and care management (Payne, 1995). Detailed guidance from central government was provided (Department of Health Social Services Inspectorate, 1991a, 1991b), which has been developed into local authority manuals and procedures about how to conduct assessments, plan care packages, draw up contracts with providers of services and monitor standards and quality. Again, the language is largely technical, standardised forms are often used, and a 'procedural model' is invoked by agencies (Coulshed and Orme, 1998, p. 27). Although the views of users and carers are to be taken into account, ultimately the decision regarding what services to provide and how will depend on availability of resources and political and ethical decisions about priorities for types of user groups and services. Indeed the Department of Health guidance states:

> to ensure consistency of resource allocation between users with similar needs, authorities or agencies may wish to issue guidelines to their staff on the levels of expenditure appropriate to different

needs. Some discretion will be necessary if flexible, individualised responses are to develop. (1991a, p. 65)

The guide goes on to state that practitioners have to balance their accountability to users and to their employing agency. It recommends that users are informed of the ways of making representations under complaints procedures if they are dissatisfied. It is acknowledged that practitioners will experience the stress of identifying needs for which no resources are available. According to Lymbery (1998, p. 875) much of the work of the social worker within care management is limited by both time and resources, leading to 'a form of practice dominated by unimaginative, routinized, bureaucratic approaches'. Indeed, research by Lewis and Glennerster (1996, pp. 140–3) demonstrates increased levels of bureaucracy and managerial control and a shift in the balance of work from counselling to administration.

These changes in the field of child protection and community care represent major shifts in the role of social workers. We have already noted the emphasis on users' rights, complaints, user involvement, starting from users' needs rather than available services and adopting multidisciplinary approaches, in Chapter 6. Some commentators argue that this represents a shift in attitude and behaviour on the part of social workers and other professionals amounting to 'a cultural revolution' (Audit Commission, 1992, p. 19). Indeed, Lymbery (2000, p. 123) argues that 'the implementation of community care has signalled a substantial setback for the professional project . . . of social work'. Yet in some ways such thinking is much less revolutionary for social workers than is being suggested. First, the values of social work have always been about 'putting the user first' and the current of 'anti-professionalism' within social work has always been strong. Second, despite the rhetoric about user-centred, needs-led services, in a time of resource shortage the reality is that economy and efficiency are often going to come before meeting the particular preferences and needs of users. The real revolution is arguably in the role that social workers are increasingly taking on as assessors, inspectors, gatherers of evidence and managers of budgets and in the fragmentation of the role of generic social worker into specialist functions with different titles. The duties required by the agency or employer are being defined in increasing detail in order to meet the ever-changing requirements of central government for quality standards (see for example, Department of Health, 1998). This leads at best to bureaucratic practice (which focuses primarily on issues of needs or risk assessment and resource allocation as determined by agency rules and procedures) and at worst to defensive practice (going by the book and denying personal responsibility). Such an approach to practice can be distinguished from the 'professional' model which focuses more on the individual worker–user relationship with guidance from the code of ethics and the 'radical' or 'committed' model which stresses individual or societal change and does not separate out the personal from the professional or agency values (see Table 7.1). While there is an increasing emphasis on the 'technical–bureaucratic' model at the present time, there are constant tensions between all three and this is part of the reason why ethical dilemmas often arise in social work – because of the many layers of duties involved. We have already noted that much social work often takes place in bureaucratic settings where social workers may be taking on both 'professional' and 'official' roles; this tension between bureaucracy and professionalism was noted in Chapter 5.

Ethics in bureaucracies: defensive versus reflective practice

Whilst some of the new managerialist developments may have been designed to reduce bureaucracy and decentralise decision-making, the growth of centrally defined schedules and procedures has in fact increased the administrative approach that is one of the hallmarks of bureaucracies. According to Torstendahl (1991, p. 37) bureaucracy is 'the social subsystem of administrative work in a specific setting'. Although the new managerialist bureaucracies may have more of a flavour of a 'contract' culture, with some flatter and more decentralised management structures (Gray and Jenkins, 1999, pp. 211–12), more specialisation and interdisciplinarity (Mullender and Perrott, 1998, pp. 69–70) and a concern with consumer responsiveness (Hugman, 1998, pp. 135–60), I would argue it still makes sense to characterise them as bureaucracies. One of the major concerns about professionals located in bureaucracies has been and still is that bureaucratic decision-making undermines moral responsibility.

Rhodes (1986, pp. 134ff.) suggests that it is based on role and legal responsibility and encourages a split between personal and professional life – freeing employees from the demands of their personal moralities. For example, she says that:

> while you might *personally* wish to give welfare recipients more money, the organisation forbids it. (p. 136)

> You may be urged to place a child in a foster home rather than a residential treatment school, because the more expensive treatment plan is viewed as 'inefficient' and 'costly'. (p. 137)

She notes the contradictions between the individualised, caring concerns of social workers and the impersonal requirements of bureaucracies, and argues that 'being a good worker may mean acting unethically' (p. 137). However, we need to ask whether it is, in fact, unethical to refrain from giving welfare recipients more money. First, if it is just a question of me personally 'wishing' to do this, is it a moral judgement at all? If this were to be a moral judgement, it would be stated in terms of the fact that welfare recipients *ought* to have more money. If we assume that moral judgements prescribe action and are universalisable, then it should commit me to action, and it would mean that other people in other areas in similar situations should be given more money. Yet if I give these people more money, others may have less; it may not be fair. If I break the rules for distributing money, then chaos will ensue. I could argue that it is in the greatest interest of the greatest number of people to stick to the rules at present because I am in an organisation that works by rules and is dealing with many people. If I decide to do this, surely I would not be acting 'unethically'. I would essentially be working from utilitarian moral principles relating to justice and fairness. It would be unethical if I *unthinkingly* always followed all agency rules and procedures; or if I *knowingly* acted unethically, using the agency rules as an excuse.

There is a tendency to assume that questions around the distribution of resources, efficiency and cost are not ethical ones. They are, and it is dangerous not to regard them as such. Seeking the cheapest service may not be an unethical decision, if it may be argued that this results in more people getting some level of service, rather than a few people getting good-quality service. It should be noted that Rhodes espouses a virtue-based ethical theory which, while consistent as a theory of ethics, does not reflect the system of morality currently predominant in social work. Working in a bureaucracy does not inevitably mean acting 'unethically'; adopting utilitarian approaches is not necessarily unethical. In fact, it is vital to see such work as very much in the sphere of the ethical, rather than the purely technical. Otherwise there is the danger that we become 'defensive' practitioners. The ethical decisions regarding resource allocation or what is to count as child abuse may have been made elsewhere (by central government or by agency managers), but that does not absolve the social worker of the responsibility to challenge these decisions if necessary. For example, we need to guard against the preoccupation which the bureaucratic approach encourages with the distribution of existing resources, and think about arguing for more resources for social services users. The social worker in a bureaucracy can and should still be a 'reflective' practitioner. In summary, we may distinguish between defensive and reflective practitioners as follows:

- *Defensive practitioners* go by the book and fulfil duties/responsibilities defined by the agency and the law. There is no need to take blame if the prescribed rules and procedures have been followed. Social workers are 'officials' or 'technicians'. Doing 'my duty' means fulfilling my obligations to the agency, rather than doing the morally right action; personal and agency values tend to be separated, and the latter tend to be adopted whilst in the role of social worker.
- *Reflective practitioners* recognise ethical dilemmas and conflicts and how they arise (for example, through unequal power relationships with users; contradictions within the welfare state; society's ambivalence towards the welfare state and social workers in particular). They are more confident about their own values and how to put them into practice; integrate knowledge, values and skills; reflect on practice and learn from it; are prepared to take risks and moral blame. There is a recognition that personal and agency values may conflict and that the worker as a person has a moral responsibility to make decisions about these conflicts.

Conclusions

In this chapter we have discussed the many layers of often conflicting duties that social workers have to balance and choose between. We have argued that the critical or reflective practitioner needs to be aware of these and to make informed ethical judgements about which duties have priority. She may have to operate within several contradictory models of social work practice and be able to recognise and hold the tensions between them. If the social worker takes on one model to the exclusion of others, then important aspects of social work practice will be ignored. If the social worker regards herself exclusively as a 'professional', ignoring the constraints imposed by the employing agency, then she may become narrow and elitist. If she wholeheartedly takes on board the technical–bureaucratic model, she may become the defensive practitioner, mindlessly following agency rules. If she sees her own personal religious or political beliefs as paramount, then she may become unaccountable to her agency or to users. To recognise and balance these layers of duties is part of what it means to be a competent practitioner. We need to recognise that personal, professional, agency and societal values are interlocking, yet in tension.

Exercise 4

Aims of the exercise – to show how the values of the individual, the agency and society may be similar and/or conflicting.

1. Think of the job that you are currently doing, or one that you have done in the past:

   - What are your main *aims* in the job?
   - What *roles* do you play?
   - Describe your major *achievements* in this job.
   - What *values* do you think underpin your work in this job (what you regard as your major achievements may help you think through what your values are).

2. Now imagine looking at your job from the point of view of the agency you are working for or used to work for:

   - What do you think the agency's *aims* are?
   - What do you think is the agency view of the *role* you are playing?
   - What pieces of work do you think the agency would *value* most?
   - What *values* do you think underpin the agency's work?

3. Now imagine looking at your job from the point of view of society as a whole, or 'the public':

   - What do you think the public regards as the *aims* of the job?
   - What *role* do you think the public regards you as playing?
   - What pieces of work do you think the public would *value* most?
   - What *values* do you think underpin the public's view of your job?

4. Are there differences between your values and those of the agency and/or society? If so, why do you think this is the case?

8

Ethical Problems and Dilemmas in Practice

This chapter will explore some of the ethical problems and dilemmas that arise in everyday social work practice about which social workers have to make decisions. First I will give a brief outline of one view of the nature of ethical decision-making in professional practice. We will then explore examples of problems and dilemmas that have been collected from both trainee and experienced social workers in the light of the discussion in the previous chapters.

Ethical decision-making

Much of social work is concerned with making decisions about how to act in particular cases: for example, whether to commit a confused woman to hospital against her will. This involves making ethical decisions or judgements. One such judgement might be: 'It is morally wrong to commit this woman to hospital against her will.' As is apparent from our discussion in Chapters 2 and 3, there is considerable disagreement amongst ethical theorists not only about the nature of ethics, but also about how judgements are arrived at and justified, and, indeed, whether ethical judgements are more akin to expressions of taste or feeling than rational prescriptions for action (for a more detailed discussion of different theories of ethics see Hudson, 1978; Lafollette, 2000). Nevertheless, in the context of professional ethics, where professionals have defined roles and responsibilities and deal with the distribution of public resources, notions of accountability, rationality and fairness are regarded as important aspects of decision-making. A view about the nature of ethical judgements which I think fits with the general context of the work of the welfare professions is summarised below. It articulates many of the preconditions for principle-based ethics, with an emphasis on rational justification with reference to principles (as articulated in Chapter 2). However, the importance of the particularity of situations, attitudes and feelings is also included, building on our discussions in Chapter 3.

1. Ethical judgements are about *human welfare* – for example, the promotion of human happiness or the satisfaction of needs (Norman, 1998, pp. 218–20; Warnock, 1967, pp. 48–72). What counts as a 'human need' will be relative to a particular society or ideological belief system and will change over time. This does not necessarily mean there are no universal values, but how they are implemented may vary according to time, place and circumstances (Ife, 1999, pp. 218–19).

2. Ethical judgements entail *action*, that is, they are prescriptive (Hare, 1952, 1963). If a social worker makes the moral judgement that the woman suffering from confusion ought not to be committed to hospital against her will, then the worker should be prepared to act on this, which might include making plans for her to stay at home and being prepared to argue the case to her family and to professional colleagues.

3. Ethical judgements about particular cases take into account the *context of the situation*, including the particular relationships and responsibilities of the people involved.

4. Nevertheless, an ethical judgement should be *universalisable,* in the sense that it should apply to all people in similar circumstances. The social worker should make the same moral judgement about another confused woman, unless it could be demonstrated that the situation was significantly different.

5. It makes sense to ask people to *justify* their ethical judgements. They may do so with reference to some general moral judgements or principles within their particular system of morality or to particular relationships and responsibilities. In this case, the social worker might refer to the principle that 'all individuals have a right to decide for themselves what they want to do' (self-determination). This in turn might be justified with reference to the principle that 'all persons should be respected as rational and self-determining beings'. Ultimately a stage is reached where no further justification can be given and certain beliefs about the nature of human welfare and needs have to be taken as given.

Alternatively, or in addition, the social worker might justify
her decision with reference to her particular relationship with
Mrs Brown, her understanding of Mrs Brown's feelings, or her
responsibilities as a social worker.

Developing the reflective practitioner: case studies from trainees

In discussing ethical dilemmas with trainee social workers, there is
often an acute sense of confusion, anxiety and guilt around the decisions social workers have to make and the roles they play. This
may arise from a lack of understanding of the nature of the social
worker's role (that it is complex and contradictory), idealism, a lack
of information about policies and procedures, or simply a lack of
opportunity to rehearse situations and learn from experience. An
important part, therefore, of the education and training of social
workers is to facilitate the development of skills in critical reflection.
Developing a capacity for critical reflection is much more than
simply learning procedures or achieving particular 'competences'.
Part of the process of becoming a reflective practitioner is the adoption of a critical and informed stance towards practice. This can only
come about through doing the practice, reflecting on it through dialogue and questioning, and changing the practice in the light of the
reflection. This links to the concept of 'praxis' and the inseparabil-
ity of theory and practice discussed in Chapter 4. The notion of the
helping professional as a reflective practitioner was developed particularly by Schön (1983, 1987) and is now an influential strand in
the literature of the caring professions (see Gould and Taylor, 1996;
Smith, 1994; Yelloly and Henkel, 1995). It is based on the notion
of the practitioner reflecting on what is happening whilst in action,
and reflecting on what happened afterwards ('reflection in and on
action'). According to Brookfield: 'Practitioners develop strategies,
techniques, and habitual responses to deal with different kinds of situations, drawing chiefly on their acquired experience and intuitive
understanding' (Brookfield, 1987, p. 156).
'Beginning' practitioners, or those with little experience, have obviously had less opportunity to gain experience and develop strategies
and responses – or what Schön calls 'theories in use'. What a beginning practitioner may regard as an ethical dilemma – a choice

between two equally unwelcome alternatives involving a conflict between ethical principles – an experienced practitioner may not. For the experienced practitioner it may be obvious that one alternative is less unwelcome than the other, or that one principle has priority over another, so she does not even conceptualise the decision as involving a moral dilemma. This does not mean that ethical issues are not involved, or that the situation should not be seen as involving an ethical problem, just that, strictly speaking, a dilemma is what confronts the worker before a decision is made. If the situation is familiar, or the worker has a clear sense of which moral principles have priority in this type of situation, then the situation will not be experienced as a dilemma, but simply a case of having to make a moral choice or decision. Thompson *et al.* (1994, pp. 4–5) distinguish between moral problems and moral dilemmas – arguing that a moral problem usually has a solution, or a possible solution. This seems to imply that a dilemma does not. However, I would argue that most of the time social workers do have to resolve dilemmas – in that they do have to take some action, even if this is deciding not to act, in which case they make a choice between the alternatives. This may be done either by making a random choice, or, more usually, after a process of reflection and research which eventually leads the worker to decide that one course of action may be better than another and therefore is the right action.

Some of the anxieties around the ethical dilemmas experienced by trainee social workers seem to be based on the following:

1. lack of training and knowledge in a new situation;
2. lack of clarity about the role of social worker, for example carer or controller, and rules attached to the role such as confidentiality;
3. lack of confidence in their own status/position, especially *vis-à-vis* other professionals;
4. narrow focus on the needs or rights of one individual user, or on one issue, without seeing the complexity of the case;
5. the complexity of the situation is seen, but found to be overwhelming.

The following cases from trainee social workers illustrate the above points. These are all examples of ethical dilemmas experienced by trainee social workers either whilst undertaking fieldwork practice, or before they joined a social work training programme (that is, when they were unqualified workers or volunteers).

1. Lack of training and knowledge in a new situation

> *Child abuse disclosure to a volunteer*: a volunteer working in a day centre was approached by a nine-year-old girl with whom she had a good relationship, saying that her father had been hitting her and she was upset. She asked if the volunteer would sit in on a meeting between the girl and her parents. The centre manager encouraged the volunteer to go ahead and provided a room. The volunteer was given no guidance on procedure. She was asked to swear confidentiality by the father at the outset of the meeting. She commented afterwards: 'in my naivety I agreed, which I later found out was a mistake'. She was told about a variety of sexual and physical abuse.

The dilemma here for the volunteer is whether she should respect the confidence and keep her promise to the girl (a Kantian approach), or break the confidence and discuss the matter with her line manager because of the serious harm that is being done to the girl (a utilitarian approach). A decision may be made by balancing the importance of respecting a confidence against what is in the girl's best interests – weighing up the immediate danger to the girl, and the likelihood of the volunteer being able to persuade the girl to tell someone else. Alternatively the volunteer may realise, or discover, that the agency she works for has a policy that all suspicions about child abuse must be reported to the line manager. She may decide that agency rules should always be followed, or that this particular rule is an important one and it is in the interests of all that it is followed. Therefore the dilemma is resolved and she should tell her line manager.

For the experienced practitioner this case may not present a dilemma at all. First, the experienced practitioner would probably have said at the outset that she could not promise confidentiality. However, assuming she had promised confidentiality because she knew the girl had something important to say and would not be able to say it otherwise, the experienced social worker would usually be much more aware of herself as an employee of an agency and would be familiar with agency rules and procedures and have worked out which ones it was important to follow. She may have worked out from past experience that confidentiality can never be absolute and in her view the best interests of the user always come first.

The learning from this experience for the volunteer is that in similar circumstances next time she would start the meeting by explaining that any information she was given might be shared with the line manager. This might not stop her feeling anxious about sharing the information she was given, but she should not feel guilty about breaking a confidence.

2. Lack of clarity about role

Mother who was working and claiming benefit: a young mother was referred to a family centre because of feelings of social isolation. During a counselling session with her key worker discussing budgeting, and the problems caused by spending any time away from her daughter, she revealed that she was claiming income support and working nights as a cleaner. The key worker posed the following questions: 'Should I ignore it? By discussing it with her am I legally condoning it? Should the matter be reported to the Department of Social Security? Should the principle of confidentiality be upheld? Is the social worker an agent of the state?'

This example shows a trainee social worker wondering about the extent to which she is 'an agent of social control' – assuming that her responsibilities to the state extend more widely than they in fact do. She does not realise that if a user has done or is doing something illegal the social worker does not automatically have to report this to the appropriate authority. Usually a social worker would only break confidentiality in these circumstances if a very serious crime was being committed or a life was in danger. While the social worker should not aid and abet a user in an illegal pursuit, discussing the matter does not necessarily entail condoning it. In fact, the social worker can make it clear that what the user is doing is illegal and cannot be condoned.

Not only would the experienced practitioner be clearer about the law, but she would probably have had time to reflect on the complex and contradictory nature of the social worker's role and know when it was appropriate to adopt a social control role, an enabling role or a caring role. She might also ask the question 'whose dilemma is it anyway?' (Bond, 2000, p. 224) and realise that it is in fact the user's own ethical dilemma, not the social worker's.

3. Feeling of lack of confidence in status/position of social worker

Treatment of a resident in an institution: Susan was a 22-year-old woman living in a residential care home for people with cerebral palsy and related disabilities who was prone to spells of depression which resulted in her crying a lot, or refusing to communicate or eat. She communicated by means of a communication board attached to her wheelchair. The trainee social worker, who had worked in the home as an unqualified care worker for four months, was told by the other staff that Susan's behaviour was due to homesickness, a crush on a member of staff and a 'predisposition towards attention-seeking behaviour'. When Susan became upset, the policy was to take her to her room, shut the door and leave her there to calm down. When the care worker talked to Susan, she said she would like to get out of the home more often, meet more people and take a course at a local college. She asked the care worker to pass this information on at the next staff meeting. When the care worker did this, Susan's request was dismissed as 'playing up' and 'nagging susceptible new members of staff'. The care worker felt that there was a culture of running the home to suit the staff who spent a large part of their time smoking and drinking coffee, while residents watched TV or sat motionless in the corridors. The care worker commented afterwards: 'I was worried that I was rocking the boat too much, that I asked too many questions and that I refused to fit into the team and their way of doing things . . . Nothing happened and shortly afterwards I left.'

This case is typical of many recounted by trainee social workers who feel powerless to challenge or change what they consider to be bad practice in not meeting the needs or respecting the rights and dignity of individual service users. In this case it is a question of not fitting in with the team norms, in other cases it may be fear of reprisals or of the power of the practice teacher or fieldwork supervisor to fail a student's placement. One group of trainees discussing issues arising from their fieldwork practice commented on the conflict between the idealism they gain during their studies and the realities of practice in the 'outside world'. It is not always clear what the standard of acceptable practice should be, and sometimes students are indeed too idealistic. Yet they also see things with fresh eyes and can disturb a cosy complacency or, even worse, a seriously neglectful or abusive situation. This case raises the question of how to challenge practice within a staff team, which may lead to making a complaint or even whistleblowing. For inexperienced workers who are not confident of the expected 'standards' or how a complaints procedure may work and may be worried about reprisals it is often difficult to take any action at all. They are left feeling that they ought to have acted, yet failed to do so. Seeking alliances with other workers, trainees and talking to college tutors may help in rehearsing the arguments and testing others' understandings of what counts as bad practice and how it can be challenged.

4. *Narrow focus on individual user/one issue*

> *Elderly couple and residential care*: Mr and Mrs Finch, aged 91 and 86, were admitted to residential care by the night duty team on a call from the warden of the sheltered accommodation where they lived. They were reported as being unable to cope with everyday domestic functions and Mrs Finch had had a fall in the night. There was pressure from the family, the warden and senior social work colleagues for them to be admitted permanently to residential care. The trainee social worker stated that when she visited them, 'Mr and Mrs Finch were suffering from impaired memory function. They could not comprehend why they had been admitted to residential accommodation, but were categoric that they wanted to return home.' She felt that 'the couple should be allowed to return home on the basis of their individual right to choose'.

The trainee social worker may well be right in this case – that the couple should be allowed to return home – but focusing on their right to choose (a Kantian approach) is only one way of looking at the issue. She might consider the extent to which they are capable of making an informed choice, as well as taking into account the rights and needs of the warden and the family. It seems as though she sees herself principally in the role of advocate for the users, whereas it is often the social worker's job to assess the whole situation and work for a solution in the best interests of all concerned (a more utilitarian approach). In stressing the principle of user self-determination, there appears to be no dilemma here for the trainee social worker. Since she knows what is the morally right course of action, what she feels she is facing is a moral problem – of how to achieve this in the face of opposition. Others might see it as a dilemma – to be resolved by taking various other factors into account, such as whether the users understand the risks attached to returning home and what level of support and responsibility is it fair to place on the warden.

5. *The complexity of the situation is seen, but found to be overwhelming*

Banning the Sun *newspaper in a residential home*: at a staff meeting at a residential unit for drug users it was decided that the unit should stop buying newspapers published by News International. The reason for this was the dispute at the time between the printers' trade unions and this publisher. The union for public sector employees, to which the staff of the unit belonged, was supporting a boycott of these papers. The initial ban was just on newspapers from the unit's funds. Subsequently a ban was extended to residents buying the *Sun* out of their own money on the grounds of not only the union dispute, but also its sexist, homophobic and racist stance and its distortions on the subject of AIDS. The trainee social worker reported that 'what initially appeared to be a straightforward dilemma when the ban was introduced as a union issue soon became a complex and deeply disturbing problem for all concerned'.

The trainee social worker, in writing up this case, raises a series of questions at the end, including asking whether social workers are agents of change, and if so where the limits of their responsibility to bring about change lie. If the *Sun* is banned, what about television programmes and pornographic magazines? Have workers the right to impose their own values on residents? It was only after much reflection and discussion afterwards that this worker came to the view that the *Sun* should not be banned, but rather the issues regarding the dispute with the unions and the prejudiced and offensive nature of much of the material in the newspaper should be discussed with residents. This would entail treating the residents as capable of making their own choices and encouraging them to participate in decision-making.

When is blame and guilt justified?
Case studies from practitioners

In experienced practitioners we would generally expect some clarity about their role as social workers, a certain confidence in acting on their own principles, and an ability to hold complexity and contradiction in the work. Indeed, when senior social work practitioners were interviewed about ethical dilemmas in their work, their responses frequently referred to difficult cases involving ethical issues and problems (particularly around lack of suitable resources or threats to service users' well-being) rather than ethical dilemmas as such. A team manager in a child care team told me of several difficult cases where other agencies had recommended courses of action with which she disagreed. Although she used the term 'ethical dilemma' frequently, it was clear that she knew what was the right course of action and was prepared to act on this. One of her examples is given at the end of this chapter.

Nevertheless, even the most experienced practitioners find themselves facing ethical dilemmas, and have feelings of guilt about the choices and actions they take. Some of this guilt and blame is necessary – if we do what we know to be morally wrong, or retreat into defensive practice, or take a decision which turns out to have a bad outcome which we could have predicted if we had thought about it more deeply. Yet some of the guilt and blame is unnecessary and unproductive, as was discussed in Chapter 1. It is easy to see how it comes about, for the nature of a dilemma is that whatever decision is made there will be some unwelcome outcomes. Usually there is a choice between two or more conflicting ethical principles, all of which we believe are important. If we can understand that this is the nature of the job, and that, for example, in a particular case, we chose to break confidentiality because another overriding principle relating to the welfare of the user was more important, then we should not regard ourselves as having acted immorally. Rather we have faced up to a difficult ethical decision. The following four case examples relate to two situations where social workers said they felt bad about the decisions they had made and wondered if they should have acted differently, and two situations where the workers knew they had made hard or uncomfortable decisions, but still felt confident that they had made the right choice. In the two cases where the workers reported feeling confident about their decisions (one of which also resulted in a bad outcome) both workers felt very clear about where they stood on a particular issue – they had thought through their positions and accepted what the consequences of their actions might be. The four case examples can be categorised as follows (names and some details have been changed to preserve anonymity):

1. The worker felt guilty because a bad outcome occurred and he was aware of the dangers and wondered if he should have done more to prevent this.
2. The worker felt her actions were morally right, despite a bad outcome, because she stuck to a deeply held moral principle.
3. The worker felt guilty because he had to compromise one of his deeply held principles.
4. The worker felt her actions were morally right, despite having to compromise one of her principles, because another principle had priority.

1. Worker felt guilty about a bad outcome

The following example was given to me by an approved psychiatric social worker, and is a case where the social worker felt he did not act in the user's best interests and felt guilty about this. The fact that there was a bad outcome to the case (the user died) no doubt exacerbated the feelings of guilt.

The user's interests versus the constraints of the agency role: the social worker described a case where he felt the drugs administered by a psychiatrist had caused a patient's physical health to deteriorate, culminating in death by pneumonia. The patient's family were concerned about whether she had been given the right treatment and whether the pneumonia had been picked up soon enough. The social worker commented: 'I thought it was the drugs that had caused her death. I didn't say it to the family. In the end you're working so much with other health professionals. I colluded.'

The social worker clearly felt quite bad about this case. He had been involved with admitting this woman to hospital originally for 28 days under the Mental Health Act. The social worker felt this was the right decision. On going to hospital she became calmer, accepted her fate and agreed to take medication. But it soon became obvious to the social worker that the medication was affecting her physically. The social worker said he felt responsible for her, as he watched her condition deteriorate as she was shipped backwards and forwards between the psychiatric and general hospitals. He did not seem sure what he could or should have done: 'It is difficult to question consultants. You can only question whether hospital is the best place, not the diagnosis and treatment.'

In hindsight, he suggested that the point at which he could have done something was after the original 28-day section ran out and it was then renewed for six months. He did have a choice at this stage regarding whether to sign the documents as an approved social worker. However, he did feel the patient needed to be in hospital, and trusted the hospital to pick up on any serious physical problems.

This case seems to have three stages. The first stage was the initial committal to hospital which the social worker felt was legally and morally justified. The second stage was the time during the treatment, including the time when the section had to be renewed, when he knew the patient was deteriorating physically, but did not do anything about it. The third stage was after her death when he had to decide whether or not to tell the relatives the truth about his own feelings relating to the cause of death. He commented that with hindsight perhaps he could have acted differently at the second stage, but it would have been difficult. Did he retreat into a kind of defensive practice? He acted within the law and according to agency rules, but was he denying some moral responsibility for the situation when he said that it was not his role to question the diagnosis? It is always a

difficult decision to go beyond the agency-defined role – to risk going
out on a limb, to challenge another professional when it is not one's
role to do so.

This is a good example of the type of tough dilemma often faced
by social workers, when no course of action has a good outcome.
The worker has to try to weigh up how much risk or harm to a
patient should be allowed before some action is taken. We can understand the social worker's inaction in this case; perhaps we would not
blame him for the patient's death. However, we might think perhaps
his own feelings of blame and guilt are justified because he did not
do what he thought was in the best interests of the patient. The
ethical issues here relate not just to the rights and interests of the
patient and the duties of professionals to promote the welfare of
patients, but to the summoning of the courage and confidence to
implement the right action. The third stage, where the question of
what to say to the relatives arose, is probably less problematic. Given
he had signed the papers for the renewal of the section and had not
challenged the consultant then or later, he no doubt felt that it was
not fair to mention his views about the drugs to the woman's family.
The situation might have been different if the social worker had
believed the psychiatrist to be incompetent and likely to put other
patients at risk.

2. *Worker did not feel guilty about bad outcome because she stuck to a deeply-held principle*

The following example was given to me by a youth worker. She
felt the case described presented a moral dilemma and she had
made a decision based on her belief in confidentiality and user self-
determination as absolute moral principles. Although the outcome
of the situation was bad, she still felt she had made the morally right
decision.

> *Confidentiality and user self-determination versus the user's inter-
> ests*: the youth worker was working in a busy youth club on a
> normal youth club evening. She was approached in the coffee bar
> by a 15-year-old girl, Jan, who was obviously in a state of distress.
> The youth worker took her into a quiet room. From that initial
> contact Jan swore the worker to secrecy. Jan revealed to the worker

over several weeks that during the past year she had been raped four times by her father and was now pregnant by him. She had also decided to commit suicide as a way out of the situation. The youth worker talked through the issues with Jan, suggesting various options for help and that suicide was not the best way out. However, Jan continued to refuse to consider any professional help, and insisted that the worker should not tell anyone. The youth worker respected her request for confidentiality. Jan did commit suicide.

Obviously this case relates to a youth worker, not a social worker. If the worker had been working for a social work agency, agency policy would require the worker to report any cases of suspected child abuse and would advise workers not to promise absolute confidentiality. The case would have been analogous to the one given earlier about the volunteer who promised confidentiality. However, in this case it seems there was no agency policy and the worker stuck to the principle of confidentiality because she personally believed it was an important one (a Kantian approach). She did not feel she had any overriding duties to her agency, nor that she should adopt a different set of principles as a youth worker than she should in her everyday life – we might suggest that she was working within the committed practitioner model. She felt that the girl, at 15, was capable of making her own decisions, and should not be treated in a parentalist way. The youth worker, in spite of the girl's suicide, felt she had acted in accordance with her moral principles and therefore that her decision not to break the confidence was right.

This is a complex case to explore. For other workers, the decision about whether to break confidence may hardly have presented a dilemma at all. Given it was a case of child abuse and there was even a slight risk of self-inflicted harm to the girl, a line manager or the social services department should have been informed. This would both cover the worker from feeling guilt if the girl did commit suicide, and would be in the girl's best interests (utilitarian considerations). Others may have seen it as a dilemma, involving the weighing up of the importance of respecting the girl's right to confidentiality and to make her own decisions about her life against the likelihood of the girl committing suicide.

I am less concerned to consider what would have been the 'right' action in this case, and more interested in the fact that this is a situation where a worker apparently did not feel guilty or responsible for a bad outcome. This type of worker is rare in social work, partly because most social workers feel they have a right not to be burdened with the responsibility for someone's death, and they adopt a much more utilitarian approach to moral decision-making by weighing up the possible outcomes of actions and being more prepared to take a parentalist view of what is in a user's best interests. It is also partly because social work agencies (and many youth work agencies) have rules and procedures designed to ensure that an individual worker does not carry the total responsibility for the outcome of an intervention. Some people may feel that the youth worker should have acted differently and was at least partly to blame for the girl's death. The youth worker was in a position of responsibility in relation to the young people in the club and had a duty to promote their welfare; to adhere rigidly to a personally-held principle of confidentiality may not have been appropriate in this context. Others may feel she was right, seeing her relationship with the girl in the context of a voluntary non-directive counselling role.

3. Worker felt guilty about compromising a principle

The manager of a day centre for people with learning disabilities described a situation where he felt he had acted 'immorally'. The reason he described his action in this way was because he had made a decision which was contrary to one of the key principles that he believed was important for social work – namely, user self-determination.

> *User self-determination versus the interests of the user and others*: John, a 26-year-old man with learning disabilities who had been attending the day centre for some time, asked if he could walk to the centre on his own, rather than use the minibus provided by the social services department. Staff of the centre judged that he was capable of doing so, and they thought that this would help him develop his life skills, self-confidence and independence. However, John's parents were extremely worried at this suggestion, feeling that John would not be able to cope. They stated categorically that they would not allow John to attend the centre if he had to make

his own way there. The centre manager reluctantly agreed that
John should continue to use the bus.

When the social worker who had been the centre manager was asked
why he came to this decision, it became obvious that he was taking
into account the views and feelings of John's parents, as well as what
he thought would promote greater self-determination for John. He
had weighed up the consequences for John and his parents of insist-
ing that John should walk to the day centre. Given that John relied
on his parents for care, they had a right to have their views heard.
Also it would not be in John's long-term interests if he stopped
coming to the day centre or if his parents were excessively anxious.
So this social worker had in effect gone through a process of weighing up the outcomes of the proposed change against the status quo
and decided that the least harm would be done if the status quo was
maintained. This social worker did not act 'unethically' – far from it
– he actually went through a very serious process of moral reasoning to come to the decision he did. What his decision shows is that
the principle of user self-determination is not the only ethical principle, or even the paramount ethical principle for social work practice. Other principles such as promoting the good of the user (which
involves other things than self-determination) and promoting the
general good (which involves people other than just the user) are also
important. If we accept utilitarianism as a theory of ethics, then
these are ethical principles. This social worker was facing an ethical
dilemma involving a conflict between ethical principles – user self-
determination versus the promotion of the greatest good of the
greatest number. In order to resolve the dilemma he had to make a
choice – and whichever choice he made would go against one of the
principles. So it was not surprising that he was left feeling dissatisfied with the outcome. However, should he feel guilty that John was
not allowed to exercise his freedom to walk to the day centre? Surely
he should not, provided he felt he had done all he could to persuade
and encourage the parents to allow a trial run. He may feel *regret*
that John has not been allowed to walk to the centre, but not guilt.
By reflecting on this and discussing it, will this worker feel any less
guilty in the future? It is hard to say, but if he accepts that user self-
determination is not an absolute moral principle, and that therefore
it can be morally right to go against that principle, it might make it

easier for him to understand the nature of the decisions he has to make.

4. *Worker did not feel guilty because she clearly prioritised her principles*

This case is about the dilemmas felt by a black woman working in a voluntary sector Asian women's project where issues of family violence and neglect came up.

The needs of black children versus the 'betrayal' of the black community: an Asian woman moved into the area where the project was based from another part of the country. She was on her own, with five children under six years old, having fled a violent husband. She felt isolated as a newcomer, was given little support from the statutory services and found it hard to cope with the children. Her husband followed her and began harassing her. Some black professionals were providing her with limited support. In the course of her work, the worker at the Asian Women's Project discovered that the woman was locking up her children in her house and going out, either to seek help, or just for a break. The worker discussed this with her, explaining why it was not an appropriate thing to do, and that the children were being put at risk. However, the woman continued to leave her children locked in the house. The worker had to warn the woman that if she continued to leave her children unattended at home she would have to report her to the social services, and the implications of this might be that the children could be taken into care.

Finally the worker decided that she must inform social services because of the potential danger to the children. The worker found this a tough decision to make, because she felt that in the past social services had treated black women very badly, and had been insensitive to the complexities of cultural and gender issues. She said: 'It was a betrayal of the black community in a sense. In the past I had campaigned about the insensitivity of social services. But on this occasion I felt I had to do it because of the risk to the children.'

The worker in this case said she did not feel guilty about what she had done. She felt it was the right decision. Having explained to the woman on several occasions that she should not leave the children on their own and having worked with her trying to sort out her domestic and financial problems, she had given the woman due warning. This seems to be a case where the worker felt regret, but not guilt.

This case highlights some of the tensions felt by black workers in a professional position. This worker commented on how a large part of her job was trying to explain to the Asian women the British laws, and the powers and roles of the various authorities and services. The women often found it hard to comprehend that neglect of and violence towards children were illegal. The social services and other agencies generally were insensitive to the needs of the Asian women, and were unwilling, or unable, to take into account the whole picture of a woman's life, including her religion and cultural background. The workers at the Asian Women's Project were in a sense mediating between the western and Asian cultures and values. Often their role was resented by members of the Asian community, particularly the men. The workers in the Asian Women's Project were concerned not just about balancing the needs and interests of different sections of the black community, but also about trying to adopt a committed/ radical approach to practice and to work from a black feminist perspective. This particular worker commented that it was important for her to be very clear about her own values and about her professional commitments. Whilst she had a strong commitment to help the Asian community, she was not prepared to cover up or ignore cases of family violence or neglect where women or children were at risk of harm. She said that she rarely felt guilt or self-blame about the actions she had taken, since she was clear where she stood. Some black workers who were more ambivalent about their professional roles, particularly statutory social workers, seemed to have a tougher time.

Ethical decision-making: a team manager's case

All the above cases relate to whether or not a social worker should have felt blame or guilt about the outcomes of their decisions or actions. We have argued that it is important that social workers come to a considered decision. At the beginning of this chapter it was suggested that making a moral judgement in a professional context should be regarded as an essentially rational process which can be

justified by the social worker. In justifying decisions, it is often useful
to make appeal to general and impartial principles, as we have done
in the previous section. Yet part of the process of decision-making
will also involve taking account of the particularities of the situation faced and the relationships with the people involved. What decision is made and whether it is implemented will also depend on the
strength of commitment, integrity and determination of the professionals involved. These factors are hard to encapsulate in brief case
studies where the details of people's lives, relationships and the feelings and views of the social workers involved are not given. I will
end the book by discussing just one example of a social work case
which raised difficult ethical issues for the team manager and social
worker involved and where some of the comments from the team
manager are incorporated to contextualise the case. It highlights the
problems and complexities of interdisciplinary working in cases
regarded as 'high risk'.

At the age of 19 Tracey was convicted of infanticide, having
stabbed to death a baby born after a concealed pregnancy. She was
given a two-year non-custodial sentence, supervised by the probation service. Cynthia, a senior mental health social worker,
worked with Tracey and her family for two years after this inci-
dent. At the age of 21 Tracey became pregnant again, to the same
young man as before, with whom she was now living. She phoned
to tell Cynthia, who was now a team manager of a child care team,
very excited. According to Cynthia, 'this was a very different situation [from last time]'. Tracey's family and partner were very supportive and a child care social worker in Cynthia's team made a
positive assessment. Although Cynthia commented that 'there
were obvious risks', particularly relating to the fact that Tracey
had remained amnesiac about the events following the birth of her
first child, and Cynthia felt that 'the birth of this child might act
as some kind of catalyst and we couldn't be sure what the reaction would be'. A plan was made for her to be admitted to the
family unit of the local hospital for assessment following the birth.
However, shortly before the birth was due, the decision was
changed. A guardian *ad litem* was appointed to safeguard the
interests of the baby. The medical staff, the probation officer and
guardian decided that it was too risky to allow Tracey and the baby
to be admitted to the family unit. According to Cynthia:

At the last moment they pulled the plug and said: 'we're not prepared to have her on this ward'. The whole thing gathered a
momentum of its own, where they were coming to conference
suggesting that Group 4 [a security firm] should be involved,
because of the risk she might pose to other mothers and children on the ward. This is a young woman who had been given
a two year probation sentence, not a custodial one, being
treated, I felt, very respectfully by the courts and with a great
deal of understanding, and had worked incredibly well with us
and had matured over that time . . . All sorts of incredible
things happened, like a professional forensic psychiatrist saw
her for an hour, and said, you know, Health were right . . . this
was a very dangerous situation.

Cynthia and the child care social worker were left having to decide
what to do at this point. She said: 'both of us felt very strongly that
it would have been completely wrong to have removed that child
and for her [Tracey] not to have had a chance'.

Ethical issues involved

1. *Rights of the service user(s)* – the Kantian principle of respect
   for persons entails that a user should be treated with respect and
   fairness and should be able to make decisions about her own life
   provided she is capable of rational and self-determining action
   and the decision does not present a serious danger to herself or
   others. In this case, Tracey's ability to remain 'rational' after the
   birth is in question, which raises the issue of the risk to the baby
   once born, and possibly other babies. It might be argued that the
   unborn baby should also be regarded as a 'service user' in this
   case, rather than just one of the 'others' involved. Certainly it
   would be the role of the social workers, as well as the guardian
   ad litem, to ensure that the rights of the unborn child were taken
   into account.
2. *The interests and welfare of the service user(s)* – what are the
   users' best interests? The principle of promoting user welfare
   arises here along with the question of whether we take account
   of Tracey's own view of her interests and welfare or what others
   think is best for her (parentalism). In the case of the unborn
   child, then we have to rely on what others think is best.

3. *The rights, interests and welfare of others* – who are the other
    parties involved (Tracey's partner, her parents, the other mothers
    and babies in the hospital ward, the hospital as a public institu-
    tion, the professionals involved – from health, probation, social
    services, the guardian) and what are their rights and interests?
    The utilitarian principle of promoting the greatest good of the
    greatest number comes in here – which entails questions of dis-
    tributive justice.
4. *Equality and justice* – how are pregnant young women, people
    with criminal convictions or psychiatric problems regarded in
    society generally and how are they treated by powerful profes-
    sionals? Is Tracey being unfairly discriminated against because
    of her past criminal conviction?

How the issues arose

These issues arose because health and social care professionals have
a duty to protect children. Their concern about the risks to Tracey's
unborn child and to other babies she may come in contact with in the
hospital leads them to propose strategies which circumscribe the
freedom of choice and movement of Tracey, her partner and her
family. Because there is no clear answer regarding how likely it is that
any harm will occur, this creates a climate of uncertainty and anxiety
and a concern amongst the health professionals and guardian about
taking responsibility for a bad outcome. As Parton (1998, p. 21) suggests, 'where the key concern is risk, the focus becomes, not making
the *right* decision, but making a *defensible* decision'. The context in
which this decision is being made can be understood in relation to
the discussion in Chapter 7 of the increasing concern with risk assessment and risk management in the role of welfare professionals.

Lines of argument

There are a number of lines of argument that might be pursued by
the social workers in coming to a decision and justifying it.

1. *Does Tracey have a right to look after her baby after its birth?* In
    normal circumstances the answer to this question would be 'yes'.

But because she killed her first baby, this right may be overridden in the interests of the rights and welfare of the child. The extent to which this right is removed or limited will depend on the answer to the second question.

2. *Is Tracey likely to harm her baby after the birth?* This is where the different professionals involved either disagree on what the risk to the child would be, and/or disagree in terms of how much risk they are prepared to tolerate. The social workers feel they know Tracey pretty well and judge that she is ready and able to care for the baby. The team leader commented:

> lots of things could weaken your resolve if we hadn't known the case as well as we did . . . despite the fact that I'd joint worked with the psychiatrist for two years with the case, this forensic psychiatrist 'expert' from London, you know, could make this judgement . . .

The other professionals seem to have greater doubts, however, with the forensic psychiatrist saying that it is a 'dangerous situation'. Furthermore, the guardian *ad litem* and the health professionals may have a lower tolerance of risk in this case than the social workers. Even if they all agree that the risk of harm to the baby in a supervised setting would be minimal, perhaps the guardian and health professionals see the worst-case scenario (death of the baby) as so bad that they feel they cannot take responsibility for a decision which allows Tracey to be assessed in the hospital unit. The guardian certainly would be acting with the child's best interests at heart. The health professionals also seem concerned about risk of harm to other babies. As O'Sullivan (1999, p. 145) comments in discussing risk assessment in social work: 'one person's risk taking can be another person's hazard'.

3. *What is in Tracey's best interests?* If there is a grave danger of her harming her newborn baby, this would have serious consequences for her in that, apart from the emotional upset it would cause her, she would be likely to receive a custodial sentence. The safest option, therefore, might be to remove the baby at birth. On the other hand, if she is not given the chance to care for the baby from the time of its birth, she would not be able to bond with it and if she was allowed to care for it subsequently, might find it difficult or be more likely to fail. It seems likely to be in

Tracey's best interests if she can be well-supervised and supported during the period after the birth, so that the baby does
not have to be removed, and the risks of harm are minimised.
4. *What are the rights and interests of the unborn baby?* Clearly once
the baby is born, it has a right to life, protection from harm and
a safe environment. Whether this environment would best be
provided by the mother and her family is the issue at stake. It
could be argued that it is in the child's interests to have conti-
nuity of high-quality care which, if the mother is capable, might
be best provided in the family of origin rather than in what might
turn out to be a series of placements.
5. *What are the rights and interests of other parties involved?*
Tracey's partner has some right to be involved in the decision-
making process about the care of his child, although he does not
seem to feature greatly in this case, apart from being described
as 'supportive'. The parents are also described as 'supportive' by
the team leader, but they were never assessed as potential alternative carers 'because there was a feeling that they could have
prevented it, had been somehow involved in the event [the previous infanticide]'. A similar view seems to have been taken
regarding Tracey's partner. The other parties who might be
affected include the other mothers and babies in the hospital
ward and this seems to have been a serious concern of the
medical staff. On the other hand, the social workers felt Tracey
posed no risk to other people's babies. She had lived quite
happily in the community for the past few years, and had done
babysitting for people. The health professionals involved were
concerned not to have to take responsibility if anything went
wrong. Their interests (which would involve protecting their own
reputations, jobs, the hospital's credibility) were to minimise the
risk.
6. *Is Tracey being treated fairly?* Cynthia, the team manager, said
she felt at times as though there was a retrial taking place:

> I felt, strongly, that given that there'd been a court hearing,
> that this young woman had been convicted of her offence, that
> had to be our starting point. She was a Schedule 1 offender,
> she'd had this desperately awful incident in her past and we
> had to work from that premise. And we couldn't reconsider

all the other possible dimensions of what might have happened on that occasion. But all the police files were got out again, the whole thing was trawled, which is not good for any pregnant young woman.

Cynthia is taking account of considerations of injustice and discrimination against Tracey on account of her past record. She does not feel this is warranted and is therefore prepared to stand up for Tracey.

The decision

Cynthia decided to recommend that social services should supervise the young woman and child from the moment of birth 'because Health wouldn't take that responsibility'. She commented that 'the Social Services Director at the time was very unhappy that we were carrying that responsibility', adding that in this case, like many others, 'the stakes are so high'. In fact, the young woman and her partner coped very well with the child (who was three and a half years old at the time of the interview) and hence the social worker felt vindicated. When asked what it was that made her feel so strongly that she was prepared to 'go out on a limb' in this case, she replied:

I think it was the understanding of the individual person and the belief that she has qualities that were necessary to parent a child and indeed to protect the child, particularly with the support of her partner who'd been long-term, and who absolutely knew what had happened before . . . But I think mainly, if I'd looked at that case on paper, I would have thought well, no wonder people are anxious, and it was mainly knowing and having assessed myself and then the new social worker having assessed the situation that gave me the confidence to feel that no way should she lose the opportunity to parent her child. But it is difficult . . . in the children and families team we have the luxury of knowing people fairly thoroughly before we have to make very far reaching decisions.

If we look at this case in terms of ethical principles, Cynthia was obviously concerned to respect Tracey as a person, to see her as an individual with the right and capacity to make her own choices and to promote her capacity to be self-determining by offering support (Kantian principles). There is no doubt that she was also concerned about the rights and interests of the unborn baby and other mothers and babies in the assessment unit, but she judged that the risks of harm to others (utilitarian considerations) were not sufficiently great to outweigh Tracey's rights and interests. But what enabled her to prioritise and implement her principles and duties in this way was her particular relationship with Tracey, her knowledge and under-standing of her situation, her professional judgement about Tracey's capabilities, her sense of fairness and justice and her determination and commitment to support this person. In other words, Cynthia's qualities or 'virtues' and her relationship of care with Tracey were important features of this situation.

Conclusions

Discussion of these case examples shows the importance of critical reflection on social work practice and the need to understand the complexities and contradictions inherent in the role of social worker. This enables social workers to understand more clearly how and why ethical problems and dilemmas arise in practice, and may enable them to be able better to defend themselves and the profession from moral attack and reduce some of the feelings of guilt, blame and anxiety in making difficult ethical decisions. Trainee social workers in particular experience a lot of confusion and anxiety about their roles, which can be reduced through reflection on ethical and value issues and relating them to social work theory and practice. The rapid changes taking place in the structure and organisation of social work services mean that it is even more important for practi-tioners to be clear about their value positions in order to resist the authoritarian, bureaucratising trends. These not only threaten pro-fessional identity and the traditional values based on respect for indi-vidual persons, but make increasingly difficult more radical and committed forms of practice which challenge both the traditional Kantian values and the utilitarian principles of the bureaucratic model.

Exercise 5

Aims of the exercise – to encourage the reader to analyse her/his practice in terms of the ethical issues involved.

Using the format adopted for analysing the last case example in Chapter 8:

1. Briefly describe an ethical dilemma experienced in your practice. Include reference to your feelings about the situation and the nature of your relationships with the people involved.
2. What were the ethical issues involved?
3. How did they arise?
4. What line of argument would you use to justify the course of action you took?

References

Abbott, P. and Meerabeau, L. (1998) 'Professionals, Professionalization and the Caring Professions', in P. Abbott and L. Meerabeau (eds), *The Sociology of the Caring Professions*, London, UCL Press, pp. 1–19.

Adams, R. (1999) *Personal Social Services: Clients, Consumers or Citizens?*, London, Longman.

Adams, R., Dominelli, L. and Payne, M. (eds) (1998) *Social Work: Themes, Issues and Critical Debates*, Basingstoke, Macmillan.

Ahmad, B. (1990) *Black Perspectives in Social Work*, Birmingham, Venture Press.

Alaszewski, A. (1998) 'Health and Welfare: Managing Risk in Late Modern Society', in A. Alaszewski, L. Harrison and J. Manthorpe (eds), *Risk, Health and Welfare: Policies, Strategies and Practice*, Buckingham, Open University Press, pp. 127–53.

Aldridge, M. (1994) *Making Social Work News*, London, Routledge.

Allmark, P. (1995) 'Can There Be an Ethics of Care?', *Journal of Medical Ethics*, vol. 21, pp. 19–24.

Amphlett, S. (1998) 'The Experience of a Watchdog', in G. Hunt (ed.), *Whistleblowing in the Social Services*, London, Arnold, pp. 65–93.

Aristotle (1954) *The Nichomachean Ethics of Aristotle*, translated by Sir David Ross, London, Oxford University Press.

Arrington, R. (1998) *Western Ethics: An Historical Introduction*, Oxford, Blackwell.

ASPS (Association of Social Workers in the Slovak Republic) (1997) *The Code of Ethics for Social Workers in Slovakia*, Bratislava, ASPS.

Association Nationale des Assistantes d'Hygiène Sociale, Assistantes Sociales et Infirmières Graduées du Luxembourg (n.d.) *Code de déontologie des professions d'assistant d'hygiène sociale et d'assistant social*, Luxembourg, ANAHSASIGL.

Association Nationale des Assistantes de Service Social (1994) *Code de déontologie des Assistants de Service Social*, Paris, ANAS.

Association suisse des professionnels de l'action sociale (ASPAS) (1999) *Code de déontologie*, Berne, ASAS/SBS.

Audit Commission (1992) *The Community Revolution: Personal Social Services and Community Care*, London, HMSO.

Australian Association of Social Workers (AASW) (1994) *Code of Ethics*, Barton, Australia, AASW.

Baier, A. (1995) 'The Need for More Than Justice', in V. Held (ed.), *Justice and Care: Essential Readings in Feminist Ethics*, Boulder, Colorado, Westview Press.

Bailey, R. and Brake, M. (eds) (1975) *Radical Social Work*, London, Edward Arnold.

Bamford, T. (1990) *The Future of Social Work*, London, Macmillan.

Banks, S. (1990) 'Doubts, Dilemmas and Duties: Ethics and the Social Worker', in P. Carter *et al.* (eds), *Social Work and Social Welfare Year-book 2*, Buckingham, Open University Press, pp. 91–106.

Banks, S. (1998a) 'Professional Ethics in Social Work – What Future?', *British Journal of Social Work*, vol. 28, pp. 213–31.

Banks, S. (1998b) 'Codes of Ethics and Ethical Conduct: A View from the Caring Professions', *Public Money and Management*, vol. 18, no. 1, pp. 27–30.

Banks, S. (1999) 'Ethics and the Youth Worker', in S. Banks (ed.), *Ethical Issues in Youth Work*, London, Routledge, pp. 3–20.

Barclay Report (1982) *Social Workers, Their Role and Tasks*, London, Bedford Square Press.

Bauman, Z. (1992) *Intimations of Postmodernity*, London, Routledge.

Bauman, Z. (1993) *Postmodern Ethics*, Oxford, Blackwell.

Bauman, Z. (1995) *Life in Fragments: Essays in Postmodern Morality*, Oxford, Blackwell.

Bauman, Z. (1997) 'Morality Begins at Home – or: Can there be a Levinasian Macro-Ethics?', in H. Jodalen and A. Vetlesen (eds), *Close-ness: An Ethics*, Oslo, Scandinavian University Press, pp. 218–44.

Bayley, M. (1989) 'Values in Locally Based Work', in S. Shardlow (ed.), *The Values of Change in Social Work*, London, Tavistock/Routledge, pp. 45–60.

Beauchamp, T. (1996) 'The Role of Principles in Practical Ethics', in L. Sumner and J. Boyle (eds), *Philosophical Perspectives on Bioethics*, Toronto, University of Toronto Press, pp. 79–95.

Beauchamp, T. and Childress, J. (1994) *Principles of Biomedical Ethics*, 4th edn, Oxford and New York, Oxford University Press.

Bell, M. (1999) *Child Protection: Families and the Conference Process*, Aldershot, Ashgate.

Bell, M. and Sinclair, I. (1993) *Parental Involvement in Initial Child Protec-tion Conferences in Leeds: An External Evaluation*, University of York.

Beresford, P. (1984) *Patch in Perspective, Decentralising and Democratising Social Services*, London, Battersea Community Action.

Berry, L. (1988) 'The Rhetoric of Consumerism and the Exclusion of Community', *Community Development Journal*, vol. 23, no. 4, pp. 266–72.

Biestek, F. (1961) *The Casework Relationship*, London, Allen & Unwin.

Bloxham, S. (1993) 'Managerialism in Youth and Community Work: A Cri-tique of Changing Organisational Structures and Management Practice', *Youth & Policy*, no. 41, pp. 1–12.

Blum, L. (1988) 'Gilligan and Kohlberg: Implications for Moral Theory', *Ethics*, vol. 98, pp. 472–91.

Bond, T. (2000) *Standards and Ethics for Counselling in Action*, 2nd edn, London, Sage.

Bouquet, B. (1999) 'De l'éthique personelle à une éthique professionnelle', *EMPAN*, no. 36, pp. 27–33.

Bowden, P. (1997) *Caring: Gender-Sensitive Ethics*, London, Routledge.

Bowie, N. (1999) *Business Ethics: A Kantian Perspective*, Oxford, Blackwell.

Bradshaw, P. (1996) 'Yes! There Is an Ethics of Care: An Answer for Peter Allmark', *Journal of Medical Ethics*, vol. 22, pp. 8–12.

Brake, M. and Bailey, R. (eds) (1980) *Radical Social Work and Practice*, London, Edward Arnold.

Brandon, D. (1976) *Zen in the Art of Helping*, London, Routledge & Kegan Paul.

Brandon, D. (1991) *Innovation without Change? Consumer Power in Psychiatric Services*, Basingstoke, Macmillan.

Braye, S. and Preston-Shoot, M. (1997) *Practising Social Work Law*, 2nd edn, Basingstoke, Macmillan.

Briskman, L. and Noble, C. (1999) 'Social Work Ethics: Embracing Diversity?', in B. Pease and J. Fook (eds), *Transforming Social Work Practice: Postmodern Critical Perspectives*, London, Routledge, pp. 57–69.

British Association for Counselling (1997) *Code of Ethics and Practice for Counsellors*, Rugby, BAC.

British Association of Social Workers (BASW) (1980) *Clients are Fellow Citizens*, Birmingham, BASW.

British Association of Social Workers (BASW) (1983) *Effective and Ethical Recording*, Birmingham, BASW.

British Association of Social Workers (BASW) (1989) *Rights, Responsibilities and Remedies*, Birmingham, BASW.

British Association of Social Workers (BASW) (1996) *A Code of Ethics for Social Work*, Birmingham, BASW.

Brock, D. (1991) 'Decision-making Competence and Risk', *Bioethics*, vol. 5, no. 2, pp. 105–112.

Brookfield, S. (1987) *Developing Critical Thinkers*, Milton Keynes, Open University Press.

Brown, H. and Smith, H. (1992) 'Assertion Not Assimilation: A Feminist Perspective on the Normalisation Principle', in H. Brown and H. Smith (eds), *Normalisation: A Reader for the Nineties*, London, Routledge, pp. 149–71.

Buchanan, A. and Brock, D. (1989) *Deciding for Others: The Ethics of Surrogate Decision Making*, Cambridge, Cambridge University Press.

Burrage, M. and Torstendahl, R. (eds) (1990) *Professions in Theory and History: Rethinking the Study of the Professions*, London, Sage.

Butrym, Z. (1976) *The Nature of Social Work*, London, Macmillan.

Campbell, T. (1978) 'Discretionary Rights', in N. Timms and D. Watson (eds), *Philosophy in Social Work*, London, Routledge & Kegan Paul.

Canadian Association of Social Workers (CASW) (1994) *Code of Ethics*, Ottawa, CASW.

Central Council for Education and Training in Social Work (CCETSW) (1976) *Values in Social Work*, London, CCETSW.

Central Council for Education and Training in Social Work (CCETSW) (1989) *Requirements and Regulations for the Diploma in Social Work*, London, CCETSW.

Central Council for Education and Training in Social Work (CCETSW) (1995) *Assuring Quality in the Diploma in Social Work – 1: Rules and Requirements for the Diploma in Social Work*, London, CCETSW.

Chamberlain, L. (1992) 'Right to See the Record', *Community Care*, 22 October, pp. 14–15.

Chambon, A. (1994) 'Postmodernity and Social Work Discourse(s): Notes on the Changing Language of a Profession', in A. Chambon and A. Irving (eds), *Essays on Postmodernism and Social Work*, Toronto, Canadian Scholars' Press, pp. 63–75.

Clark, C. (1995) 'Competences and Discipline in Professional Formation', *British Journal of Social Work*, vol. 25, no. 5, pp. 563–80.

Clark, C. (1999) 'Observing the Lighthouse: From Theory to Institutions in Social Work Ethics', *European Journal of Social Work*, vol. 2, no. 3, pp. 259–70.

Clark, C. (2000) *Social Work Ethics: Politics, Principles and Practice*, London, Macmillan.

Clark, C. with Asquith, S. (1985) *Social Work and Social Philosophy*, London, Routledge & Kegan Paul.

Community Care (1999–2000) 'Comment: A New Century of Uncertainty', *Community Care*, no. 1303, 16 December 1999–12 January 2000.

Cooper, D. (1993) *Child Abuse Revisited: Children, Society and Social Work*, Buckingham, Open University Press.

Corden, J. and Preston-Shoot, M. (1987) *Contracts in Social Work*, Aldershot, Gower.

Corrigan, P. and Leonard, P. (1978) *Social Work Practice under Capitalism: A Marxist Approach*, London, Macmillan.

Coulshed, V. and Orme, J. (1998) *Social Work Practice*, 3rd edn, Basingstoke, Macmillan.

Counsel and Care (1992) *From Home to a Home*, London, Counsel and Care.

Crisp, R. (ed.) (1996) *How Should One Live? Essays on the Virtues*, Oxford, Oxford University Press.

Crisp, R. and Slote, M. (eds) (1997) *Virtue Ethics*, Oxford, Oxford University Press.

Croft, S. and Beresford, P. (1989) 'Decentralisation and the Personal Social Services', in M. Langan and P. Lee (eds), *Radical Social Work Today*, London, Unwin Hyman, pp. 97–121.

Curnock, K. and Hardicker, P. (1979) *Towards Practice Theory: Skills and Methods in Social Assessments*, London, Routledge & Kegan Paul.

Dalley, G. (1992) 'Social Welfare Ideologies and Normalisation: Links and Conflicts', in H. Brown and H. Smith (eds), *Normalisation: A Reader for the Nineties*, London, Routledge, pp. 100–11.

Dalrymple, J. (1993) 'Advice, Advocacy and Representation for Children', *Childright*, July, no. 98, pp. 11–13.

Dalrymple, J. (1995) 'It's Not As Easy As You Think! Dilemmas and Advocacy', in J. Dalrymple and J. Hough (eds), *Having a Voice: An Exploration of Children's Rights and Advocacy*, Birmingham, Venture Press, pp. 105–22.

Dansk Socialrådgiverforening (1997) *Etiske Principper i Socialt Arbejde*, Copenhagen, Dansk Socialrådgiverforening.

Davies, M. (ed.) (1997) *The Blackwell Companion to Social Work*, Oxford, Blackwell.

Davis, M. (1999) *Ethics and the University*, London, Routledge.

Day, L. (1992) 'Women and Oppression: Race, Class and Gender', in M. Langan and L. Day (eds), *Women, Oppression and Social Work*, London, Routledge, pp. 12–31.

Deleuze, G. (1988) *Spinoza, Practical Philosophy*, San Francisco, City Lights.

Dent, M. (1999) 'Professional Judgement and the Role of Clinical Guidelines and Evidence-based Medicine (EBM): Netherlands, Britain and Sweden', *Journal of Interprofessional Care*, vol. 13, no. 2, pp. 151–64.

Department of Health (1988) *Protecting Children: A Guide for Social Workers Undertaking a Comprehensive Assessment*, London, HMSO.

Department of Health (1995) *Looking After Children: Good Parenting, Good Outcomes*, London, HMSO.

Department of Health (1998) *Modernising Social Services: Promoting Independence, Improving Protection, Raising Standards*, London, HMSO.

Department of Health (1999) *Framework for the Assessment of Children in Need and their Families (Consultation Draft)*, London, DoH.

Department of Health Social Services Inspectorate (1991a) *Care Management and Assessment: Managers' Guide*, London, HMSO.

Department of Health Social Services Inspectorate (1991b) *Care Management and Assessment: Practitioners' Guide*, London, HMSO.

Deverell, K. and Sharma, U. (2000) 'Professionalism in Everyday Practice: Issues of Trust, Experience and Boundaries', in N. Malin (ed.), *Professionalism, Boundaries and the Workplace*, London, Routledge, pp. 25–46.

Dominelli, L. (1988) *Anti-Racist Social Work*, Basingstoke, Macmillan.

Dominelli, L. (1996) 'Deprofessionalising Social Work: Anti-Oppressive Practice, Competencies and Postmodernism', *British Journal of Social Work*, no. 26, pp. 153–75.

Dominelli, L. (1997) *Anti-Racist Social Work*, 2nd edn, Basingstoke, Macmillan.

Dominelli, L. and McLeod, E. (1989) *Feminist Social Work*, Basingstoke, Macmillan.

Donati, P. and Folgheraiter, F. (eds) (1999) *Gli operatori sociali nel welfare mix. Privatizzazione, pluralizzazione dei soggetti erogatori, managerialismo: il futuro del servizio sociale?*, Trento, Italy, Erickson.

Downie, R. (1971) *Roles and Values*, London, Methuen.

Downie, R. (1989) 'A Political Critique of Kantian Ethics in Social Work: A Reply to Webb and McBeath', *British Journal of Social Work*, vol. 19, pp. 507–10.

Downie, R. and Calman, K. (1994) *Healthy Respect: Ethics in Health Care*, 2nd edn, Oxford, Oxford University Press.

Downie, R. and Loudfoot, E. (1978) 'Aim, Skill and Role in Social Work', in N. Timms and D. Watson (eds), *Philosophy in Social Work*, London, Routledge & Kegan Paul, pp. 111–26.

Downie, R. and Telfer, E. (1969) *Respect for Persons*, London, Routledge & Kegan Paul.

Downie, R. and Telfer, E. (1980) *Caring and Curing*, London, Methuen.

Doyal, L. and Gough, I. (1991) *A Theory of Human Need*, Basingstoke, Macmillan.

Durham County Advocacy Project (1993) *'Speaking Up' in County Durham: First Steps in Developing Advocacy*, Durham, DCAP.

Edwards, P. (1998) 'The Future of Ethics', in O. Leaman (ed.), *The Future of Philosophy: Towards the Twenty-First Century*, London, Routledge, pp. 41–61.

Edwards, S. (1996) *Nursing Ethics: A Principle-based Approach*, Basingstoke, Macmillan.

England, H. (1986) *Social Work as Art*, London, Allen & Unwin.

Etzioni, A. (1969) *The Semi-Professions and Their Organisation*, New York, Free Press.

Etzioni, A. (1995) *The Spirit of Community*, London, Fontana.

Etzioni, A. (1997) *The New Golden Rule: Community and Morality in a Democratic Society*, New York, Basic Books.

Farley, M. (1993) 'Feminism and Universal Morality', in G. Outka and J. Reeder (eds), *Prospects for a Common Morality*, Chichester, Sussex, Princeton University Press, pp. 170–90.

Feinberg, J. (1973) *Social Philosophy*, Englewood Cliffs, New Jersey, Prentice-Hall.

Fellesorganisasjonen for Barnevernpedagoger, Socionomer og Vernepleiere (FO) (1998) *Yrkesetiske prinsipper og retningsliner*, Oslo, FO.

Fook, J. (1993) *Radical Casework: A Theory of Practice*, Sydney, Allen & Unwin.

Foucault, M. (1984) 'On the Genealogy of Ethics: An Overview of Work in Progress', in P. Rabinow (ed.), *The Foucault Reader*, Harmondsworth, Penguin, pp. 340–72.

Foucault, M. (1999) 'Social Work, Social Control, and Normalization: Discussion with Michael Foucault', in A. Chambon, A. Irving and L. Epstein (eds), *Reading Foucault for Social Work*, New York, Columbia University Press, pp. 83–97.

Frankena, W. (1963) *Ethics*, Englewood Cliffs, New Jersey, Prentice Hall.

Franklin, B. (1989) 'Wimps and Bullies: Press Reporting of Child Abuse', in P. Carter *et al.* (eds), *Social Work and Social Welfare Yearbook*, Milton Keynes, Open University Press, pp. 1–14.

Freidson, E. (1994) *Professionalism Reborn: Theory, Prophecy, and Policy*, Chicago, Ill., University of Chicago Press.

Freire, P. (1972) *Pedagogy of the Oppressed*, London, Penguin.

Giddens, A. (1998) *The Third Way: The Renewal of Social Democracy*, Oxford, Polity Press.

Gilligan, C. (1982) *In a Different Voice: Psychological Theory and Women's Development*, Cambridge, Mass., Harvard University Press.

Gould, N. and Taylor, I. (eds) (1996) *Reflective Learning for Social Work*, Aldershot, Arena.

Graham, M. (1999) 'The African-Centred Worldview: Developing a Paradigm for Social Work', *British Journal of Social Work*, vol. 29, pp. 251–67.

Gray, A. and Jenkins, B. (1999) 'Professions, Bureaucracy, and Social Welfare', in J. Baldock *et al.* (eds), *Social Policy*, Oxford, Oxford University Press, pp. 191–217.

Greenwood, E. (1957) 'Attributes of a Profession', *Social Work*, vol. 2, no. 3, pp. 44–55.

Gyford, J. (1991) *Citizens, Consumers and Councils*, London, Macmillan.

Hadley, R. and McGrath, M. (eds) (1980) *Going Local: Neighbourhood Social Services*, London, Bedford Square Press/NCVO.

Hadley, R. and McGrath, M. (1984) *When Social Services are Local: The Normanton Experience*, London, Allen & Unwin.

Halmos, P. (1978) *The Faith of Counsellors*, London, Constable.

Hanford, L. (1994) 'Nursing and the Concept of Care: An Appraisal of Noddings' Theory', in G. Hunt (ed.), *Ethical Issues in Nursing*, London, Routledge, pp. 181–97.

Hanvey, C. and Philpot, T. (eds) (1994) *Practising Social Work*, London, Routledge.

Hare, R. M. (1952) *The Language of Morals*, Oxford, Clarendon Press.

Hare, R. M. (1963) *Freedom and Reason*, Oxford, Clarendon Press.

Harris, N. (1987) 'Defensive Social Work', *British Journal of Social Work*, vol. 17, pp. 61–9.

Harris, N. (1994) 'Professional Codes and Kantian Duties', in R. Chadwick (ed.), *Ethics and the Professions*, Aldershot, Avebury, pp. 104–15.

Harvey, D. (1990) *The Condition of Postmodernity*, Oxford, Blackwell.

Healy, K. (2000) *Social Work Practices: Contemporary Perspectives on Change*, London, Sage.

Hollis, M. (1977) *Models of Man*, Cambridge, Cambridge University Press.

Hollis, M. and Howe, D. (1990) 'Moral Risks in the Social Work Role: A Response to Macdonald', *British Journal of Social Work*, vol. 20, pp. 547–52.

Holmes, J. (1981) *Professionalisation – a Misleading Myth? A Study of the Careers of Youth and Community Work Courses in England and Wales from 1970 to 1978*, Leicester, National Youth Bureau.

Hong Kong Social Workers Association (1998) *Code of Practice*, Hong Kong, HKSWA.

Horne, M. (1999) *Values in Social Work*, 2nd edn, Aldershot, Hants, Wildwood House.

Howe, D. (1987) *An Introduction to Social Work Theory*, Aldershot, Hants, Wildwood House.

Howe, D. (1991) 'Knowledge, Power and the Shape of Social Work Practice', in M. Davies (ed.), *The Sociology of Social Work*, London, Routledge.

Howe, D. (1992) 'Child Abuse and the Bureaucratisation of Social Work', *The Sociological Review*, vol. 40, no. 3, pp. 491–508.

Hudson, B. and Macdonald, G. (1986) *Behavioural Social Work: An Introduction*, London, Macmillan.

References   193

Hudson, W. (1978) *Modern Moral Philosophy*, London, Macmillan.
Hugman, R. (1991) *Power in Caring Professions*, London, Macmillan.
Hugman, R. (1998) *Social Welfare and Social Value*, Basingstoke, Macmillan.
Hunt, G. (ed.) (1998) *Whistleblowing in the Social Services: Public Accountability and Professional Practice*, London, Arnold.
Hursthouse, R. (1997) 'Virtue Theory and Abortion', in D. Statman (ed.), *Virtue Ethics: A Critical Reader*, Edinburgh, Edinburgh University Press, pp. 227–44.
Husband, C. (1995) 'The Morally Active Practitioner and the Ethics of Antiracist Social Work', in R. Hugman and D. Smith (eds), *Ethical Issues in Social Work*, London, Routledge, pp. 84–103.
Ife, J. (1997) *Rethinking Social Work: Towards Critical Practice*, Melbourne, Longman.
Ife, J. (1999) 'Postmodernism, Critical Theory and Social Work', in B. Pease and J. Fook (eds), *Transforming Social Work Practice: Postmodern Critical Perspectives*, London, Routledge, pp. 211–23.
Illich, I. *et al.* (1977) *The Disabling Professions*, London, Marion Boyars.
International Federation of Social Workers (IFSW) (1989) *Comparaison des formations d'assistants sociaux dans les pays membres de la Communauté Européenne*, Brussels, IFSW.
International Federation of Social Workers (IFSW) (1990) *Social Workers in the European Community: Training–Employment–Perspectives 1992*, Brussels, IFSW.
International Federation of Social Workers (IFSW) (1994) *The Ethics of Social Work – Principles and Standards*, http://www.ifsw.org/4.4.pub.html
Irish Association of Social Workers (IASW) (1995) *Code of Ethics of the Irish Association of Social Workers*, Dublin, IASW.
Irving, A. (1994) 'From Image to Simulacra: The Modern/Postmodern Divide in Social Work', in A. Chambon and A. Irving (eds), *Essays on Postmodernism and Social Work*, Toronto, Canadian Scholars' Press, pp. 21–32.
Jackson, J. (1994) 'Common Codes: Divergent Practices', in R. Chadwick (ed.), *Ethics and the Professions*, Aldershot, Avebury, pp. 116–24.
Jameson, F. (1991) *Postmodernism or, The Cultural Logic of Late Capitalism*, London, Verso.
Japanese Association of Social Workers (1992) *Code of Ethics*, Tokyo, JASW.
Jeffs, T. and Smith, M. (1994) 'Young People, Youth Work and a New Authoritarianism', *Youth and Policy*, no. 53, pp. 1–14.
Johnson, T. (1972) *Professions and Power*, London, Macmillan.
Johnson, T. (1984) 'Professionalism: Occupation or Ideology?', in S. Goodlad (ed.), *Education for the Professions: Quis Custodiet . . . ?*, Guildford, Society for Research into Higher Education and National Foundation for Educational Research/Nelson.
Jones, P. (1994) *Rights*, Basingstoke, Macmillan.

194 *References*

Jordan, B. (1975) 'Is the Client a Fellow Citizen?', *Social Work Today*, vol. 6, no. 15, pp. 471–5.

Jordan, B. (1989) *The Common Good: Citizenship, Morality and Self-Interest*, Oxford, Blackwell.

Jordan, B. (1990) *Social Work in an Unjust Society*, Hemel Hempstead, Harvester.

Jordan, B. (1991) 'Competencies and Values', *Social Work Education*, vol. 10, no. 1, pp. 5–11.

Kant, I. (1964) *Groundwork of the Metaphysics of Morals*, New York, Harper & Row.

Katz, I. (1995) 'Approaches to Empowerment and Participation in Child Protection', in C. Cloke and M. Davies (eds), *Participation and Empowerment in Child Protection*, London, Pitman, pp. 154–69.

King, M. and Trowell, J. (1992) *Children's Welfare and the Law: The Limits of Legal Intervention*, London, Sage.

Knight, T. and Caveney, S. (1998) 'Assessment and Action Records: Will they Promote Good Parenting?', *British Journal of Social Work*, vol. 28, pp. 29–43.

Koehn, D. (1994) *The Ground of Professional Ethics*, London, Routledge.

Kuhse, H. (1997) *Caring: Nurses, Women and Ethics*, Oxford, Blackwell.

Kutchins, H. (1991) 'The Fiduciary Relationship: The Legal Basis for Social Workers' Responsibilities to Clients', *Social Work*, vol. 36, no. 2, pp. 106–13.

Lafollette, H. (ed.) (2000) *The Blackwell Guide to Ethical Theory*, Oxford, Blackwell.

Langan, M. (1993) 'New Directions in Social Work', in J. Clarke (ed.), *A Crisis in Care? Challenges to Social Work*, London, Sage/Open University Press, pp. 149–67.

Langan, M. and Lee, P. (eds) (1989) *Radical Social Work Today*, London, Unwin Hyman.

Lansdown, G. (1995) 'Children's Rights to Participation: A Critique', in C. Cloke and M. Davies (eds), *Participation and Empowerment in Child Protection*, London, Pitman, pp. 19–38.

Le Grand, J. and Bartlett, W. (eds) (1993) *Quasi-Markets and Social Policy*, Basingstoke, Macmillan.

Leighton, N. (1985) 'Personal and Professional Values – Marriage or Divorce?', in D. Watson (ed.), *A Code of Ethics for Social Work: The Second Step*, London, Routledge & Kegan Paul, pp. 59–85.

Leonard, P. (1997) *Postmodern Welfare: Reconstructing an Emancipatory Project*, London, Sage.

Levinas, E. (1989) 'Ethics as First Philosophy', in S. Hand (ed.), *The Levinas Reader*, Oxford, Blackwell, pp. 75–87.

Levy, C. (1976) *Social Work Ethics*, New York, Human Sciences Press.

Levy, C. (1993) *Social Work Ethics on the Line*, Binghampton, New York, Haworth Press.

Lewis, J. and Glennerster, H. (1996) *Implementing the New Community Care*, Buckingham, Open University Press.

Lishman, J. (ed.) (1991) *Handbook of Theory for Practice Teachers in Social Work*, London, Jessica Kingsley.

Lister, R. (1991) 'Citizenship Engendered', *Critical Social Policy*, no. 32, pp. 65–71.

Løgstrup, K. (1997) 'On Trust', in H. Jodalen and A. Vetlesen (eds), *Closeness: An Ethics*, Oslo, Scandinavian University Press, pp. 71–89.

Long, A. and Harrison, S. (1996) 'Evidence-based Decision-making', *Health Service Journal*, vol. 106 (11 January), pp. 8–11.

Lukes, S. (1987) *Marxism and Morality*, Oxford, Oxford University Press.

Lund, B. (1999) 'Ask Not What Your Community Can Do for You': Obligations, New Labour and Welfare Reform', *Critical Social Policy*, vol. 19, no. 4, pp. 447–62.

Lymbery, M. (1998) 'Care Management and Professional Autonomy: The Impact of Community Care Legislation on Social Work with Older People', *British Journal of Social Work*, vol. 28, pp. 863–78.

Lymbery, M. (2000) 'The Retreat from Professionalism: From Social Worker to Care Manager', in N. Malin (ed.), *Professionalism, Boundaries and the Workplace*, London, Routledge, pp. 123–38.

Lyotard, J.-F. (1984) *The Postmodern Condition: A Report on Knowledge*, trans. G. Bennington and B. Massumi, Manchester, Manchester University Press.

McBeath, G. and Webb, S. (1990–1) 'Child Protection Language as Professional Ideology in Social Work', *Social Work & Social Sciences Review*, vol. 2, no. 2, pp. 122–45.

McBeath G. and Webb, S. (1991) 'Social Work, Modernity and Post Modernity', *Sociological Review*, vol. 39, no 4, pp. 745–62.

McDermott, F. (1975) 'Against the Persuasive Definition of Self-determination', in F. McDermott (ed.), *Self-Determination in Social Work*, London, Routledge & Kegan Paul, pp. 118–37.

Macdonald, G. (1990) 'Allocating Blame in Social Work', *British Journal of Social Work*, vol. 20, pp. 525–46.

MacIntyre, A. (1985) *After Virtue: A Study in Moral Theory*, 2nd edn, London, Duckworth.

MacIntyre, A. (1999) *Dependent Rational Animals: Why Human Beings Need the Virtues*, London, Duckworth.

Malin, N. (2000) 'Professionalism and Boundaries of the Formal Sector: The Example of Social and Community Care', in N. Malin (ed.), *Professionalism, Boundaries and the Workplace*, London, Routledge, pp. 7–24.

Marshall, T. (1963) 'Citizenship and Social Class', in *Sociology at the Crossroads and Other Essays*, London, Heineman, pp. 67–127.

Marshall, T. (1972) 'Value Problems of Welfare-Capitalism', *Journal of Social Policy*, vol. 1, pp. 15–30.

Marx, K. (1963) *Early Writings*, edited by T. Bottomore, London, Fontana.

Marx, K. and Engels, F. (1969) 'Manifesto of the Communist Party', in L. Feuer (ed.), *Marx and Engels: Basic Writings on Politics and Philosophy*, Glasgow, Collins/Fontana, pp. 43–82.

Mayer, J. and Timms, N. (1970) *The Client Speaks*, London, Routledge & Kegan Paul.

Mendus, S. (1993) 'Different Voices, Still Lives: Problems in the Ethics of Care', *Journal of Applied Philosophy*, vol. 10, no. 1, pp. 17–27.

Mill, J. S. (1972) *Utilitarianism, On Liberty, and Considerations on Representative Government*, London, Dent.

Millerson, G. (1964) *The Qualifying Associations: A Study in Professionalisation*, London, Routledge & Kegan Paul.

Mintzberg, H. (1979) *The Structuring of Organisations*, Englewood Cliffs, New Jersey, Prentice-Hall.

Moffet, J. (1968) *Concepts of Casework Treatment*, London, Routledge & Kegan Paul.

Moon, D. (1988) 'Introduction: Responsibility, Rights and Welfare', in D. Moon (ed.), *Responsibility, Rights and Welfare: The Theory of the Welfare State*, Boulder, Colorado, Westview Press, pp. 1–15.

Morales, A. and Sheafor, B. (1986) *Social Work: A Profession of Many Faces*, Boston, Mass., Allyn & Bacon.

Mullender, A. and Perrott, S. (1998) 'Social Work and Organisations', in R. Adams, L. Dominelli and M. Payne (eds), *Social Work: Themes, Issues and Critical Debates*, Basingstoke, Macmillan, pp. 67–77.

Mullender, A. and Ward, D. (1991) *Self-Directed Groupwork: Users Take Action for Empowerment*, London, Whiting & Birch.

Nagel, T. (1976) 'Moral Luck', *Proceedings of the Aristotelian Society*, Supplementary vol. L, pp. 137–51.

Nagel, T. (1979) 'The Fragmentation of Value', in T. Nagel, *Mortal Questions*, Cambridge, Cambridge University Press, pp. 128–41.

National Association of Social Workers (NASW) (1996) *Code of Ethics*, Washington, DC, NASW.

National Consumer Council (1993) *Getting Heard and Getting Things Changed*, London, NCC.

Nederlanse Vereniging van Maatschappelijk Werkers (NVMW) (1999) *Beroepscode voor de maatschappelijk werker*, Utrecht, NVMW.

New Zealand Association of Social Workers (NZASW) (1993) *Code of Ethics*, Dunedin, New Zealand, NZASW.

Newcastle upon Tyne Social Services Department (n.d.) *Policy and Procedure in Relation to Access to Information*, Newcastle, Newcastle City Council.

Newell, P. (1991) *The UN Convention and Children's Rights in the UK*, London, National Children's Bureau.

Noddings, N. (1984) *Caring: A Feminine Approach to Ethics and Moral Education*, Berkeley and Los Angeles, University of California Press.

Norman, R. (1998) *The Moral Philosophers*, Oxford, Clarendon Press.

O'Connor, J. (1973) *The Fiscal Crisis of the State*, New York, St Martin's Press.

Offe, C. (1984) *Contradictions of the Welfare State*, London, Hutchinson.

Okin, S. (1994) 'Gender Inequality and Cultural Difference', *Political Theory*, vol. 22, pp. 5–24.

Ordine Nazionale Assistenti Sociali (1998) *Codice Deontologico Degli Assistenti Sociali*, Rome, ONAS.
Osborne, T. (1998) 'Constructionism, Authority and the Ethical Life', in I. Velody and R. Williams (eds), *The Politics of Constructionism*, London, Sage, pp. 221–34.
O'Sullivan, T. (1999) *Decision Making in Social Work*, Basingstoke, Macmillan.
Outka, G. and Reeder, J. (eds) (1993) *Prospects for a Common Morality*, Chichester, Sussex, Princeton University Press.
Øvretveit, J. (1997) 'How Patient Power and Client Participation Affects Relations Between Professions', in J. Øvretveit, P. Mathias and T. Thompson (eds), *Interprofessional Working for Health and Social Care*, Basingstoke, Macmillan, pp. 79–102.
Parsons, T. (1959) 'The Professions and Social Structure', in *Essays in Social Theory*, New York, Free Press.
Parton, N. (1989) 'Child Abuse', in B. Kahan (ed.), *Child Care Research, Policy and Practice*, London, Hodder & Stoughton/Open University.
Parton, N. (1991) *Governing the Family: Child Care, Child Protection and the State*, Basingstoke, Macmillan.
Parton, N. (1997) 'Child Protection and Family Support: Current Debates and Future Prospects', in N. Parton (ed.), *Child Protection and Family Support: Tensions, Contradictions and Possibilities*, London, Routledge, pp. 1–24.
Parton, N. (1998) 'Risk, Advanced Liberalism and Child Welfare: The Need to Rediscover Uncertainty and Ambiguity', *British Journal of Social Work*, vol. 28, pp. 5–27.
Parton, N. (1999) 'Reconfiguring Child Welfare Practices: Risk, Advanced Liberalism, and the Government of Freedom', in A. Chambon, A. Irving and L. Epstein (eds), *Reading Foucault for Social Work*, New York, Columbia University Press, pp. 101–30.
Parton, N. and Small, N. (1989) 'Violence, Social Work and the Emergence of Dangerousness', in M. Langan and P. Lee (eds), *Radical Social Work Today*, London, Unwin Hyman, pp. 120–39.
Parton, N., Thorpe, D. and Wattam, C. (1997) *Child Protection, Risk and the Moral Order*, Basingstoke, Macmillan.
Patel, S. (1995) 'Advocacy Through the Eyes of a Young Person', in J. Dalrymple and J. Hough (eds), *Having a Voice: An Exploration of Children's Rights and Advocacy*, Birmingham, Venture Press, pp. 1–18.
Payne, C. (1994) 'The Systems Approach', in C. Hanvey and T. Philpot (eds), *Practising Social Work*, London, Routledge, pp. 8–21.
Payne, H. and Littlechild, B. (eds) (2000) *Ethical Practice and the Abuse of Power in Social Responsibility: Leave No Stone Unturned*, London, Jessica Kingsley.
Payne, M. (1989) 'Open Records and Shared Decisions with Clients', in S. Shardlow (ed.), *The Values of Change in Social Work*, London, Routledge, pp. 114–34.

Payne, M. (1995) *Social Work and Community Care*, Basingstoke, Macmillan.

Payne, M. (1997) *Modern Social Work Theory: A Critical Introduction*, 2nd edn, Basingstoke, Macmillan.

Pierson, C. (1998) *Beyond the Welfare State? The New Political Economy of Welfare*, Oxford, Polity Press.

Pincus, A. and Minahan, A. (1973) *Social Work Practice: Model and Method*, Itasca, Illinois, Peacock.

Pinker, R. (1990) *Social Work in an Enterprise Society*, London, Routledge.

Plamenatz, J. (1966) *The English Utilitarians*, Oxford, Blackwell.

Plant, R. (1970) *Social and Moral Theory in Casework*, London, Routledge & Kegan Paul.

Popple, K. (1995) *Analysing Community Work*, Buckingham, Open University Press.

Ragg, N. (1977) *People Not Cases*, London, Routledge & Kegan Paul.

Ramon, S. (ed.) (1991) *Beyond Community Care: Normalisation and Integration Work*, London, Macmillan.

Raphael, D. (1981) *Moral Philosophy*, Oxford, Oxford University Press.

Rawls, J. (1973) *A Theory of Justice*, Oxford, Oxford University Press.

Rea, D. (1998) 'The Myth of the Market in the Organisation of Community Care', in A. Symonds and A. Kelly (eds), *The Social Construction of Community Care*, Basingstoke, Macmillan, pp. 199–207.

Rhodes, M. (1986) *Ethical Dilemmas in Social Work Practice*, Boston, Mass., Routledge & Kegan Paul.

Rice, D. (1975) 'The Code: A Voice for Approval', *Social Work Today*, 18 October, pp. 381–2.

Roberts, R. (1990) *Lessons from the Past: Issues for Social Work Theory*, London, Routledge.

Roger, J. (2000) *From a Welfare State to a Welfare Society: The Changing Context of Social Policy in a Postmodern Era*, Basingstoke, Macmillan.

Rogers, C. (1951) *Client-Centred Therapy: Its Current Practice, Implications and Theory*, London, Constable.

Rogers, C. (1961) *On Becoming a Person: A Therapist's View of Psychotherapy*, London, Constable.

Rojeck, C. and Collins, S. (1987) 'Contract or Con Trick', *British Journal of Social Work*, vol. 17, pp. 199–211.

Rojeck, C. and Collins, S. (1988) 'Contract or Con Trick Revisited', *British Journal of Social Work*, vol. 18, pp. 611–22.

Ronnby, A. (1992) 'Praxiology in Social Work', *International Social Work*, vol. 35, pp. 317–26.

Ronnby, A. (1993) 'The Carer Society and Ethics', unpublished paper, Department of Social Work and Humanities, Mid-Sweden University, Östersund.

Rosenau, P. (1992) *Post-modernism and the Social Sciences: Insights, Inroads, and Intrusions*, Princeton, New Jersey, Princeton University Press.

Ross, W. (1930) *The Right and the Good*, Oxford, Clarendon Press.

Rossiter, A., Prilleltensky, I. and Walsh-Bowers, R. (2000) 'A Postmodern

Perspective on Professional Ethics', in B. Fawcett, B. Featherstone, J. Fook and A. Rossiter (eds), *Practice and Research in Social Work: Postmodern Feminist Perspectives*, London, Routledge, pp. 83–103.

SABSWA (n.d.) *Code of Ethics*, Johannesburg, SABSWA.

Sartre, J.-P. (1969) *Being and Nothingness*, translated by Hazel Barnes, London, Methuen.

Schön, D. (1983) *The Reflective Practitioner: How Professionals Think in Action*, New York, Basic Books.

Schön, D. (1987) *Educating the Reflective Practitioner. Towards a New Design for Teaching and Learning in the Professions*, San Francisco, Jossey-Bass.

Shah, N. (1989) 'It's Up to You Sisters: Black Women and Radical Social Work', in M. Langan and P. Lee (eds), *Radical Social Work Today*, London, Unwin Hyman, pp. 178–91.

Shaw, W. (1999) *Contemporary Ethics: Taking Account of Utilitarianism*, Oxford, Blackwell.

Sheldon, B. (1995) *Cognitive-behavioural Therapy: Research, Practice and Philosophy*, London, Routledge.

Shenton, F. (1999) *Evaluation of County Durham 'Investing in Children Initiative'*, Durham, University of Durham.

Siegrist, H. (1994) 'The Professions, State and Government in Theory and History', in T. Becher (ed.), *Governments and Professional Education*, Buckingham, Society for Research into Higher Education and Open University Press, pp. 3–20.

Singapore Association of Social Workers (n.d.) *Code of Ethics of the Singapore Association of Social Workers*, Singapore, SASW.

Slote, M. (1992) *From Morality to Virtue*, New York, Oxford University Press.

Smart, J. and Williams, B. (1973) *Utilitarianism: For and Against*, Cambridge, Cambridge University Press.

Smith, M. (1994) *Local Education: Community, Conversation, Praxis*, Buckingham, Open University Press.

Solomon, R. (1992) *Ethics and Excellence*, Oxford, Oxford University Press.

Solomon, R. (1997) 'Corporate Roles, Personal Virtues: An Aristotelian Approach to Business Ethics', in D. Statman (ed.), *Virtue Ethics: A Critical Reader*, Edinburgh, Edinburgh University Press, pp. 205–6.

Soulet, M.-H. (ed.) (1997) *Les transformations des métiers du social*, Fribourg, Editions Universitaires Fribourg Suisse.

Southon, G. and Braithwhaite, J. (2000) 'The End of Professionalism?', in C. Davies *et al.* (eds), *Changing Practice in Health and Social Care*, London, Sage, pp. 300–7.

Spicker, P. (1988) *Principles of Social Welfare*, London, Routledge.

SSPCR (Association of Social Workers in the Czech Republic) (1995) *Ethical Code of Social Workers in the Czech Republic*, Prague, SSPCR.

SSR (Swedish Union of Social Workers, Personnel and Public Administrators) (1997) *Yrkesetiska Riktlinjer för Socionomer*, Stockholm, SSR.

Stalley, R. (1978) 'Non-judgmental Attitudes', in N. Timms and D. Watson (eds), *Philosophy in Social Work*, London, Routledge & Kegan Paul.

Statman, D. (1997) 'Introduction to Virtue Ethics', in D. Statman (ed.), *Virtue Ethics: A Critical Reader*, Edinburgh, Edinburgh University Press, pp. 3–41.

Strawson, P. (1959) *Individuals*, London, Methuen.

Swidler, A. (1986) 'Culture in Action: Symbols and Strategies', *American Sociological Review*, vol. 51 (April), pp. 273–86.

Tam, H. (1998) *Communitarianism: A New Agenda for Politics and Citizenship*, Basingstoke, Macmillan.

Taylor, D. (1989) 'Citizenship and Social Power', *Critical Social Policy*, no. 26, pp. 19–31.

Taylor, D. (1991/2) 'A Big Idea for the Nineties'? The Rise of the Citizens' Charters', *Critical Social Policy*, no. 33, pp. 87–94.

Thomas, T., Noone, M. and Rowbottom, T. (1993) *Confidentiality in Social Services*, London, CCETSW.

Thompson, I., Melia, K. and Boyd, K. (1994) *Nursing Ethics*, 3rd edn, Edinburgh, Churchill Livingstone.

Thompson, N. (1991) 'Putting Theory Into Practice: A Study of Practice Records', *Journal of Training and Development*, vol. 1, no. 4, pp. 55–60.

Thompson, N. (1992) *Existentialism and Social Work*, Aldershot, Hants, Avebury.

Thompson, N. (1993) *Anti-Discriminatory Practice*, Basingstoke, Macmillan.

Thompson, N. (2000) *Understanding Social Work: Preparing for Practice*, London, Macmillan.

Toren, N. (1972) *Social Work: The Case of a Semi-Profession*, Beverley Hills, Calif., Sage.

Torstendahl, R. (1991) *Bureaucratisation in Northwestern Europe 1880–1985: Domination and Governance*, London, Routledge.

Tronto, J. (1993) *Moral Boundaries: A Political Argument for an Ethic of Care*, London, Routledge.

United Nations (1959) *Declaration of the Rights of the Child*, reprinted in P. Newell (1991) *The UN Convention and Children's Rights in the UK*, London, National Children's Bureau, pp. 182–3.

Urmson, J. (ed.) (1975) *The Concise Encyclopedia of Western Philsophy and Philosphers*, London, Hutchinson.

Veatch, R. (1999) 'Abandoning Informed Consent', in H. Kuhse and P. Singer (eds), *Bioethics: An Anthology*, Oxford, Blackwell, pp. 523–32.

von Bertalanffy, L. (1971) *General System Theory: Foundations, Development, Application*, London, Allen Lane.

Warnock, G. (1967) *Contemporary Moral Philosophy*, London, Macmillan.

Warnock, M. (1998) *An Intelligent Person's Guide to Ethics*, London, Duckworth.

Watson, D. (1985) 'What's the Point of a Code of Ethics for Social Work', in D. Watson (ed.), *A Code of Ethics for Social Work: The Second Step*, London, Routledge & Kegan Paul, pp. 20–39.

Webb, S. and McBeath, G. (1989) 'A Political Critique of Kantian Ethics in Social Work', *British Journal of Social Work*, vol. 19, pp. 491–506.

Webb, S. and McBeath, G. (1990) 'A Political Critique of Kantian Ethics in Social Work: A Reply to Prof. R.S. Downie', *British Journal of Social Work*, vol. 20, pp. 65–71.

Whitley, C. (1969) 'On Duties', in J. Feinberg (ed.), *Moral Concepts*, Oxford, Oxford University Press, pp. 53–9.

Wicclair, M. (1991) 'Patient Decision-Making Capacity and Risk', *Bioethics*, vol. 5, no. 2, pp. 91–104.

Wilding, P. (1982) *Professional Power and Social Welfare*, London, Routledge & Kegan Paul.

Wilkes, R. (1981) *Social Work with Undervalued Groups*, London, Tavistock.

Wilkes, R. (1985) 'Social Work: What Kind of Profession?', in D. Watson (ed.), *A Code of Ethics for Social Work: The Second Step*, London, Routledge & Kegan Paul, pp. 40–58.

Wilmot, S. (1997) *The Ethics of Community Care*, London, Cassell.

Winch, P. (1958) *The Idea of a Social Science and its Relation to Philosophy*, London, Routledge & Kegan Paul.

Wittgenstein, L. (1967) *Philosophical Investigations*, Oxford, Blackwell.

Yelloly, M. and Henkel, M. (eds) (1995) *Learning and Teaching in Social Work: Towards Reflective Practice*, London, Jessica Kingsley.

Index